STILL
WITH THE
MUSIC

Karl Jenkins

STILL
WITH THE
MUSIC

My Autobiography

KARL
JENKINS

with SAM JACKSON

First published 2015 by
Elliott and Thompson Limited
27 John Street, London WC1N 2BX
www.eandtbooks.com

ISBN: 978-1-78396-137-5

All pictures supplied from the Jenkins' family archive.
Page 10: (bottom) David Williams/Warner Classics; page 11: (top) Chris Leslie, (bottom) John Swannell/Warner Classics; page 12: (top) Jan Potgieter, University of Johannesburg; page 14: (top) John Suett, (bottom) Charles Green; page 15: June Mendoza; page 16: (top) Rhys Frampton

Every effort has been made to trace copyright holders for material used within this book. Where this has not been possible, the publisher will be happy to credit them in future editions.

9 8 7 6 5 4 3 2 1

A catalogue record for this book is available from the British Library.

Typesetting: Marie Doherty
Printed in the UK by TJ International Ltd.

For my family:
Carol, Jody, Rosie, Astrid and Minty
and in memory of those departed

CONTENTS

A few years ago now, I was visiting Swansea market, happily wrapped up in a world of my own. Suddenly, my daydreaming was interrupted when, out of nowhere, one of the very Welsh cockle-vendors from my home village of Penclawdd shouted, 'Kaaarl! Still with the mew-sic?'

1

BEGINNINGS

*M*any people have careers in music, but not so many have what amounts to four – four consecutive careers, spanning fifty years, using the same twelve notes. It took me many years as a musical tourist to discover what I was good at. I arrived at my natural musical habitat with *Adiemus*, *The Armed Man: A Mass for Peace* and the works that followed. I seem to have made such a significant connection, through my music, with people from all over the globe that I thought it might justify my writing this book. The getting there is not without interest, too, and is, of course, the path that led me to where I am now.

One day in May 2015, on returning to London from some concerts in Kazakhstan, I went to our studio to see my son and collect the company mail. There was a letter from the Cabinet Office. It read:

The Prime Minister has asked me to inform you that having accepted the advice of the Head of the Civil Service and the Main Honours Committee, he proposes to submit your name to the Queen. He is recommending that Her Majesty be

graciously pleased to approve that the honour of Knighthood
be conferred upon you in the Birthday 2015 Honours List.

However, my beginnings were far more humble. I was born in Neath,
South Wales, on 17 February 1944. My childhood was full of love and
laughter, but recently it's dawned on me that before I was even out of
my teens, I had experienced more tragedy in the first few years of my
life than most of my contemporaries would experience in their first
few decades. This is something I'll return to in the pages that follow.
For now, though, allow me to share what it was like growing up in
this beautiful part of Wales in the 1940s and 1950s.

The Jenkins family had made its home in the coastal village of
Penclawdd, nestling between an imposing hill (known as the Graig) on
the one side and the Bury estuary, on the stunning Gower Peninsula,
on the other – a location that later gained some status as the first place
in the United Kingdom to be officially designated an area of outstanding natural beauty. I was the first and only child of my parents, David
and Lily. Although I might not have had a very large nuclear family, I
vividly remember being surrounded by many aunts, uncles and close
friends in this tight-knit community.

Penclawdd was, and is, famous for its cockles. They were collected
'out on the sands', when the tide had receded, and brought back in
sacks to the factories, either by horse-drawn cart or by donkey. Most
cockle-pickers were women, and many balanced the sieves, used for
riddling the cockles, on their heads. Seeing them walk through the
village, with their donkeys loaded with sacks of cockles beside them,
was quite an alien sight for a British community. An ancillary task was
the collection of seaweed of the laver variety – *Porphyra umbilicalis* – to
make laverbread.

At one time, Penclawdd had been a thriving industrial village with
a tin works. It also had a dock and ships that used to 'to and fro' from

Cornwall, taking coal from the pits nearby and bringing back tin for processing. This modest village had seven pubs on the estuary front (all within the space of a mile), three Nonconformist chapels and one church. By the time I arrived, only three pubs had survived, but the chapels and church remain to this day.

One of the pubs that had fallen into disuse, the New Inn, had been converted into the cottage home of my mother's parents. Around a decade before I was born, my grandmother had died when, along with eight other cocklewomen, she drowned on the sands in the Bury estuary. The sudden death of a family member, especially in such horrendous circumstances, is something that can never be forgotten. Many of my relatives were still living with their deep loss at the time of my birth.

In happier times, my maternal grandmother – Margaret Ann – used to go by train to the bigger towns further east every Saturday to sell cockles. In Newport, she met a Swedish sailor – one Carl Gustavus Edward Pamp. He was smitten with her, and she with him. They eventually married and settled in Penclawdd, raising three children: Axel, Ida and Lily. My grandfather was always known to me as Morfar, which is Swedish for 'mother's father'. Swedes sensibly have a different name for each grandparent. Morfar was a real character, and often used to stand on the 'ship bank' and sway, as if he were riding the rolling sea. Back in Sweden, his three sisters owned a ladies' clothes shop in Gävle, north of Stockholm. Their grandfather, Lars, had been Head Gardener to the King of Sweden, and their brother Axel a ship's captain who had gone down with his ship.

I remember an occasion when Morfar's sisters, none of whom had married, came to visit from Sweden. He retired early one night, which was very unlike him. The sisters sent my cousin upstairs to see if he was all right but he wasn't there. Morfar had gone out through the window, down a ladder, and over to the Ship and Castle pub.

He certainly liked a drink. He was also a hoarder: on one occasion I needed some empty matchboxes for a project at junior school and he gave me fifty.

One of the earliest memories I have of my contented childhood is of the little car Morfar, who was extremely clever with his hands, made for me. I can still feel the thrill of being able to sit in this bright red car, steer it and pedal along. Somehow it had acquired a Wolseley badge on the bonnet. I was in awe of Morfar's many talents, which even extended to the skilful pickling of a multitude of vegetables. We never went short of pickled gherkins in our family.

The other side of the family was 100 per cent Welsh. As was the case with my mother's relatives, they too had faced tragedy before I was born. My grandfather, William Jenkins, was killed underground when a colliery wall fell on him. He was survived by my grandmother, Mary Ann, and their five children: Thomas Charles (who died very young); my aunt Evelyn Mary; Alfryn James, who was lost over Berlin as a Lancaster bomber pilot with an all-Welsh crew in 1944; William Ivor; and my father, Joseph David, who was often known simply as Dai or Dai Bach ('Little David').

The house where I began life was called Min-Y-Dwr, meaning 'edge of the water'; unsurprisingly, it was on the estuary front. Despite being named after my grandfather, I was always Karl with a 'K' – not for any profound reason, it turns out, but simply because my parents preferred the spelling. As far as I know, our existence as a little family of three was initially a simple but very happy one. However, soon after I was born, my mother contracted tuberculosis and her health began to deteriorate. I later learned that, sadly, she had initially been misdiagnosed. When I was aged two, it was decided that she and I should go and live in Sweden for a while, where it was thought the air might benefit her. My father, a schoolteacher, stayed behind in Wales and came out to join us only during school holidays. Despite being just two years old at the time, I can remember flying out from Northolt in a Dakota aircraft. The first sounds I uttered were Swedish, which my mother spoke fluently; alas, all gone now. Her health did not improve, so we returned. My mother died before I was five.

While I will always be able to recall my father's warmth and compassion, any knowledge of my mother is based largely on what others have told me. What I do remember, though, is how confused I was at the time of her passing. Emotions weren't really talked about in those days; I don't believe this was something particular to Wales, but more a question of what was deemed appropriate in the late 1940s. When my mother died, I was staying with my aunt Ida and uncle Cliff. As they put me to bed one night, I looked at my uncle and simply asked, 'Where's Mammy?' His response was short and to the point: 'She's in heaven.' No one had yet told me my mother had died and I had no *real* idea of what heaven was. I was just four years old, staying in a house that wasn't my home. The first I knew of my mother not being there for me any more was when Uncle Cliff made this brief, unexplained comment. In retrospect, it seems a very callous and stupid thing to say to a four-year-old, even though I realise it was not deliberate but probably uttered in panic.

Astonishing as it may seem nowadays, after that point I was largely left on my own to deal with any grief I may have felt. I was taken on the six-mile journey home to Penclawdd; I didn't attend my mother's funeral, and nothing was ever explained. Nowadays, people talk of the importance of reaching 'closure' after any kind of trauma but in the 1940s that was a wholly alien concept. I didn't find the traditional mourning process to be helpful at all: seeing friends and relatives wearing black for days on end only prolonged my sadness and, I suppose, prevented me from being able to move on from that dark time in my young life.

My abiding memory of this entire period, beyond feeling

confusion over why my mother was no longer there, was of our new home. My father and I moved out of the house we had lived in as a family of three, swapping places with Ivor and his wife Llewella, and taking up residence with my grandmother and aunt, so that the two women could look after us. Benson Cottage became the place I would call home from the age of five until I left Penclawdd for university. Despite the sadness of family bereavement, I had a wonderfully carefree childhood with my dad, our cat Sparky, our budgie Kiki, my Aunty Ev and my mam – short for *mamgu*, Welsh for 'grandmother'. It was by no means a stoic existence: within the confines of society at the time, our family was very open and warm. There were many women in my life, all of whom felt sorry for me as an only child with no mother – and all of whom I called 'aunty', even when they were not related to me. Aunty 'Fanw (Myfanwy), for example: she lived next door and she's still there, aged ninety-seven.

My father, born and raised in the village, went to Gowerton Boys' Grammar School, three miles up the road, which I also attended many years later. He went on to Caerleon College, near Newport, where he trained to be a teacher. Everyone tells me that he was an outstanding rugby player. He played as a stand-off half for the 'All Whites' (Swansea) while still at school. Mam once told me how he returned home one Boxing Day in a sorry state, having broken his collarbone in a match against London Welsh on their annual tour of the principality. My father could also, reputedly, clear his own height in the high jump – but then he was not very tall. I did see him play cricket for Penclawdd though, on the 'Rec'.

My father was to be the greatest influence in my life, both personally and musically. He was multi-talented: a photographer who 'did weddings' at weekends, a teacher of art and pottery, a producer of school plays, but above all he was a musician. His instruments were the piano, which he also taught, and the organ.

It has been suggested to me that I must have inherited my father's creativity; and if these things are indeed genetic, then this could be the case. But my dad had a far wider skill set than I have. Whereas my interests have always by and large been confined to music, he had the most extraordinarily broad range of hobbies, and a real desire for knowledge, too. His creative thirst was all expressed at an amateur, local level, but it was none the poorer for that. I'm proud of the fact that my father was respected and revered by a great many people. Even nowadays, former pupils of his come up to me to say what a great teacher he was. It's a wonderful thing to hear.

When my father went to the chapel to practise the organ, I often went with him. As my musical confidence grew, having started piano with him, I would sometimes play a little myself but generally I went simply to listen. My father's passion was the music of Bach.

Many family groups had nicknames. Ours was 'the Baswrs', an anglicised plural of the Welsh word *baswr*, meaning 'bass', due to a preponderance of good male singing voices in the extended family.

The link between religion and society in my little part of South Wales was very strong, and its importance should not be underestimated. Everyone attended one of the chapels and there was often quite fierce yet ultimately trivial rivalry between the different congregations. My family was very Christian, in the traditional sense: they were Nonconformist Methodists who followed the rules. They would wear their Sunday best, without fail, and alcohol would virtually never pass their lips – the only exception being a cheeky sherry at Christmas. They all had a living faith as well, though; it wasn't only about rules and regulations. My father was very devout: I used to ask him sometimes, later in life, why he had never remarried, but he was always of the firm belief that he would see my mother again, in 'the afterlife'.

There were two musical Jenkins families in the village and in our chapel. There was my father and I, and there was the family descended from William Jenkins 'Pen y Lan', the sobriquet deriving from the 'top of shore' area where he lived. My father eventually succeeded William's nephew Gwynfor as choirmaster and organist, the position becoming vacant on the death of the incumbent.

The two families did intermarry at one point when William Jenkins's niece Gwen married my uncle Alfryn, who had played the viola. When I composed *For the Fallen*, which takes as its text the Laurence Binyon poem, for the 2010 Festival of Remembrance at the Royal Albert Hall, I dedicated the piece to Alfryn, the pilot who had died in the Second World War. It begins with a viola solo in homage to him.

Some of my musical education came through Tabernacle Calvinistic Methodist Chapel. We would go there three times every Sunday, and the place had a very profound impact on me. As for the rest of my studies, I had an extremely positive experience of school, beginning at Penclawdd Infants. I sat next to John Ratti, whose father Ernesto (known by the more prosaic name of Ernie) was one of the many Italians who had come to South Wales and opened cafes, or betting shops. In his cafe Ernie used to serve what the locals called 'frothy coffee', which was, of course, cappuccino. He had a massive Gaggia coffee machine and he also made exceptionally good ice-cream. In common with the other Italians and Germans already living in the United Kingdom, Ernie had been interned during the war. I can recall Gwynfor Jenkins bringing tears to this lovely man's eyes by intoning parts of the Latin Mass to him in Ratti's Café.

Penclawdd Infants was followed by Penclawdd Junior, where I still sat next to John Ratti. We used to take the bus through the village to the 'west end' where the school stood. The bus stop was outside 'Morgans the Forge' and the blacksmith would often be shoeing the cockle and farm horses there in the morning. I can still smell the sizzling moment when he placed the red-hot shoe on the animal's hoof and see the resulting cloud of smoke.

John Ratti always was a joker. His father's cafe had a window display of confectionery including Cadbury's chocolates. To avoid them melting in the sunshine, they had cardboard innards. One April Fools' Day John happily gave them to the teachers.

The headmaster at junior school was the same Gwynfor Jenkins. He had a useful sideline in hot weather making ice cubes on a stick and selling them for a penny (an 'old penny', of course, with 240 to a pound). Gwynfor was a good musician and introduced us to the tonic sol-fa technique for sight singing: *do, re, mi, fa, sol, la, ti, do.*

As a child, I took part in *Cymanfa Ganu* (congregational singing festivals) and was exposed to that raw style of four-part hymn singing that definitely was to be a lasting influence on me. The local community took these festivals seriously, and that attitude was infectious. People often say that Wales is a musical nation and, to a certain degree, it is; but it's really only singing that the Welsh like. I doubt that the knowledge of classical music in Wales is particularly extensive, at least no more so than anywhere else, but it's certainly true that the Welsh are a cut above the rest of the UK when it comes to the ability to sing in four-part harmony.

At chapel, there was also the annual oratorio concert when the choir would perform a work such as Handel's *Messiah* or Mendelssohn's *Elijah*. These were not, by any means, parochial affairs. The Morgan Lloyd Orchestra was hired and soloists often came from London. (Morgan, once a prodigy, had studied at the Royal Academy of Music, where I was later to go.) As young artists some now-famous names including Dame Janet Baker, Raimund Herincx, Philip Langridge and Heather Harper appeared, and much later, after I had left, a young baritone named Bryn Terfel Jones.

When my father became organist and choirmaster, he transcribed the whole of Fauré's *Requiem* into tonic sol-fa for the choir since this was the only system they could read, not the 'old notation', as what we generally know to be printed music was called.

It was quite a vibrant tradition. The other big chapel, Bethel, performed annual oratorios as well and, for these occasions, choirs used to join together to swell the numbers, setting their customary tribal rivalry aside. Oratorios were known as 'books', so a question might be asked about a conductor: 'What book is David taking next year?' There was even an 'oratorio of the oratorios' called *Comforting Words*, consisting of the most popular movements from a selection of them. Whether the libretto made any sense I do not know.

A once local 'girl' sometimes featured in these oratorio performances: Maureen Guy, the daughter of a coal miner, who had attended Bethel Chapel, Gowerton Girls' Grammar School and the Guildhall School of Music. She had become a mezzo-soprano of distinction, singing at Stravinsky's eightieth birthday celebrations, with the composer conducting his *Oedipus Rex*. She is also one of the Rhinemaidens on Georg Solti's iconic 1960s recording of Wagner's *Ring Cycle*. My father took their wedding photographs when she married, at Bethel Chapel, the tenor John Mitchinson. She died in 2015.

Growing up in Penclawdd, there were so many characters in the village, many with nicknames: there was 'Dai Kick' (the rugby stand-off half who would never pass the ball); 'Mrs America' (she'd been there once); 'Paris Fashions' (she liked to dress well); 'Selwyn Flat Roof' (his house had one); 'Jumper' (as a boy I was told it was because he was good at the long jump, but later learned it was because he had twenty children). Then there was Ivor Rees the cobbler, who had only one hand, and at the Memorial Hall cinema there was 'usherette' Sergeant Lord, a retired policeman, whose role was not to show customers to their seat but to shine his torch in people's faces to stop them talking or throwing sweet wrappers at the screen.

My father's cousin, Griff Griffiths, was both barber and undertaker, leading to inevitable comparisons with Sweeney Todd. We had a Dai Bun (a baker) and a Dai Brush (a painter and decorator), Morgan Morgans known as 'Morgans Twice', Willie Jones 'the French' (he saw action there in the First World War), 'Leonard the Coal' and 'Gwyn the Milk'.

When Gwyn the Milk did the rounds for his customary free Christmas drink, it was the only time in the year that he took off his cap. His bald head was two shades: a dark weather-beaten face with a snow-white pate. He used to deliver his milk with Tommy the horse and a cart, with his dog Peter in tow. I remember when his milk was delivered in churns and dispensed by a jug; after all, this was a time when farmers like Gwyn actually milked their own cows and sold their own milk. When pasteurisation came in, Gwyn always insisted that the bottled milk he got back from the dairy was his very own. He had such a long milk round and such a slow method of delivery that we always had our milk in the afternoon – and, in summer, very warm milk it was too.

Perhaps my favourite character of all is Will Hopkins, who played the double-bass. His nephew, Glynn Rees, was responsible for the first television set I ever saw. Glynn worked in London for one of the early television manufacturers, and he assembled a set for his uncle. Being hard of hearing, Will used an enormous ear trumpet. He had his favourite chair and he would not budge from it. Because of the way the aerial had to be positioned, the television set would work only in a certain part of the room. For many years, Will, with his ear trumpet, watched television in the mirror hanging on the opposite wall. I wonder if it affected how he saw certain aspects of life.

Life at school, meanwhile, carried on. I used to walk the mile home but often my father, having finished his day teaching at around the same time, would collect me on his bike, which had a child seat fixed on the crossbar. For the last year or so at junior school, I was in the eleven-plus 'scholarship class' and too big for the crossbar. This class was not selective. Some families didn't want their offspring even to attempt to gain a place at the grammar school. They would go on to Penclawdd Secondary Modern and leave to work at fourteen.

Our teacher, Ivor Davies, was a very strict disciplinarian of the old school and a bachelor, brandishing a cane that he was not loath to use. He sometimes took us outside for 'physical jerks', exercising in the schoolyard, still wearing his blue serge suit and trilby, and flexing his cane. He was also well known in the area for delivering dramatic Victorian monologues such as Kipling's 'You're a Better Man Than I Am, Gunga Din'.

My best friends out of school were the brothers Jeff and Brent Rees. Jeff was older than me and Brent was younger. The orchard of their garden backed onto Benson Cottage and we spent hours in this magical place. One winter we built an igloo. We compacted snow quite thickly in a circle and placed some corrugated tin sheets over the top to serve as the base of a roof before covering that with more snow. It was still standing in April, long after the snows had gone. We also constructed a tree house with some planks and rope. It was probably not very safe but we had enormous fun. Sadly, Jeff perished in a motor accident in his early twenties and Brent took his own life not long after. I sometimes spent time with two other brothers, Geoffrey and Ian Nichols, who also lived in Benson Street. In a bizarre coincidence, Ian, while still a young man, was also killed on the road, in a motorcycle accident.

I recall playing cricket in Benson Street, the wicket being drawn on the door of 'Uncle' Haydn's garage. The Christian names Haydn and Handel were quite common in Wales at that time, no doubt taken from the composers of the popular oratorios *The Creation* and *Messiah*.

I had also joined the Boy Scouts, which met in Dunvant, a village some five miles away. Six of us used to travel, by bus once a week, from Penclawdd, to learn skills such as semaphore signalling, Morse code, first aid, and igniting a fire without matches to make 'twist' (cooking dough wrapped around a stick). How useful those skills were in the 20th century was somewhat questionable but it was immense fun and I did gain my Scouts 'Musician' badge as well. What I did not enjoy, however, were the feelings of homesickness that pervaded at this time. I remember the very first occasion I really missed home: our Boy Scouts troop went camping in Oxwich, a beautiful bay in South Gower. The feeling of loneliness and isolation at that time was all encompassing; around that point, I was always worrying about my loved ones if they weren't with me, feelings that persist to this day, undoubtedly stemming from the loss of my mother.

Two other friends from those days at school were Spencer Howells, the son of the chapel caretaker, and Gillian Matthews. Spencer went on to have a blistering academic career, with periods of study at both Cambridge and Oxford Universities, before becoming a research scientist.

I was determined to have someone accompany me when I began exploring jazz at the piano, so I removed the strings from an old banjo and converted it into a side drum so that Spencer could play along after chapel on Sunday nights. The banjo has a skin-headed soundbox, just like a drum. We had a defunct TV aerial, so I cut out two pieces of the thin hollow aluminium tubes into which I hammered some bristles from a brush, thus producing a pair of 'jazz brushes'. Spencer later bought a snare drum. Much later I was best man at his wedding.

Gillian (my first 'girlfriend', when we were six) eventually married Tony Small, who is now a very close friend of mine. He is a fine trumpeter who was destined to stay two years ahead of me at the same five academic institutions, from Penclawdd Infants and Junior

Schools, through Gowerton Grammar and Cardiff University to the Royal Academy of Music in London.

All the way through my youth, I enjoyed playing the piano, my father having taught me from the age of six, but I was never more than adequate, despite passing some early Associated Board examinations with distinction. Having a parent as a teacher is not necessarily a good idea, since there is an inevitable familiarity there that somehow compromises the pupil–teacher relationship; what's more, I hadn't yet found my 'real' instrument, the one that would perfectly suit me.

Because I had started school early, I had two attempts at the eleven-plus scholarship, passing the second time, and in September 1956 I began at Gowerton Boys' Grammar School. I might have been at a new school, but some things remained reassuringly the same. Happily, I was still sitting next to John Ratti.

2

THE TEENAGE YEARS

*D*uring the late 1950s and early 1960s, my days were punctuated with the three-mile bus journey from Penclawdd to Gowerton Boys' Grammar School. It was a place of academic, sporting and musical achievement and excellence, with a catchment area covering the whole of the Gower Peninsula, together with some other villages towards Swansea in the east and Loughor Bridge in the west. Loughor Bridge was the gateway to Carmarthen and west Wales; at one time, it was very busy on Sundays since on the Glamorgan side the pubs were open and on the Carmarthen side they were not.

There were about sixty boys in the annual intake, divided into two forms. I later came to love it there, but at first I found it extremely difficult to cope with the new surroundings. I started to develop a stammer, and I felt paralysed by it. Reading aloud in class was torture. I was always looking ahead to calculate what passage would come my way and what letter the text would start with. Ws were horrendous; As OK. It took two years for the stammer to disappear. In the context of a lifetime, I realise that's not very long, but it always caused me great anguish.

Some other issues also surfaced during this pre-pubescent period, without doubt caused by the same demon I was subconsciously dealing with: the death of my mother. I was prone to blushing and when discussions took place, whether formal or informal, regarding one's mother, as inevitably surfaced occasionally, my stomach churned and I felt like crawling into a hole. I somehow felt ashamed – not a healthy consequence. I suppose I've been introverted and taciturn ever since.

I was homesick, which in retrospect seems an absurd thing to say since we were all, as grammar school boys, day students. I even had family to hand in that my Aunty Ev, who had raised me with my grandmother and my father since my mother had died, was working in the school kitchen as a cook.

Over time, though, the issue receded. I lost my stammer and I began to appreciate what was on offer at Gowerton – and beyond. Aunty Ev had very much become my surrogate mother; and I, her surrogate son. She had been widowed in the 1930s and had no children. A wonderfully warm and caring woman, she was extremely popular. She also had a good soprano voice and sung both in the chapel choir and in the mixed choir that had started in the village and of which my father was the accompanist. At Christmas lunch in Gowerton School, Aunty Ev used to dress up as Santa and give the embarrassed all-male staff, sitting at the head table, a gift and a kiss.

She was quite a character. Many years later, Jody, my son, and I were about to sit down with her to watch, on television, a rugby international involving Wales. She was then well into her eighties and soon began dozing off in her chair. She suddenly opened one eye and said, 'Wake me up if there's a fight!'

Morfar had died when I was ten, and my Swedish great aunts, Lily, Hilda and Mia, were to leave this world during my teenage years and shortly beyond. So I went over to Sweden to attend three separate funerals during the next ten years or so. The eldest, Lily, the only one with any real English, went first. They all lived well into their nineties but none of them married, leaving me bereft of any Swedish relatives, and of the possibility of becoming bilingual, which never developed beyond fledgling status.

I should mention the question of language in Wales. It was pretty much a lottery as to whether one was Welsh-speaking or not. If a child came from a Welsh-speaking family, it was almost certain that the offspring would speak some Welsh as well. To what extent often depended on whether or not Welsh was the first language of one of the parents. Some families spoke only English; some, only Welsh; and others mixed them up, using both. One could almost draw a diagonal line across Gower from Llanmadoc (at the northern end of the iconic three-mile Rhossili Bay) in the north-west, to Swansea in the south-east. South of that line was a land of agriculture and farming with sandy beaches, dramatic cliff scenery, coastal caves – and virtually no Welsh spoken. North of that line was an area of salty marshes and with an industrial past where Welsh was spoken, but not universally. Incredibly, many celebrated English-language actors came from a relatively small area around Swansea: Richard Burton, Ray Milland, Anthony Hopkins, Siân Phillips, Michael Sheen, Catherine Zeta Jones and, of course, the poet Dylan Thomas, who wrote in English. Neither I nor any of my friends spoke Welsh. My father could, to a certain extent, but no one else in the family was even close to being bilingual, let alone trilingual. Whether my Swedish-speaking mother spoke some Welsh, I don't know.

I came from a generation where learning Welsh was neither actively encouraged nor compulsory in schools. There was even a school of thought, which had some currency at the time, that speaking Welsh could 'hold one back'. This sentiment, I should add, was not universally held but the general perception was that English was the language of opportunity and the future.

I therefore took French and Latin for O level, instead of what some would consider should have been my mother tongue. The situation has since changed, with the Welsh language becoming compulsory in schools. Today, most young people in the principality are indeed bilingual, with some schools teaching all subjects through the medium of Welsh. Indeed, the actual building I attended is now such a Welsh school. Wales is officially a bilingual country and I regret not learning the language.

Today, I associate Gowerton School with so many happy memories. The music department was, quite simply, amazing. Sadly, it puts what is available nowadays in schools to shame and is an indictment of what has happened to music education in this country. The music teacher was C. K. (Cynwyd King) Watkins, and many fine musicians went through his hands. Alun Hoddinott, the composer, was one such. Hoddinott taught me composition and orchestration at Cardiff University, where he was a lecturer and, later, head of department.

Early class music lessons at Gowerton were relatively basic and general – more like music appreciation – since all boys took the subject, but once one decided to study music at O level, that all changed. Lessons then entailed harmony, some counterpoint, aural training, music history, form and analysis. Astonishing as it may seem in today's relatively impoverished educational world, every orchestral instrument was on offer, with tuition provided by expert peripatetic teachers. Moreover, both the use of the instrument and the lessons were completely free of charge. Of course, if a child showed a degree of aptitude for playing, parents were then encouraged to buy an instrument for their child so that the school instrument was then available for a new entrant. But a lack of money was never ever a barrier to opportunity.

It both saddens and angers me that in the 21st century a great many British children are never afforded the opportunity to get anywhere near a musical instrument, or even to sing. There must be thousands of people who are innately good musicians but are not aware of it, since they escaped what has become a very small net. I sometimes record in Helsinki with Finnish singers, and the educational structure there is beyond compare. All children learn to read music, sing and play; many have very little talent but at least they are given the chance to find out whether they do or not. This approach, more importantly, can foster a love of music. I realise that Finland is a small country with a population of 5 million but we shouldn't be in the state that we are.

It was not just the grammar schools in Wales that offered free instrumental tuition: this was true of secondary modern schools as well, such as Penclawdd, where my father was deputy head. Coincidentally, my wife had similar opportunities in Leicestershire where there was also a vibrant music education policy. In 2013 I was involved in a radio debate about cuts in Wales when it was decided to end peripatetic instrumental teaching in Gwent schools. A question was raised in respect of Germany, where they were *increasing* such funding in difficult economic times. Germany saw it as 'investing in the cultural future of the country'; if only we did the same in the UK. But I understand, at the time of writing, that cuts are now being introduced there as well. It is also a well-established fact that the learning of music helps skills in other areas. In addition, playing with others, as in a group or an orchestra, instils 'old-fashioned' virtues: loyalty, team spirit, discipline. This is why I would always recommend, if a child shows an aptitude for the piano, that he or she learns another instrument as well so that they can share the experience of music making with others, in an ensemble or an orchestra. Piano playing can be a lonely business but it is a great springboard for all music skills.

The peripatetic teachers my contemporaries and I encountered had ample credibility as instrumentalists in their own right. The cello, for example, was taught by Antonio Duvall, who had played in the orchestra of La Scala, Milan. I was somewhat ambivalent about what instrument I should try but my father, mindful of my growing ability on the recorder, suggested the oboe, the instrument he loved above all others. I had already started to play the recorder to a decent standard while at junior school, and the fingering, as with all woodwind instruments, is similar, so once I managed to make a sound, I could actually play some music.

My oboe teacher was Vincent Hanny, who, at that time, was playing in theatres in the area. We had one-to-one instrumental lessons once a week but they were rotated through the timetable so that we didn't always miss the same academic lesson. Even so, in a school that prided itself on its musical prowess, some teachers were very condescending when one had to go and ask permission for leave of absence for a music lesson – a battle that one could have done without. However, some of the teachers actually played in the school orchestra. Glyn Samuel, a physics teacher, was a flautist, and George Bowler, the Latin master, played double-bass. Bowler's lessons were a toss-up between learning some Latin or him regaling his captive audience with his war exploits with Field Marshal Montgomery, 1st Viscount Montgomery of Alamein, KG, GCB, DSO, PC (he never failed to reel those letters off). Every morning, the school orchestra would play for assembly – and once I was a half-decent oboist, a favourite piece of mine was Schubert's 'Unfinished' Symphony, since it has a fine oboe solo in the opening movement. For tuning up, C. K. Watkins had composed a clever little ditty called *The Enemy*, subtitled 'Give us an A', played on the piano, with a repeated A and changing harmonies underneath.

Come Christmas time, there were concerts involving the orchestra and choir and, as a woodwind group, we sometimes played for school productions of Shakespeare plays. We also (as English literature students) undertook school trips to the Royal Shakespeare Company at Stratford upon Avon. I saw Paul Scofield's *King Lear* there. Many years later, I discovered that my future wife, who went to school in Leicestershire, had been on a school trip that season to the same play.

Five years behind me, playing the cello, was Dennis O'Neill, who was later to become one of the world's leading tenors. We sometimes had guest musicians give recitals to the school: one was David Mason, a trumpeter who, in 1967, gained some fame by playing the piccolo trumpet solo on the Beatles' 'Penny Lane'.

As one became gradually more proficient, there was an established route to be negotiated to the National Youth Orchestra of Wales (NYOW), or the 'Nash' as it was called. The Welsh really do like abbreviations. The progression was the West Glamorgan Youth Orchestra (the 'West Glam'), the Glamorgan Youth Orchestra (the 'Glam') and then the 'Nash'. Attending the West Glamorgan Youth Orchestra was a logistical nightmare for me: it was held on Friday evenings in Neath and it involved two bus journeys. Getting there was possible but the return, via Swansea, meant I couldn't get home, since the second bus service on the return leg had stopped running by then. We didn't own a car; I went a couple of times but it proved too much of a trek.

My first rehearsal was scary. The first oboe player hadn't turned up that evening so I had to sight read a piece that I hadn't heard and which began with a fearsome oboe solo: the Overture to *The Italian Girl in Algiers* by Rossini. It was a shock but I think I got away with it. Just.

The Glamorgan Youth Orchestra was residential and met three times a year. These courses were held at Ogmore, South Glamorgan, on the coast. The place was a county educational establishment that had been some kind of military barracks in the past. We slept in long dormitories, two for boys, one for girls, and we had sectional rehearsals by day with full orchestral rehearsals in the evening.

I vividly recall the sheer weight of sound around me in the very first rehearsal when we struck up with the opening bars of Handel's *Water Music*. It was incredibly exciting, suddenly feeling part of something on a grand scale, with dozens of other like-minded young people who were also eagerly exploring this music for the very first time. There would always be a concert at the end of the course in one of the towns of Glamorgan – never in Swansea or Cardiff, though, since they each had their own youth orchestra. Russell Shepherd, the County Music Organiser, was our conductor; he was an excellent musician but he could be a bit of a fusser. My favourite memory of 'Shep' was when, during a power cut in the middle of a full rehearsal, our principal cellist Wayne Warlow lit a match. 'Get out, you madman!' Shep screamed at him. 'You'll burn us in our beds!'

By this stage of my childhood, school was progressing well and I was usually in the top three or four come the end of the year. In the third year, we had to make choices regarding our O levels and take the arts or science route. I took arts but there was one anomaly even so. I had to make a choice between art (as in painting) or music. This seemed most odd to me. As well as music, I also loved sport, particularly athletics, at which I represented the school at county level. The long jump and the triple jump were my events. My enthusiasm for sport manifested itself in regular trips to Swansea with my father to watch the rugby.

When I was about sixteen, two important things happened. Firstly, my grandmother (Mam) died. She was a fine woman, the head of the family as I was growing up. She could look quite severe with her hair drawn back in a bun but she had a great sense of humour, was an excellent cook and had raised me with Aunty Ev and my father. Mam was the first deceased person I had ever seen. She had passed away in her sleep; I kissed her, said goodbye, and reflected on what a special part she had played in my life. The second moment of significance – and, thankfully, it was a far happier one – was that I then had an epiphanic moment at school when I heard jazz for the first time. Some of the more senior boys I knew from the orchestra were playing this strange and wonderful music on a record-player in the music room during a lunch break. The actual artist was the black Canadian pianist Oscar Peterson, and I was mesmerised. From that point onwards, I would be hooked on jazz, becoming avid in my reading about this music. I slowly built up a record collection to complement the classical one my father was building at home, and I also bought a tenor saxophone. This instrument, again, has similar fingering to the oboe and recorder, so I was soon up and running, trying to play along with some of the jazz LPs I'd bought.

As an art teacher, my father had graduates with him from time to time for teacher training. One such was David Randall Davies – also from Penclawdd – a very fine artist, who, although not a musician himself, had a passion for music. Together he and my father built a hi-fi system that sounded fabulous. They bought the mechanical units such as the actual speakers and amps but then housed them in acoustically designed but home-built cabinets. This was the time when stereo was first becoming available to the public. We had a stereo demonstration LP that included the sound of a train 'going through the front room'. This seemed to impress visitors more than any music that was played.

As I moved into the heart of my teenage years, I soon found out about girls – or, more accurately, one particular girl by the name of Janet Williams. Janet was also from Penclawdd and went to Gowerton Girls' Grammar School, which was about three hundred yards from the boys' school. Many lads had girlfriends there and we used to squeeze through a gap in the fence and wander over in the lunch break, to chat through the railings. It always seemed to me to be akin to visiting jail. I was with Janet for quite a while, until my early twenties. However, that relationship was doomed from the day her mother said, 'If you want to marry my daughter, you'll have to give up the music!'

I was still sitting next to John Ratti, since we broadly took the same subjects for O level, one of which was Geography. He was still a joker. It was a particularly humid day and the lesson happened to be about humidity. The teacher (a not particularly pleasant man called Gilbert Davies) asked the class why the day was so oppressive and unbearable. John Ratti nudged me saying, 'Tell him it's because we have a geography lesson today.' So, foolishly eager to oblige, my hand shot up and I answered accordingly. I was dismissed and banned from geography lessons for two weeks.

In 1962 I entered the sixth form, taking A levels in Music, English Literature and History. Initially there were three music students alongside me: John Weeks (flute), Wynne Edwards (trombone) and Derrick Cousins (horn). Like me, they were all were in the Glamorgan Youth Orchestra. Then Derrick decided to run away from home; I've no idea why. His family was Salvationist and he played tenor horn in the local Salvation Army band. I heard nothing about him for years and then learned that he had turned up in Canada.

Wynne Edwards had a terrible problem in that he used to have blackouts that lasted a few minutes. He would go ashen white and his body would freeze and become statue-like, even when he was standing up. There was no intimation as to when this would happen and he didn't know himself. If it happened during a music lesson 'Watty' (C. K. Watkins) would whisper and tell us to pretend nothing was happening. I don't know why, since poor Wynne was oblivious to it himself. It was darkly comedic, if rather cruel, that if it happened as we were leaving school and he was standing, boys would hang their satchels or coats on him. Wynne is no longer with us. He died young, no doubt because of his illness. No one ever explained what the problem was but it must have been a neurological disease of some kind. He wanted to be a teacher but was denied a place at teacher training college because of this medical problem.

Apart from studying together, we were also, by then, in the 'Nash', which for us Welsh boys represented the apotheosis of our ambition and attainment. In fact, it is the oldest national youth orchestra in the world, founded in 1945. I only ever knew of one Welsh boy or girl who went instead to the National Youth Orchestra of Great Britain, and that was bassoonist Bob Codd, but that was probably because he went to school in Bristol. We met when we began the first year of university together. The NYOW used to meet every summer in Llandrindod Wells in mid-Wales; after a week or so of rehearsing we undertook a concert tour of Wales, which always included a performance at the National Eisteddfod – wherever it was taking place that year. (Ingeniously, the Eisteddfod is held in a movable pavilion that alternates between South and North Wales on an annual basis.) Our instrumental tutors were, in the main, from the London orchestras – and for us woodwind players it was clarinettist Stephen Waters. He performed in the Brain Ensemble with the legendary horn player Dennis Brain and his oboist brother Leonard Brain, who later was to teach me at the Royal Academy of Music. The NYOW also ran a B orchestra and that course ran concurrently with the main orchestra but didn't give concerts. The programme was the same. Some excellent players went through the ranks, many eventually joining major London orchestras, but two in particular made an impression on me: Roy Gillard and Terence 'Drac' Johns. They were both from the village of Hirwaun but for some reason they went to different schools, Drac in Glamorgan (so I already knew him from the 'Glam') but Roy across the county line in Brecon, so the NYOW course was the first time I met him.

I don't know quite why Terence Johns was called Drac (short for 'Dracula'). Some say it was because he only came out at night. He had high cheekbones and black hair, and he was one of those charismatic people to whom others used to gravitate. He too, like me, went on to the Royal Academy of Music, eventually joining the Royal Philharmonic Orchestra. Drac later became Principal Horn in the London Symphony Orchestra, during the ensemble's flamboyant days with conductor André Previn. He then ran a pub in Brecon, which turned out to be not such a good idea, before moving up to Scotland where he resumed playing the horn.

Later, violinist Roy Gillard would on occasion lead both the London Philharmonic Orchestra and the Philharmonia Orchestra. The first time I heard him play was when he was about twelve. When we arrived for the NYOW course, the A and B orchestras played together for the first rehearsal; you can imagine how many players there were. In an orchestra, the strings (violins, violas, cellos, basses) sit two by two, sharing the same music and stand. Each pair is called a desk. Roy was at the back somewhere, twenty desks or so away from the podium. Our conductor was Clarence Raybould. There was a particularly difficult passage for the violins, and Clarence asked the leader to play it. He then went back through every desk, player by player, asking them to play the same passage. He eventually came to Roy, and when he had played the passage there was a resounding cheer. Raybould then moved everyone (apart from the leader) back a place so young Roy was on the front desk from then on.

Another member, who was principal viola, was John Cale, who was to become well known in rock circles due to his association with Lou Reed and the Velvet Underground. We sometimes had jazz jam sessions in our 'down time'; Drac was a good improviser and Wayne Warlow, cellist from the Glam, a mighty fine bass player. Wayne was multi-talented and played the oboe as well. John Cale came along with his Dave Brubeck songbook and played something from that. This seemed odd to me since we were supposed to be improvising. He also wrote some classical avant-garde pieces, once presenting a chart that, among other things, had a photo of a swastika and a lavatory pan stuck onto it. We were meant to improvise, depicting the said object through what we played.

Meanwhile, A levels were approaching – and, at school, our teachers were as interesting as some of the topics we had to study. Take the history teacher, Moir Gilchrist. He had a habit of pushing out his tongue, like a snake, which, inevitably, led to the boys counting each execution, and betting on the total during a lesson – not that money changed hands. My English teacher was Gilbert Bennett, a lovely man and an inspirational teacher. Thanks to him, I can still recite the opening of Chaucer's *Canterbury Tales* in Middle English. He also did BBC radio commentaries on Welsh rugby internationals.

I had applied to three or four universities to read music but really wanted to go to only Cardiff, which had an outstanding music department. I gained an A in music, along with a B and C in my other subjects, so I was on my way.

3

BEYOND PENCLAWDD

*I*n 1963, the Beatles released their first album (*Please, Please Me*), *Lawrence of Arabia* was one of the year's most popular films, and the nation's favourite TV shows ranged from *The Avengers* to *The Flintstones*. It was also the year President Kennedy was assassinated. In Cardiff, meanwhile, I was starting my Bachelor of Music degree course.

The university was set in a particularly attractive part of the city called Cathay's Park. The National Museum of Wales was there and the area almost had a Parisian look to it, with its wide, tree-lined avenues. Professor Joe Morgan was the head of the faculty, and the universally excellent lecturers were Alun Hoddinott, David Evans, and two unrelated Bruces: Ian and Robert. I had played a piece by the latter with the National Youth Orchestra of Wales: it had the rather wacky title of *The Dong with the Luminous Nose*, as it was a musical depiction of the Edward Lear poem.

The course was very academic, and I quickly immersed myself in everything it offered: harmony, counterpoint, fugue, orchestration, music history, figured bass, composition and much more. Looking back, it's funny to think that this was the 'Swinging Sixties'. My love of my subject, and being into jazz, did genuinely mean that much of the social change that was taking place in the West almost passed me by. I was aware of it, and I enjoyed Beatles albums when they were released – but the whole social-upheaval element was relatively lost on me. Similarly, while I can remember situations where drugs were available and offered to me, I've never partaken of an illegal substance, beyond one drag of a joint (which, to be honest, did absolutely nothing for me – so I quickly decided to experiment no further). There have been periods of my life when I've taken too much alcohol, I'll admit, but the 'sex, drugs and rock 'n' roll' revolution was certainly not something I found myself swept up in.

In that first year in Cardiff, there were about fifteen of us studying music and I had three mates in particular: Roger Parker from Willenhall in Staffordshire played the trombone but was also an excellent jazz pianist; Howard Rees, whose father was the vicar of Ferryside in Carmarthenshire, and who played the clarinet; and the aforementioned bassoonist Bob Codd, the son of two doctors from Aberdare. Apart from the degree course, lessons were also offered on whichever instrument one played, usually by members of the BBC National Orchestra of Wales, then called the BBC Welsh Orchestra. I was very fortunate to have the principal oboist, Philip Jones, as my tutor.

On Wednesday afternoons, we had a tutorial that always focused on Palestrina counterpoint. Palestrina was an Italian Renaissance composer of sacred music whose work, by common consent, is seen as the apotheosis of polyphonic music of this period. Many years later, I quoted from his setting of *L'Homme armé (The Armed Man)* in the 'Christe Eleison' section of my work, *The Armed Man: A Mass for Peace*. This class was conducted in groups of three and was the only lecture or tutorial for which we had to wear our gowns. I attended this class with Roger and Bob; our tutor, Professor Joe Morgan, used to sit at his desk and effortlessly read and correct our exercises upside-down – no mean feat when dealing with the rather complex music of Palestrina. He could be quite dour, though. There was a TV series on at the time, involving comedians Peter Cook and Dudley Moore called *Not Only . . . But Also*. There was one sketch where Moore, who had actually been an organ scholar at Oxford and a jazz pianist, was playing a piano when it was lowered into the Thames. Professor Morgan was really put out and upset by this and declared indignantly, 'Did you see what they did to that piano on that programme?'

The university had a resident string quartet led by a Chilean violinist called Alfredo Wang; he used to swan about in a cloak and a broad-rimmed black maestro's hat. It was said that when he took a bath he always kept his left hand out of the water so as not to soften the calluses on his fingers. George Isaacs was the cellist, and the viola player was Gordon Mutter (who had given up playing in orchestras because they were too loud). The second violinist, James Barton, played left handed, which was really unusual and oddly uncomfortable to watch. They performed every Tuesday evening at the Reardon Smith Lecture Theatre (part of the National Museum of Wales) and students, although it was not compulsory, were expected to attend. Sometimes I missed the concerts because of my own unofficial jazz rehearsals but Joe Morgan, out of thirty or forty music undergraduates across the three-year course, always knew exactly who wasn't there and would remark on it during the subsequent lecture one had with him. Orchestration was with Alun Hoddinott, every Saturday morning at 9 a.m. It was not unknown for him to turn up for the lecture in his dinner jacket from the night before! He was a brilliant musician, and I learned so much from him.

During the first year at Cardiff University music students also had to study a language (which could be English). The popular line was to take the Italian option since the rumour was one would pass whatever standard one achieved. Not so. There was a handful of music students in this Italian class, but the remainder comprised forty or so language undergraduates who were reading French, Spanish or Portuguese as their main language. The class went from scratch to A-level standard in the one year. A few of us, not surprisingly, failed. This didn't matter in itself, although I wished I had made a better fist of it since Italy is now my favourite country to visit. In retrospect it was a mad decision. It meant that, moving into the second year, one had to opt for a 'Mains', not an 'Honours' degree. I've not heard of this anywhere else. The work was the same. The classes were the same. I had the option of repeating year one but I didn't see the point in that. All it meant was that the degree would not be classified, however well I did. It was somewhat irritating to those of us in the same boat, since we had not gone there to learn Italian.

Student accommodation in the university halls of residence was quite limited so, for my freshers year, I stayed in 'digs'. Leighton (the musician son of Gwynfor Jenkins) had trodden the same scholastic path: Penclawdd, Gowerton, and music at Cardiff. He put me in touch with his old landlady, a Mrs Copp, who had no vacancies but her friend, a Mrs Richards, did. The house was in the Victoria Park area of Cardiff and necessitated a trolley-bus ride to the university. A fellow lodger was a student from Carmarthen. He was redoing the same pharmaceutical exam for the third time. It became clear why when he asked me, 'What do they mean when they ask you to write a critical essay?' An evening meal was included in the rent and it was usually quite dreadful but, with the same menu on specific days each week, I knew what lay ahead. Mrs Richards would cook it earlier in the day and leave it warming in the oven; the trick was to get back before she did and flush it down the lavatory.

The former Labour leader, Neil Kinnock, and his future wife, Glenys, were one year ahead of me. Neil, always interested in politics, not surprisingly became President of the Students' Union. I, meanwhile, never really caught the political bug as a student. Back home, the whole family regarded themselves as Labour. It was ingrained. Labour, as it says on the tin, was for working-class people. Like many, I've gradually moved more to the centre ground of politics, as had the Labour party until 2010. While I would never want to criticise my family, who gave me a wonderful upbringing, I did find it odd that no one ever questioned their own political views (it was a case of 'we always have') but it was a different time then when socialism was socialism (not that many knew what the word meant) and unequivocally a better deal for the 'working class', and not just in South Wales. In the 2015 general election, the constituency of Gower became Tory for the first time in 109 years.

I've had a few heated debates about politics over the years. I remember very well a staunch Labour councillor who I bumped into at a friend's house where we were all watching a cricket match. Out of nowhere, he pointed at the team playing England, the West Indies, and remarked, 'I've always hated the black man.' I immediately challenged him; he simply repeated it. When I asked him how on earth he reconciled those views with his politics he looked genuinely puzzled. This particular case was an extreme example. I ultimately concluded that many of the people who labelled themselves socialists merely wanted a political badge to wear, but the councillor's attitude was a view more born of ignorance and lack of intelligence rather than pure racism. He had never even encountered a black person.

My closest friend during my three years in Cardiff was Roger Parker, the trombone player and excellent jazz pianist. While at university, I decided to change from tenor to baritone sax. There was less competition, as fewer musicians played the instrument, and at that time I was particularly enamoured with the playing of the famous American baritone sax player Gerry Mulligan. Quite early on, I discovered that the university had a Jazz Appreciation Society, so I made myself known. I met Robert (Bob) Jones, who was reading French and who also happened to be in my Italian class. He played jazz piano and, in fact, had gone to school in Aberdare with horn player Drac. Apart from us students, there were quite a few jazz musicians around – some who had been to the university and some from the town itself. Up until then, the Jazz Appreciation Society was just what the name implies. There had been no live jazz music there, so in the main it consisted of listening to records. That changed when we arrived, since, apart from those already mentioned, we also welcomed into our fold Jeff Cook (a double-bassist and ex-student who worked for the Prudential insurance company – the 'Pru') and a drummer by the name of Ieuan Thomas, who was reading English. We therefore had a quorum for a decent band.

Renamed 'Jazz Club', our sessions initially took place in the refectory of the Students' Union in Dumfries Place. The porter of the establishment was an abrasive cockney by the name of George Lambert; he did everything by the book. Since jazz is improvised, it's difficult to predict the duration of any jazz piece. On one occasion, a vibraphone player called Russ Jones was in full improvisational flight. A vibraphone needs electrical power to help create the sound but when 10.30 p.m. came, George strolled up to the stage and literally pulled the plug on him. Such sessions later moved to Park Place where the university concert venue was situated, and we started inviting guests down from London. One of the first was the Stan Tracey Quartet who performed his *Under Milk Wood* suite based on the Dylan Thomas radio play. The bass player was Jeff Clyne, with whom I would later work in London.

In the second year, I left Victoria Park and shared a flat, in Newport Road, with Bob Jones, before Roger, Howard and I took another flat at 5 Piercefield Place in Splott – an area of Cardiff where the journalist John Humphrys, whom I was soon to encounter in person, hails from. The rent collector used to appear on Saturday. We called him 'Cog' since every time he called, apologetically, for the rent he invariably said, 'I'm just a cog in this machine!' Many years later, I would compose a tune called *Splot!*, largely inspired by my memories of a very happy time there.

It was now the mid-1960s, and I was soon to meet an excellent guitarist named Tony Earnshaw, whose father was the timpanist in the BBC Welsh Orchestra. We 'jammed' together quite often, and he suggested he borrow his father's car and we go up to London to Ronnie Scott's Jazz Club. This was when it was in Gerrard Street, Soho. Ronnie was one of the doyens of British jazz: a tenor saxophone player, he was a true pioneer and had once had a band called the Jazz Couriers where he shared the 'front line' with fellow tenor player Tubby Hayes. Tubby had been a child prodigy and many consider him to be Britain's finest ever jazz musician. It was his new quintet that we went to see. The car took four, so drummer Ieuan Thomas came along with a friend of his, the aforementioned John Humphrys, who was then working on the *Western Mail* newspaper just before moving to BBC Wales.

The best jazz musician in Cardiff was, by a long way, the pianist Bernie Thorpe – a maths lecturer at the university. He came from Newcastle and had played with some musicians there who were known throughout the UK. One was the trumpeter Ian Carr, of whom more later. The premier jazz venue in the city was the Ghana Club on Bute Street. Known locally as Tiger Bay (where the singer Shirley Bassey comes from), this multicultural area encompassed Butetown and Cardiff Docks and was the red-light district of the city. In earlier times it had been very rough, even dangerous; by the 1960s, much of its reputation had faded but it still had an edge. The Ghana Club was a bar, but one night a week it became a jazz club, run by Johnny Silva, whose family owned the place. Johnny was a bass player (who played a lot of 'wrong' notes) and the house trio comprised of Bernie, Johnny and a variety of drummers. Many guests came down from London, musicians with whom I would later work, such as saxophonists Ray Warleigh and Dick Morrissey. Dick was a prodigiously talented improviser; self-taught, he never did learn to read music properly, but he was an amazing musician.

By this time we pretty much had a regular jazz quintet, for which I was writing most of the material. In my final year, we entered the UK Inter-University Jazz Competition. What one might call the 'serious rock' revolution had then not yet been established so the music of students, in so far as there was one at all, was jazz. At one of the college 'hops' the band was the John Dankworth Orchestra, perhaps the top 'big band' in the UK at the time and essentially a jazz band. During my teenage years, pop had been mainly white rock 'n' roll: Bill Haley and the Comets, and Elvis Presley from the US; Tommy Steele and Cliff Richard in the UK. Lonnie Donegan was a 'trad(-itional) jazz' banjo player who also sang. The fact that he had a hit with 'Does your chewing-gum lose its flavour on the bed post overnight?' gives some indication of what was around then.

The semi-final of the Inter-University Competition was held at the University of Sussex in Brighton. Lynton Naiff, who I would later get to know well in London, led a very good trio from Sussex. Trumpeter Ian Carr was the judge and we, with Sussex, went through to the final at Queen Mary University in London's East End. The judge this time was Jimmy Deuchar, who had been playing with the Tubby Hayes Quintet when we made our pilgrimage to Ronnie Scott's. We were ecstatic when it was revealed that the Cardiff University Jazz Quintet had won the competition. I think what swayed it for us was the fact that we played all original material, mainly written by me, whereas the rest performed jazz 'standards'.

We were also fortunate in that when visiting American jazz artists undertook a UK tour, they always played at the Capitol in Cardiff. Somewhat unusually, it was a cinema but it had a stage, so it doubled as a concert venue. I had a quite surreal experience one night: we had seen the Duke Ellington Orchestra play and much later that evening, Roger Parker and I were walking across Canton Bridge, spanning the River Taff. We saw two black men, sporting trilbies, on the bridge, approaching us through the drizzle, clearly lost. They turned out to be two living legends of jazz, from the Ellington band, alto saxophonist Johnny Hodges and baritone saxophonist Harry Carney. We had a chat (Carney a delight, Hodges dour) and helped them on their way.

Other American musicians we saw at the Capitol during my time there included my first jazz hero Oscar Peterson, singer Ella Fitzgerald, the bands of Count Basie and Stan Kenton and the piano great, Erroll Garner. A man of short stature, legend had it that he always sat on three or four Manhattan telephone directories on top of the piano stool, when he played. He did!

By now I had, broadly speaking, two great musical loves: classical and jazz. Since that time I have always resisted categorising music, certainly in terms of worthiness. My 'classical' upbringing had been nurtured by my father, both as a teacher with regard to the theory and history of music and also by him guiding me through his large LP collection. I suppose the mainstay of the collection were Austro-Germanic composers such as Bach, Haydn, Mozart and Beethoven, with a smattering of the French (Debussy, Ravel, Fauré) and some Russians (Tchaikovsky, Rachmaninov, Prokofiev and Stravinsky), with one-off works such as Bartók's Concerto for Orchestra. The only obvious genre that was missing was that of opera. We also had quite a few recordings of oboe concertos: by Albinoni,

Telemann, Cimarosa, Mozart and Richard Strauss, and the Bach Concerto for Violin and Oboe. I was immersed in these sounds from a very early age.

In addition, my father and I attended concerts together and were regular visitors to the Swansea Festival. I remember Witold Rowicki conducting the Warsaw Philharmonic Orchestra at the Brangwyn Hall in Swansea: sitting behind the orchestra, I was fascinated by his every move. The Polish composer Witold Lutosławski dedicated his Concerto for Orchestra to him. The Brangwyn Hall has an amazing sound for orchestral music: much like the Wiener Musikverein, home to the Vienna Philharmonic Orchestra, it is but a box, built before acoustic engineers got their hands on designing concert halls, but the sound is fantastic.

My interest in jazz had begun at school on first hearing Oscar Peterson. By reading and listening, I assimilated the music and started 'feeling out' chords at the piano. In that sense I was self-taught – but then, I firmly hold the belief that jazz cannot really be taught, just as I believe composition cannot be taught. In both, one can learn struc-ture and the basic tenets of method and style, but creating something that moves others emotionally is some kind of gift that one is born with. Since the jazz that grabbed me was 'modern jazz', that is where I started, in mid-history so to speak.

Jazz was born in the early 1900s in the US but what is known as 'modern jazz' began in New York in the 1940s, when a coterie of musicians – most of them black – began to experiment with more chro-matic harmony than had hitherto been used in the medium. The most important figures were Charlie Parker (saxophone), Dizzy Gillespie and Miles Davis (trumpet) and Thelonious Monk (piano). By the time I was approaching my late teens, Miles Davis had been forming a series of iconic bands and almost directing the course of the music singlehandedly. By judicious use of outstanding sidemen (musicians in a band other than the band leader), Davis changed the way rhythm sections (piano, double-bass, drums) played – and in the late 1950s he introduced jazz that was more modal (based on scales other than major or minor) with two iconic albums: *Milestones* and *Kind of Blue*.

For a simple explanation, think of modes as being a run of white notes on the piano. Playing eight consecutive white notes on the piano, from any one to its octave (eight notes) above, produces a mode. Playing between another note and its octave produces a different mode. Modes predated major and minor scales by hundreds of years. There is only one mode that is identical to a scale and that is from C to C, which forms the scale of C major while also being the Ionian mode. To form what we know as scales, we generally (other than for C major) have to introduce some black notes. Notes not belonging to the scale in which a passage of music is written are called chromatic notes.

At this time, coming through the Miles Davis Quintet was a man who some consider to be the greatest jazz musician of all time: the tenor saxophonist John Coltrane. He explored and extended the harmonic language of the music to a stage where it could go no further, with his later *Giant Steps* solo recording. Apart from formulating a harmonic style that had never been heard before in jazz, Coltrane also developed a sound that was hard and aggressive, and yet had a serene beauty as well. When improvising, he piled scale patterns on top of each other in a style known as 'sheets of sound', a description credited to critic Nat Hentoff (a rare occasion when a critic got something right). 'Trane's clones became legion. Every saxophone player on the planet seemed either to copy him slavishly or simply to give up. And all tenor players subsequently sounded like him.

The paradox was that 'modal' jazz was often more chromatic than what had gone before, since the music was not really modal in the sense of adhering to the prescribed scale. The improvisers, especially Coltrane on later solo albums, would pile chromaticism on top of chromaticism when improvising; it freed them from the shackles of a given chord progression by offering them a simple bass line on which they could pile their own flights of fancy. Much of it was more chromatic than hitherto, but it was a chromaticism of choice by the soloist over a simple ostinato bass or tonal centre, and not a chromaticism dictated by the chord progression of a tune with many shifting harmonies.

The *Kind of Blue* recording is acknowledged as being one of the great jazz albums of all time. Recordings of jazz are the equivalent to the 'full scores' of the classical world, since that is all we have. The music is transient, of the moment, and much has been lost by its improvisatory nature. *Kind of Blue* featured some of the greats of the music, notably Miles Davis, 'Trane, Julian 'Cannonball' Adderley and pianist Bill Evans, who I was privileged to meet a few years down the line when he came to Ronnie Scott's with his own trio. A musician of genuine genius, Bill Evans is the only one mentioned so far who was Caucasian, and one of perhaps only two white players (the other being saxophonist Stan Getz) who might be considered a jazz great.

To my mind, the history of jazz mirrors in one century that of classical music over many centuries – up to a point, at least. Simple beginnings, leading to increased use of chromaticism, nowhere left to explore, excursions into 'free jazz' (where improvisations were totally free and not based on any prescribed chord progression) and fusion with other genres, such as rock. A jazz performance is both predictable and unpredictable at one and the same time: when a piece is played, one knows what chord will sound at any given moment during the future course of that performance, but the improvisation at that point is where the magic and unpredictability lies.

The only music I ever composed for pleasure at this time was jazz. To me, jazz was everything that what passed for classical contemporary music wasn't. It was vibrant, exciting, had a tremendous sense of time, energy and rhythm; it was improvisatory and it was, and ever will be, *tonal*. In other words, it was based around a 'tonal centre' or in specific keys (as is all commercial music and all Western classical music up to the 20th century), as opposed to being atonal. A certain amount of charlatanism pervaded what passed for some – though by no means all – contemporary music. There were, and still are, many 'emperors with new clothes', but there was little in the way of memorable music that people wanted to hear again. Many composers could not 'hear' what they were writing. This style of music was jokingly called 'squeaky-gate'. No melody, no harmony; some composers themselves did not know when their music was being played correctly. To illustrate my point, a good friend of mine used to play in the BBC Symphony Orchestra. They played the same piece by a well-known composer, now deceased, on two separate occasions. The first time, the composer himself conducted it and the piece was performed to his satisfaction. Some time later, Pierre Boulez, whose musicianship is legendary, while rehearsing the piece with the same set of parts, found many notes in the orchestral parts that did not correspond to those in the score.

As far as contemporary classical composition was concerned, one was expected to write in this prescribed style of dissonance. I had no particular style, or 'voice' as it is called, at this time and for my degree I wrote a setting of three psalms for choir and orchestra. As with all students' degree scores, it is probably available for perusal in the Cardiff University library but I wouldn't recommend anyone looking it up. I haven't!

I was at home when the degree results came through and I was to phone my father, at his school, with whatever news arrived. Education was greatly cherished in the community and a university degree was the pinnacle of that. It meant a job, a career, a future, and it would be in music. We did not hear until quite late in the afternoon that I had graduated, by which time my father had left school and was cycling home. When he came through the door, I told him I was a B.Mus. He went into the living room, broke down and wept. A wave of compassion swept over me and I hugged him. There was always a special bond between us: he the single parent of a child who, in turn, had no siblings. My mother was always idolised by the many 'aunts', real and otherwise, who enveloped me while growing up. 'She was too good to live' was the phrase I often heard used to describe her. My dad was on his own and couldn't share this moment with her and me. I still sense a massive gap in the continuity of my life, in that it seems to be in two distinct parts, with Aunty Ev the only partial link because she saw and loved both Carol, my wife, and Jody, my son. But my parents seem to have occupied a different world in a different age, and light years away from my son and grandchildren, so there is no correlation between the two. It is as though I have had two lives.

I graduated with a Bachelor of Music degree in 1966. Unsure of what to do or where to go next, I had applied to the Royal Academy of Music in London for postgraduate studies and was accepted. The summer of that year was to prove pivotal in my life and my career path. The first Jazz Summer School took place at Barry Training College, South Wales, so I enrolled. Tutors included members of the Don Rendell–Ian Carr Quintet. Many young players came down from London, including Frank Ricotti (vibes and saxophone), who, thirty years later, played some percussion on my *Adiemus: Songs of Sanctuary*. Even BBC Wales dropped by, with John Humphrys interviewing me. One tutor was the jazz composer and bass player Graham Collier, who told me to get in touch when I came up to the Academy.

I was daunted, yet very excited, by what awaited me in London. My musical journey was now in full flow, and I couldn't wait to embrace the next part of it.

4

THE LURE OF LONDON

Whatever success I've enjoyed in recent years, I take nothing for granted, and if anyone were to ask me about my background or my class, I would still instinctively reply that the Jenkins family is, historically, a working-class one. That was certainly our way of life in Penclawdd: after all, despite the fact that my father was a teacher (a respectable, middle-class profession) and he had no mortgage to pay, he still resolutely refused to purchase a car. 'What would I need one of those for?' he would ask, on the regular occasions when I questioned why we still went everywhere on the bus or the train. However, I've always considered musicians, all 'artists' for that matter, as being beyond definitions of class – and another glorious facet of life as a musician is that there is no generation gap between any of us.

Prior to the age of twenty-one, I had never lived outside Wales. While I was growing up, we rarely travelled anywhere far afield – the only exception being the occasional bus tours to Switzerland that a colleague of my father, Miall Davies, used to organise, and of course I had been to Sweden several times. When I moved to London to study at the Royal Academy of Music, I was ready to embrace everything the capital had to offer. My first residence in London, while I looked for somewhere more permanent to live, was a hotel in Sussex Gardens, Paddington. A Welshman, Mr Carpenter and known as 'Carpi', ran it. I don't know why there are so many Welsh establishments in that area; it must be either because it is where the Welsh disembark, if they arrive by train, or because it is the nearest point from which to effect a rapid escape back to the 'land of their fathers'!

I eventually rented a house – 3 Glebe Road, Barnes – which was owned by a Mr Hyman Kaner. He seemed to be a writer of detective fiction since many of his paperbacks were strewn around the house. They had rather dated, quaint titles: one that sticks in the mind, even to this day, is a tome by the name of *Hot Swag*. My housemates were bassoonist Bob Codd, who was undertaking similar postgraduate studies as me but at the Royal College of Music, and Roger Parker, who took a music teaching post in London.

Not long after we moved in, someone wandering by heard Bob practising the bassoon and, suitably impressed, rang the doorbell. He happened to be a saxophone player by the name of Nigel Nash. We were looking for another person to share the rent so rather trustingly we gave him a room. Nigel was trying to escape some woman who kept ringing him up. Very early one morning, I heard the one and only phone in the house, which was downstairs. Since it remained unanswered for several minutes, I went down. The phone was smothered in overcoats and blankets in a futile attempt to muffle the sound, with Nigel hiding behind a door as though the receiver could see him. A very good saxophone player, though not an outstanding improviser, Nigel progressed to playing with the BBC Radio Big Band.

At first, the Royal Academy of Music tried to compel me to take the more theoretical subjects that I had already covered to a higher level for my degree, such as harmony and counterpoint. Since I was there primarily to study the oboe, with Leonard Brain, I resisted, but it took weeks for me to extricate myself from these tutorials. I completed the year, gaining the LRAM (Licentiate of the Royal Academy of Music) diploma.

That first term was also unforgettable for a monumental tragedy that happened in the Welsh valleys in the village of Aberfan, near Merthyr Tydfil. On 21 October 1966, due to a build-up of water, a coal tip started to slide and, with catastrophic consequences, enveloped part of the village and Pantglas Junior School in particular. A total of 116 children and 28 adults perished either by being crushed or suffocated. The year 2016 sees the premiere of a new work of mine, commemorating the fiftieth anniversary of that tragedy.

Happier memories of those first few months in London include a conversation with Graham Collier, who asked me to join his eponymous septet. Graham was a bass player but his main claim to fame was as a jazz composer. Essentially, he was quite an affable person but he could be difficult on occasion, which probably stemmed from an unhappiness or frustration that he was gay but hadn't at that point 'come out'. Bear in mind that this was just before the Sexual Offences Act of 1967, when homosexuality was decriminalised. The Graham Collier Septet used to rehearse in the basement of the Troubadour Coffee House, Earls Court – and it was there, at my first rehearsal, that I first met someone who would become a very good friend: a drummer called John Marshall. We were to play together in three bands as well as various offshoots, and we were to later share a flat.

Graham's band consisted of four 'front-line' instruments (alto and baritone saxes, trumpet, trombone) and a rhythm section that had guitar instead of the more usual piano. There were some phenomenal jazz players in the band at various times, particularly Ken Wheeler (trumpet and composer), Mike Gibbs (trombone and composer) and Stan Sulzmann (saxes). Incidentally, Stan Sulzmann is the saxophone player on the *Poirot* TV theme, the use of the instrument in this context no doubt stemming from the fact that the saxophone was invented by a 'real' Belgian, Adolphe Sax, in 1846. Much of Graham's writing was based on scales or modes rather than chord progressions; he saw a kindred spirit in George Russell, an American jazz composer who had written a rather intense book called *The Lydian Chromatic Concept of Tonal Organization*.

I played on two albums of Graham's. The first was *Deep Dark Blue Centre* (1967): the title was a sentiment of Graham's, with which I concur, in that he believed jazz should never lose that 'deep dark blue centre', the core of the genre that stemmed from its origins in 'the blues'. The second recording was *Down Another Road* (1969). On occasion, Graham allowed sidemen to write something for the 'big band' that he sometimes put together. 'Down the Road' was a piece that I composed in 5/4 time (the same time signature as *Take Five*, associated with Dave Brubeck). The whole point of it was that it had a 'funky' repetitive chord pattern over an ostinato bass figure. Graham then wrote *Down Another Road* and even *The Third Road*. Each subsequent 'road', with more involved time changes, moved further away from my original concept and swung less and less. I don't think he ever saw the point!

Graham did write some odd pieces: *The Wrestlers* (inspired by sculptures by Barbara Hepworth) involved the four front-line play-ers being divided into two pairs; each pair in turn battled in a joint improvisation before self-appointing a winner. The other pair fol-lowed in similar vein, before the two reluctant finalists battled to find who was triumphant. It didn't really work with self-effacing jazz musicians. It was more a case of 'After you; no, after you; no, please I insist; no . . .' To be fair, there had been a precedent for this kind of thing. At one time 'cutting contests' were part of the jazz trad-ition, mainly in the US. A group of front line musicians (often tenor players) would get together with a rhythm section, sometimes playing at breakneck tempos in an effort to outdo one another. There was no self-appointed winner though, unlike in Graham's creation.

Graham was a reluctant bass player. With the larger ensemble he occasionally put together, he would direct and bring someone in to play bass. However, on one occasion, the septet was doing a gig out of town. I travelled in Stan Sulzmann's Mini with Graham and his double-bass (yes, it *is* possible). We were playing opposite Frank Ricotti's quartet that had the brilliant Chris Laurence on bass – and, during our set, Graham attacked the bass with more gusto than usual, and the tailpiece, which fastens the strings to the bottom of the instrument, collapsed. We carried on for a few bars, minus bass, when a crouching Chris Laurence surreptitiously slid his instrument onto the stage from the wings. Graham picked it up and continued. Apparently, the bass was taken to the dressing room and laid on a table like a corpse, where Chris effected a temporary repair with a spare bass string. Chris later told me that the temporary repair was still holding, and hadn't been permanently fixed, several weeks later. On the way back to London, Graham suddenly ordered Stan to stop the car. He wasn't feeling well and went off into the night, across the fields, to do whatever he had to do. He came back, carrying bits of detritus and other matter on his shoes into the car. Stan wasn't too happy. As we started off again the headlights picked up the sign signifying the name of the place we were passing through: Colliers End, a village in Hertfordshire.

During this period with Graham, I was invited over to Hamburg to work with the NDR (Norddeutscher Rundfunk or North German Radio). They ran a permanent 'big band' but also brought musicians together from Europe to rehearse for a week and then broadcast a concert, before an audience. The first visit was for an 'East–West' programme where four Polish musicians joined forces with a few from the West (this was when the Iron Curtain was still down). The second was for a project by the virtuoso French jazz pianist Martial Solal who had written a piece for his trio with cello and oboe, a kind of chamber jazz piece. The third and final time was with Graham and his septet, augmented by extra players to perform an especially composed work of his.

Graham did much good work such as giving young aspiring musicians a start, and also as an educator in jazz. We undertook, at various times, a series of school concerts where he presented a history of jazz. This entailed a lecture by Graham, interspersed with examples of the music from various periods of jazz history, played by the band. Mike Gibbs wrote most of the arrangements; he and Graham had been at Berklee together. The Berklee College of Music in Boston was the only establishment that specialised in jazz and what the snooty brigade would term 'light' music as opposed to 'serious' music. To my mind, all music is serious business. Two other future friends and colleagues were later to pass through there: Neil Percy, principal percussionist with the London Symphony Orchestra, and the hand drummer Zands Duggan. Graham later ran the jazz course at the Royal Academy of Music. I went along to something or other there one night when I hadn't seen him for a few years. The first thing he said to me was, 'I'm an OBE now!'

In 1969 my father died, which was a hugely traumatic experience for me. I was appearing at the Antibes Jazz Festival in the south of France with Graham Collier, and we were relaxing on the beach when a message came through for me to contact the British Consulate in Nice. It was lunchtime, so we had to wait a while before we could get through on the phone – but instinctively, I knew what it was about. Call it a premonition, second sight, or whatever, but I was convinced this concerned my father, who had suffered a heart attack the previous year, and I knew it was not good news.

Graham made the phone call with a few of us at his side; he turned to me and confirmed my worst suspicions. The next few minutes were a blur. The consulate made flight arrangements and I left a few hours later to fly from Nice to Heathrow, before taking a train from Paddington to Swansea where I was met by a family friend, David Randall – the artist who had done his teacher training with my father. The funeral followed and my father was laid to rest with my mother in the churchyard in Penclawdd.

My father had been the most influential figure in my life, from both a personal and musical perspective, and I never really got over the loss. Since I was then a jazz musician, of sorts, he didn't live to see how I returned to classical music, making it fundamental to my eventual career. It saddens me that neither my father nor my Aunty Ev know about the later chapters in my life. I know it would have made them both so proud, and I would have loved to experience that with them.

The autumn of 1969 also saw a musical change: Graham Collier was changing his line-up and I was approached by Ian Carr, who had been a judge at the Inter-University Jazz Competition in my final year at Cardiff. He suggested we 'do something together' and form a band.

The first and immediate decision as part of that first conversation was to co-opt John Marshall, my closest friend in jazz and a fantastic drummer. I can't recall the exact sequence but we soon had Ray Warleigh (a brilliant alto saxophonist from Australia who has settled here) and bass player Jeff Clyne (a stalwart of the London jazz scene who had played with Ronnie Scott and Tubby Hayes). Like many jazz double-bass players then, Jeff had started playing electric bass as well. We also wanted an electric guitar player who 'crossed over' into rock as well as being a core jazz specialist. The first occupant, Bernie Holland, left pretty soon after he started; he just didn't turn up to a BBC *Jazz Club* broadcast. We heard later that he had met some mates with an alternative, more attractive offer as to how to spend the time – it must have been some offer, whatever it was. He was replaced by Chris Spedding: more of a session and rock guitarist than an out-and-out jazz musician, but his approach perfectly suited the type of music we were now playing. Before we had actually got going there had been some discussion about the name. I recall 'Crucible' as being one in the hat but we settled on 'Nucleus'. I'm afraid Ian has rewritten history to a certain extent, in that the story now generally presented is that he formed the band and that it was his vision and project. He came to me, so in that sense it *was* his idea, but that first incarnation was always meant to be a co-operative approach, which it was from a creative perspective.

Nucleus appeared at a time when there were significant changes happening in jazz – mainly to do with rhythm. Without being too technical, jazz hitherto had been music played to a 'swing' rhythm, based on triplet quavers, but now there was a movement towards incorporating rock rhythms, using 'even' quavers. This hybrid genre became known as jazz-rock. Other bands adopting this approach were Soft Machine (a group that John and I would later join) and, more significantly, jazz icon Miles Davis.

Incidentally, Miles Davis was responsible for my living in north London for the first time. In 1968, having dropped into Ronnie's, Davis heard the British bass player Dave Holland and immediately offered him a job. Dave dropped everything and went to America, leaving most of his possessions behind in his flat in Hornsey Lane near Highgate – a flat he shared with my friend John Marshall. I moved in with John, inheriting, among other things, some jazz LP records and a book on orchestration by the film composer Henry Mancini. That same year, John met the lovely Maxi (Maximilliana Augusta Egger) from Munich, and they married in August 1969. Maxi is an extraordinarily warm person and I continued to live there, with them, until I met Carol.

There was some unease within Nucleus as to the ratio, rhythmically speaking, of jazz to rock; Ray Warleigh, concerned with what he believed to be the prevalence of rock music, soon left, to be replaced by another Antipodean: Brian Smith from New Zealand, on tenor and soprano saxophone. However, the fact that one of the greatest jazz musicians of all time was also going a similar way reinforced any wavering convictions. Miles Davis released *In a Silent Way* in 1969 and *Bitches Brew* one year later. Incidentally, Ian Carr, a cultured and educated man who had read English at Newcastle University, later wrote what is considered to be the definitive biography of Davis, and was a frequent broadcaster on jazz.

Nucleus soon made its mark with this revised line-up. At the time, various national broadcasting companies sent a band to a competition as part of the Montreux Jazz Festival and, in 1970, the BBC dispatched us. We won, the prize being a performance at the Newport Jazz Festival (Newport, Rhode Island, US, not Wales) in the same year. It was a wonderful experience. We shared the festival bill with people such as the Adderley Brothers and Louis Armstrong. I also recall meeting Dill Jones there: he was a Welsh pianist who had emigrated to the US many years before and had become established as a noted mainstream musician.

Earlier that year we made our first recording – 'Elastic Rock' – in London, and then, in the same year (and perhaps too soon after the first), 'We'll Talk About It Later'. The first album took its title from a composition of mine that reflected the elasticity of the genre in which we were playing. The striking album cover was an image of another kind of 'elastic rock': molten lava. I composed half the material for that debut album, including the tracks '1916', 'Elastic Rock', 'Torrid Zone' and 'Stonescape'. The name of the second album came about because when someone suggested discussing the title, another member of the band commented, 'We'll talk about it later.' Problem solved. I again composed the greater part of the music, including 'Song for the Bearded Lady', 'Lullaby for a Lonely Child', 'We'll Talk About It Later' and 'Oasis', while also co-writing a couple of other tracks.

In the early 1970s, our guitarist Chris Spedding left the band. Chris had a morning recording session in London and Nucleus had an evening concert in Leeds. Ian said he'd never make it in time; Chris insisted he would. So we took a 'dep' (substitute). We had started playing when Chris walked in; he stood at the front, listened to the first number, then drove back to London. He always thought Ian was a bit schoolmasterly.

We undertook a German tour with another guitar player, Ray Russell. We were in Wiesbaden and for some reason Ray was returning to the UK by train, but he wouldn't travel until he had seen and approved the engine. We eventually ran out of guitar options, so we added a second keyboard player. Hywel Thomas – who I first knew as a clarinettist from the National Youth Orchestra of Wales – came in for a while but we settled on Dave MacRae, another New Zealander, who had been playing with American drummer Buddy Rich's band.

In 1971, I arranged and co-wrote an album by singer Linda Hoyle. She had been in a band called Affinity (managed, like Nucleus, by Pete King) and the organist was Lynton Naiff, from the Sussex University trio. I wrote most of the music; Linda the lyrics. On reflection, 1971 was a busy year: I was also involved in recordings for *Jesus Christ Superstar* by Andrew Lloyd Webber (on piano), *Tumbleweed Connection* by Elton John (on oboe) and *All Things Must Pass* by George Harrison (on sax). The last was unusual in that there was no

THE LURE OF LONDON

music written down. George sang a riff (a short repeated phrase) to four saxophones, of which I was one, and which was to be played on cue, and that was that. I recall mega producer Phil Spector being present. This was in Abbey Road Studio 3. Working with Andrew, I had no idea how famous he would go on to become. *Jesus Christ Superstar* was his first truly major musical; until that point, he was a relative unknown. Similarly, Elton John was by no means a 'name'. He was, quite simply, another musician who was hiring me for some freelance work, for which I was grateful – although in hindsight, I could have perhaps charged a slightly higher fee!

Around the same time, I could also occasionally be seen as a member of the band Centipede – so named because it consisted of fifty musicians, hence a hundred legs. It had been formed in 1970 by the 'free jazz' composer and pianist Keith Tippett. Much fuss was made of the fact that it was such a massive ensemble but of course, in 'classical' terms, such an aggregation is normal. Players were drawn from various bands: Keith's Sextet, Soft Machine, Nucleus and King Crimson. We recorded an album, *Septober Energy*; it all sounded like organised chaos and the whole experience was surreal. We did some university gigs in the UK and flew to Rotterdam and the Alhambra Theatre in Bordeaux (for some reason I played this venue on quite a few occasions with various bands: Soft Machine, Ronnie Scott, Nucleus). Even the chartered flights were mad: we had an American tenor player, Gary Windo, who insisted on getting out his instrument and playing on the aircraft, in the aisle. An extended improvisation of raucous 'free jazz' is the last thing needed at 30,000 feet.

I also toured the south of France with Ronnie Scott's Octet. Their baritone sax player, John Surman, had left and a replacement was needed for the tour. It was an amazing band: Ray Warleigh and Ronnie on saxes, Ken Wheeler on trumpet, the trombonist Chris Pyne, pianist Gordon Beck, bass player Ron Mathewson and drummer Tony Oxley. I went to my one and only race meeting in Marseilles, in a lovely setting, with Ronnie and a couple of the band. Ronnie was known to like a flutter, and there was a horse running called Jazz News. It had to happen. Ronnie put a pile of money on it; it came last.

I did a couple of other gigs with that band, one at a Jewish school near Reading. It was a Ronnie Scott connection, he being Jewish, and we all had to wear kippah skullcaps. I wonder what my Welsh Methodist friends would think of that. Ron Aspery (from a remarkable trio called Back Door) was 'depping' (standing in) for Ray on alto saxophone. No alcohol was allowed at the gig, but Ron smuggled in some cans of lager in his saxophone case. From that day, an alcoholic beverage was known to him as a 'Reading'. Ron, a brilliant player I often used on commercials during a later stage of my career, sometimes brought a 'Reading' along to the studio, in the form of red wine, disguised as a bottle of Ribena. Sad to say, he died of a stroke in 2004.

On the subject of Ronnie Scott, he had an unintended yet pivotal role to play in ensuring I would enjoy over forty years of happy marriage – and counting. His club, Ronnie Scott's, of which more shortly, opened in 1959. It was run by Ronnie and Pete King and came to be considered the premier jazz club in the world, even by Americans – most certainly one reason being that it was run by musicians and not shady nightclub owners. It was at Ronnie's club that I went on my very first date with a lovely young girl called Carol Barratt. In between stays in Barnes and Highgate, I briefly shared a flat with Trevor Herbert – a trombone player I had known from my Glam and Nash orchestra days. He had come to London to study at the Royal College of Music and, shortly after leaving the flat we shared, Trevor moved in to 197 Westbourne Grove above an antique shop: Terence Morse and Son. On the top floor lived a chef, Richard Shepherd,

THE LURE OF LONDON

who was soon to open Langan's Brasserie with the entrepreneur Peter Langan and the actor Michael Caine. Far more importantly, though, on the second floor lived a musician Trevor wanted me to meet. I did; and we're still joined at the hip, forty-six years later. In 2011 I wrote *The Peacemakers*, which I dedicated to her. The dedication reads: 'Finally, a special thank you to fellow composer, librettist, inspiration, best friend, personal peacemaker and wife of forty years, Carol Barratt.' Which sums it up, really. The forty years of marriage are now forty-three.

Carol was born in the small Midlands village of Church Gresley on 16 February 1945, so our birthdays are on consecutive days. She attended Ashby-de-la-Zouch Girls' Grammar School and her best friend at school, and ever since, was Joan Clamp, who played the oboe. They were both in the Leicestershire Schools Symphony Orchestra (Carol playing violin) and they then attended the Royal College of Music together. As Joan Whiting, she went on to play with the BBC Symphony Orchestra and then, for the rest of her playing career, with the London Philharmonic Orchestra. In fact, she is 'Gabriel's Oboe' on *The Mission* film soundtrack composed by Ennio Morricone.

Carol took first-study composition jointly with piano, and second-study violin. On certain mornings she took the same bus to college as that icon from another age, the conductor Sir Adrian Boult, who used to doff his hat to her. Having left the RCM, Carol was both the first woman and the first composer to win the prestigious Martin Music Scholarship, awarded by the Philharmonia, which enabled her to study with the eminent composer Elisabeth (Liz) Lutyens (daughter of architect Sir Edwin Lutyens). When we met, Carol was lecturing at Southlands Teacher Training College and at a special centre established by the Inner London Education Authority for particularly gifted music students.

Our first date was at Ronnie Scott's, to see the American drummer Shelley Mann and his group. It was the night before Good Friday so the club had early closure, at midnight, which was the law then – a fact I'd overlooked. Although it's certainly the case that our relationship developed slowly at first, I can say without doubt that I was instantly attracted to Carol. She had a bright and funny personality but she was also a very interesting young woman, and we shared the same tastes in music. Carol is one of those people who has an intuitive feel for things – so when I introduced her to Ronnie's, and she immediately agreed it was a great place to go, I knew we were meant to be.

Our second date was at the 'old' Highgate Cemetery (as opposed to the 'new' one where Karl Marx is buried). It was quite scary there and in the centre stood a mausoleum and various other tombs set in a circle. Hammer Films was a production company that cornered the market in horror movies, which they sometimes shot at Highgate, in a ready-made spooky set. In fact, composer Liz Lutyens, whom I got to know through Carol, scored quite a few of these films: *Dr Terror's House of Horrors*, *Theatre of Death* and *The Skull* being just a few of them.

I was quite intrigued by cemeteries and Carol and I have visited a fair few, especially those of musicians: Mahler (Grinzing, Vienna); Richard Strauss (Garmisch); Stravinsky (Venice, with Diaghilev nearby); Debussy and Fauré (Paris), and Composers' Corner in the Zentralfriedhof (Central Cemetery) in Vienna. Here you can find a stellar cast, including Schubert, Brahms, Schoenberg, Beethoven, Czerny, Ligeti and Salieri, as well as a memorial to Mozart (who was buried elsewhere in a mass grave). Also remembered here is a hero of mine from a different field: the jazz composer and keyboard player Joe Zawinul who made a career in the US but who was Austrian-born and had studied at the Vienna Conservatory and then at Berklee.

Incidentally, Diaghilev lived in fear of dying in water and he wouldn't go on boats. I wonder whether he knew he would be buried in Venice.

The Richard Strauss 'pilgrimage' was to more than a grave, though. Carol and I had peered through the hedge of the villa in the Bavarian town of Garmisch-Partenkirchen once before, only to be driven off by a man with a dog and a gun. Carol meekly exclaimed, 'But we're his biggest fans', but not before I procured a leaf from the hedge, which I later pressed in a book. It was said that the house, quite near the Austrian border, was built on the royalties from Strauss's opera *Der Rosenkavalier*.

The second visit, which included the one to his grave, was more organised and our son, a budding musician, was with us. I was a member of the Richard Strauss Society of Great Britain, which put me in touch with its counterpart in Germany. This led to a telephone conversation with Strauss's grandson who was a medical doctor in the town. The house is not generally open to the public but visits can be arranged by appointment. It was fascinating and had been left as though the great man had just slipped out: the bedroom with the grand piano, the desk where he worked, the living room, the kitchen with a laid table. *Der Rosenkavalier* translates as *The Knight of the Rose*, and part of the story involves the presentation of a silver rose. I gave Carol a silver rose on our twenty-fifth wedding anniversary. Who said romance is dead?

Composers' houses also featured on some our trips: that of Rimsky-Korsakov in St Petersburg; the Wagner House in Tribschen, on Lake Lucerne, where the *Siegfried Idyll* was composed and performed as a present to Wagner's wife, Cosima; the Sibelius house in Ainola, Finland, and far too many in Vienna to mention, including some buildings that had been home to Mozart, Beethoven, Schubert and Haydn. Rimsky-Korsakov's dwelling had a novel way of keeping the wooden floors gleaming: visitors had to wear cloth overshoes, thus polishing the floor while moving around the museum.

Back to our initial courtship. Within a short period of time, I had left Highgate behind and moved in with Carol. I kept this fact quiet from my family back home, unsure of what they might think of us co-habiting – or, rather, being only too sure of what they would think. The official story back home was that we lived in adjacent flats. By that time, my father had passed away, but my Aunty Ev was still very much with us. In the mid-1970s, Carol and I continued to live at 197 Westbourne Grove for a couple of years before taking out a mortgage on a flat just off Barnes Common at 3 Melina Court, Gipsy Lane. My father had left me some money, enough for this deposit. It was a new build and the property was on the market for £17,000. How times have changed. I gladly used the money for our first property but, if I'm honest, I loved the idea of using it on a motor. I had learned to drive in Paddington after meeting Carol, often navigating Marble Arch on my lessons: a very formidable area to practise being behind the wheel. My first car was a yellow Fiat 850 Coupé, before part exchanging that for a blue Lotus Europa which had two seats, a sexy shape, and was extremely fast. There was one major drawback, however: whenever it rained, water seeped into the car where the windscreen met the fibreglass body.

Carol and I once took the Lotus to Europe, on one of our Italian Soft Machine tours. We loaded the luggage in the front compartment, since the car was mid-engined, and the rev counter went haywire while the engine idled very fast. I rang the dealer, whose first and only question was 'Have you put luggage in the front luggage compartment?' He had obviously seen this problem before. Apparently, the weight presses on the throttle cable, causing it to rev. The solution was to lower the idling speed and then, when the luggage was removed, to increase it again. The engine often kept misfiring if I drove for extended periods in traffic, and I was forever cleaning and changing spark plugs. I had accumulated forty-eight spark plugs in the garage at Gipsy Lane at one point, when I needed only four!

Had I been wild, free and single, I might well have spent a sizeable proportion of my income (which wasn't much then) on cars. Happily, however, Carol and I were very much in love, we were soulmates, and after five years together, we decided to marry. Our wedding was definitely not traditional: we eschewed the idea of a big crowd, a church service and a white dress, instead opting for a brief ceremony at East Sheen Registry Office on 19 December 1973. A few friends attended and John Marshall was best man. One of the first things we did, having moved, was buy a dog. We were besotted with West Highland Terriers, found a breeder and bought Sam, our first 'Westie'.

Our first trip as a married couple was down to Wales, with Sam, to tell Aunty Ev the news of our marriage. She was overjoyed, despite Carol being 'a stranger to the village'. They had often met, of course, and had a genuine, deep affection for each other. Carol's parents, May and Tom, were pleased as well, although they seemed to show little real interest in her career – something that certainly frustrated me. When Carol had a big feature in the *Sunday Times* colour supplement regarding her groundbreaking *Chester's Piano Books* and rang her mother to tell her, the response was 'But we don't take the *Sunday Times*!'

The fact that Carol and I didn't have a big wedding ceremony did aggrieve some people: Carol's relatives in the Midlands, in particular, really felt that they had missed out. It was important to me, however, that it remained a low-key affair. Having lost a lot of people to death when I was young, I was always rather afraid of commitment. I didn't want to get too close to people, for fear of how I would then feel should I lose them. Initially, I wasn't fussed about getting married; it was only because the ceremony would be small scale that it seemed to be less of a momentous decision. Of course, nearly fifty years on,

I'm now well aware that a wedding is about far, far more than that one day alone, but at the time, this was very significant for me – and a potential barrier to tying the knot. Thankfully, as ever, Carol was very amenable and not at all conventional, and, so long as we married, she was happy. I didn't want to have a wedding; I've now been very happily married for decades. At first, I didn't want children; we now have a wonderful son Jody, an amazing daughter-in-law in Rosie, and two grandchildren, Astrid and Minty, whom I adore. I was dead against the idea of getting a dog; after that, we had three of them!

After graduating from the Royal College of Music, Carol was advised by Liz Lutyens to take a brass quintet she had written to Sheila McCrindle, who looked after composers at Chester Music, the music publishing house. Rex Billingham ran the educational side of the firm; he was later to leave music to study law, eventually becoming a judge. Rex commissioned Carol to write a series of three piano tutors for children but from a novel perspective: that of a composer. Robin Boyle, the managing director, was very supportive and saw that Carol was ideally suited to undertake this since, apart from studying both piano and composition, she has an incredibly fertile imagination and great empathy with the children she taught.

These were the first piano tutors to be produced in full colour and the books appeared between 1975 and 1977. We had come to know Wendy Hoile, sister of singer Linda Hoyle (who adapted the spelling for her stage name), very well. Wendy also sang and wrote songs but her main skill was as an illustrator. Apart from her talent, being on the same wavelength as Carol made her the obvious choice to illustrate the series. Thus the character Chester the Frog was born, around whom the lessons evolved. With the success of these publications, a great deal of ancillary material was produced as well, including music puzzles, flash cards and manuscript books. Carol and her editor at the time, Naomi Saxl, cobbled together a set of music puzzles. It caused great amusement when it won the Radcliffe Award for Graphic Design in Music Publishing since neither of them were designers. Carol was also undertaking workshop tours to Canada, the US, Singapore and Australia. This was a very exciting and stimulating time for both of us, as our careers really began to take shape and then develop in a very heartening way. Our Aunty Ev was so proud. She once thumbed through the manuscript book – which, apart from Chester the Frog on the cover, had nothing but page after page of the five lines of the music stave inside – before turning to my wife saying, 'There's a clever girl you are, Carol!'

The Chester series entitled *Chester's Piano Books* proved exciting for young people and no one found piano lessons boring with Chester the Frog. The series is still selling well after forty-odd years. In all Carol has written over 84 music publications and was actually published by Boosey & Hawkes before I was, including her *Bravo* series for all instruments. Many years later, on a recording session with the National Youth Choir of Great Britain, Carol, who was producing with me, was introduced to the choir by someone from the organisation who asked the choristers if any of them knew of the *Chester's Piano Books*. A really impressive number raised their hands. Over the years to come, Carol and I would always be each other's touchstone; checking out ideas and asking advice about all manner of things musical – the luxury of having an in-house freebee editor 24/7!

To this day, I love Carol dearly, and we still have an enormous amount of fun together. Without wanting to draw too trite a comparison, I also had a long-standing soft spot for Ronnie Scott's Jazz Club, a very different place nowadays.

During my years in and around jazz music, Ronnie's became a nocturnal home for me. Ronnie Scott, a tenor saxophonist, was the doyen of British jazz. His first club, which he opened with fellow sax player Pete King, who by that point had retired, was a central part of the thriving, Bohemian district of Soho in London. Later, Ronnie and Pete opened in bigger premises in Frith Street but the 'Old Place', as it was now officially called, in Gerrard Street continued to flourish as a home for young jazz musicians. Frith Street, meanwhile, quickly became the destination to hear celebrated guest performers from America.

This had been a battle at first, due to the antediluvian, intransigent views of the Musicians' Union that operated an 'exchange' system: when an American musician worked here, a UK musician had to go to the US – and they didn't really need British musicians there. The MU took the view that a visiting American was doing a British player out of a job, displaying no comprehension that these visiting players were icons of the genre and 'one-offs', not arriving to play at a dinner-dance. When the exchange system was eventually resolved, the first American guests were generally tenor saxophone players. Some of the greatest appeared: among them Ben Webster, Coleman Hawkins, Stan Getz and Sonny Rollins. Apparently, Stan Getz was particularly difficult to deal with: Ronnie always maintained his sciatica was caused by bending over backwards to please him! This predilection for tenor players was understandable since that was the instrument Ronnie and Pete played, and they were now in a position to invite their heroes to play at their own club.

When Nucleus was formed, Pete King became the band's manager, so we often appeared at the club and I hung out there, paying no entrance fee – which, to be fair, was reduced for musicians anyway on production of a union card. Pete could be somewhat abrasive, as most musicians would testify, but if you were 'family' he displayed a

softer, gentler side. There was also a doorman at the club called Jeff
Ellison. He could be difficult too. One night Max Bygraves (a well-
known television variety artist) turned up with his son, who was
apparently a drummer, to see Buddy Rich, the celebrated American
drummer, leading his big band. The 'house full' notice was up but
Bygraves tried to 'blag' his way in. He persisted for several minutes
before exclaiming, 'Don't you know who I am?' Jeff Ellison stared at
him for several seconds before calmly responding with 'I know who
you are, Mr Bygraves, and may I take this opportunity to say that I've
f***ing hated you for years?'

Jimmy Parsons also worked there for a while, as part of the club's
management company, before leaving to work in PR for Radio
Luxembourg. A forerunner of pirate radio, Radio Luxembourg
broadcast to the UK in English. Rather grandly, it had offices in
Mayfair, where Jimmy was based. As a sideline, he secured a record-
production deal with Pye Records and, over a period of a few years,
I worked on some projects with Jimmy, as arranger and co-producer
on albums by Georgie Fame and Marti Caine, among others.

When Jimmy was at Ronnie Scott's he asked me to 'dep' in a
band, Sweet Water Canal, for one gig. The plan was to drive to the
venue, do the gig, and drive back. That was fine, except the gig was
in Geneva. 'Scottish George', who carried out maintenance and various ancillary tasks at the club, drove us. All I remember of the trip
was George getting the transit van stuck in the tramlines in Geneva,
and in a prohibited zone at that. A huge commotion ensued with the
police involved – and all the while George was helpless with laughter.
I have no recollection of what Jimmy was up to during all this, but
we remained close friends for many years. He passed away in 2012,
and is still much missed.

On reflection, I spent hundreds of evenings at Ronnie's, but my
most treasured memory – beside my first date with Carol, of course

– is of the conversation I had with Bill Evans, considered to be one of the finest jazz pianists who ever lived. He had played on the celebrated *Kind of Blue* album by Miles Davis – the best-selling album in jazz history – and he was appearing at the club with his trio. I have never approached my heroes, in no small part because most of them are dead, but downstairs at Ronnie's, adjacent to the lavatory, was a bar. I looked in, and Evans was sitting there. There were only the two of us in the room, so we started talking. Since we were both taciturn and introverted it went slowly at first but he was really friendly and opened up. He said he found it 'challenging' to adjust his piano accompaniment to suit, to his satisfaction, the disparate soloists: tenor sax player John Coltrane, 'Cannonball' Adderley on the alto sax, and Miles Davis on trumpet. He also said that never did they envisage, at the time, how influential *Kind of Blue* would become, although they were extremely pleased with the result. Bill Evans had a beautiful way of voicing chords, which many found to be redolent of the French Impressionist composers Ravel and Debussy, and it was a sheer joy to spend a few minutes alone in his presence, hearing about his approach to making music. When Miles Davis had first hired Bill Evans, he took some flak from black players for choosing a white pianist – but he always did what he believed to be in the best interests of the music.

Apart from the advertised visiting artists, there were many surprises at Ronnie's. In September 1970, I saw rock guitarist Jimi Hendrix give his last public performance, a night or so before he died, sitting in with Eric Burden's band War on two songs: 'Mother Earth' and 'Tobacco Road'. It sounded good but I was never in the 'Hendrix is a genius' camp. On another occasion, Stevie Wonder performed on harmonica with Roland Kirk, two blind improvisers trading solos. Kirk was a black American saxophonist who played mainly tenor but had also found two hybrid saxophone instruments, in a junk shop, called the 'manzello' and the 'stritch'. In addition, Kirk played the flute, using expressive vocal techniques such as growling through the instrument, and he was quite a sight. All of Kirk's instruments hung around him on neck slings for ease of access since, of course, he couldn't see. He sometimes played two saxes at once, although he was then limited to one-hand fingering on each, and he was about the first wind player I heard to employ circular breathing. This is a technique whereby, when one needs an intake of breath, air is forced through the instrument, using the cheek muscles, while at the same time a breath is taken in through the nose. At its best, this is a seamless process with no wavering in the sound produced by the instrument. The normal club hours were 9.30 p.m. to 3 a.m. – and one night, it was advertised that Kirk would play tenor sax for three hours non-stop, not taking the instrument out of his mouth. Starting at around 3 a.m., he proceeded to play continuously until 6 a.m. Phenomenal. I'm sure the rhythm section was more tired than he was.

Ronnie Scott's Jazz Club was somewhere I felt very at home: a place where kindred spirits would meet, and it is a place that holds very special memories for me. By the early 1970s, though, I was looking to spread my musical wings beyond the jazz world, as part of a journey that continues even to this day.

5

SOFT MACHINE

*S*oft Machine, often known simply as 'the Softs', was originally a rock band from Canterbury, named after the book *The Soft Machine* by William S. Burroughs, where 'soft machine' is a generic name for the human body, so we're all 'soft machines'. During the 1970s, the band played a pivotal role in my career, and many of my most interesting musical memories date from my time with it. Soft Machine had been formed in 1966 by a quartet of musicians, one of whom was the drummer and vocalist Robert Wyatt. Robert later left to form his own band, Matching Mole (its debut album cover had two identically dressed moles, facing each other), a clever name since *machine molle* means 'soft machine' in French and Softs had been extremely popular in France. Tragically, in 1973, inebriated at a party in Maida Vale, Robert fell from a fourth-floor window and was left a paraplegic. He had eventually been replaced in Softs by Nucleus drummer John Marshall. When saxophonist Elton Dean left (Elton John had apparently appropriated his name after they had been in a band, Bluesology, together) I also joined. Softs, by now, had essentially become a jazz-fusion band, with much improvising and with no vocals. The remainder of the quartet comprised bassist Hugh Hopper – who had been a roadie with the band, would you believe – and keyboard player Mike Ratledge.

I had first jammed with the group in a Paris club, some time before. Mike Ratledge had a Hohner Pianet keyboard placed on top of his Lowry organ so we turned that around to face the other way and I played that while standing up. I can't remember anything about the music that night, but I do remember two things about the 'set'. First of all, drummer Robert Wyatt took off *all* his clothes before playing, and secondly, the band inserted earplugs. This was obviously going to be loud.

Mike had a unique sound on the organ: it is rare for someone to have an immediately identifiable sound, a signature sound unlike anyone else, but he did. Unlike most jazz or rock organists, who played the Hammond organ, Mike played a Lowry, and by combining this with a 'fuzz' pedal, which distorts the sound, a unique and interesting effect was created.

The sound of the entire band was an immensely appealing one to me, and I was delighted to be invited to join such a forward-looking group. At that time in my life, I would have described myself as an improvising 'jazzer', but I was also keen to explore further the fusion of different musical styles. That was on offer in abundance with Soft Machine, with the added bonus of the band already being well known before I got involved. In the early days, Softs had performed in the UFO Club in London with Pink Floyd. Some years later, we shared the bill again at Finsbury Park Astoria in a benefit gig for Robert Wyatt.

Soft Machine's relatively widespread appeal wasn't primarily down to radio airplay or mass-market coverage. Rather, the band's popularity grew from the grass roots up. The early incarnation was beloved by critics; later ones, less so. Perhaps they thought we were destroying the band's heritage by playing jazz. Prior to my joining the line-up, Softs had toured America for six months with Jimi Hendrix, which clearly helped boost their profile. It always struck me that there were relatively few women at our gigs; the adoring fans were primarily hirsute blokes in questionable clothing.

My first rehearsal with Softs was in a warehouse rehearsal space in St Katharine Docks, just east of Tower Bridge and the Tower of London. Mike Ratledge lived near me, off Westbourne Grove, in the now expensive area of Notting Hill, better known for the 1999 film of the same name rather than the race riots of 1976. I had already been to Mike's flat a few times to familiarise myself with the repertoire: he was writing most of the material then, with much of it in unusual time signatures. I was playing baritone and soprano sax, oboe and piano. My being a multi-instrumentalist seemed to confuse some and I was once listed as two people: Bari Sop (oboe) and Karl Jenkins (piano). I made my first album with the band, *Soft Machine Six*, in 1973, and it won the Jazz Album of the Year Award. A year later, the band was voted 'Best Small Group' in a poll by *Melody Maker* magazine. There were categories for all the usual instruments but there was also one called 'Miscellaneous Instrument'. This is where those who played any old oddball instrument were dumped; I won that category on oboe both that year and the next.

Both Mike Ratledge and I each played, among other things, a Fender Rhodes electric piano. Mike used to stab at the keys, whereas I had a softer touch, with the result that he often broke some tone bars that had to be replaced and tuned before gigs. We both used an Echoplex: a box, using tape, to create a delay in the sound. One could set the speed and the length of delay, and also the decay, and by using one each, we could set up multiple patterns. We also dabbled in what is now known as 'minimalism', before the phrase (attributed to Michael Nyman, whom I knew at this time) was coined but which we then called 'pattern pieces', a term I borrowed from Carol when describing some pieces she was then writing for classical piano. Terry Riley's *Rainbow in Curved Air*, a work and recording in this genre by the American composer that dates from 1969, gained some prominence at this time, in both rock and classical circles.

I also played a Minimoog synthesiser: it was monophonic, and therefore enabled the playing of only a single note and not chords. Crucially, though, the Minimoog was portable and did not necessitate the use of 'patch chords', which meant plugging cables to re-route and change sounds or effects. Like everything else high tech, early synthesiser models were huge, some filling a room, although they inevitably became more compact as time passed. Many years later, when I was writing music for commercials, an executive from Saatchi & Saatchi turned up to one of the sessions. He had with him one of the early mobile phones. The handset was the size of a brick but there was more to it than that: a lead led to the battery pack, which was housed in something the size of a suitcase hanging around his neck. He looked ridiculous but he, no doubt, saw himself as someone very important.

Minimoogs are iconic and highly prized nowadays, especially since they can be adapted to be controlled by a 'MIDI' computer programme (MIDI is the acronym for 'musical instrument digital interface). I also played a Logan 'string machine' that did just that: simulate orchestral strings, albeit not very well. In retrospect, the huge fuss these instruments created at the time was far too over the top. They could never have replaced the beauty of real stringed instruments and the vast spectrum of articulations available to a composer or arranger, but the Musicians' Union was convinced they would take work away from string players, so they tried to ban them from recording sessions.

Soft Machine was not a band that carried lighting or any effects unless they came with the gig. Similarly, we didn't dress for performances; denim was pretty much de rigueur then. While we might not have been adventurous with our attire, we were always on the lookout for new ways of approaching music: Mike had acquired a VCS3 (Voltage Controlled Synthesiser), a generator of electronic effects and processor of external sounds, on which he played some crazy sound design type solos, and John Marshall hit on an idea that made the drum solos rather interesting. I don't know whether the first time was by accident or design but he would regularly shake some talcum powder on his snare drum. As the solo progressed, framed by an array of gongs, strung on a rack behind him, John became enveloped in a white cloud, ending with him looking like a ghost.

My first proper Softs gig was in La Rochelle in Brittany as part of a French tour. I had been in Switzerland with Carol, so we drove from Geneva across France in my little yellow Fiat 850. There were no east–west motorways in France then; plenty north–south, but none east–west. It was a horrendous drive: we had problems finding fuel; a swarm of wasps came into the vehicle on one occasion, and it took over fourteen hours in total. Poor Carol, but then she's never been a complainer! Other journeys were far less adventurous: Soft Machine did the usual UK gigs at universities and festivals, such as Reading. Further afield, twice a year we toured Italy playing theatres in the major cities in the New Year, and coastal venues in the summer. Most Italian tours were organised by two brothers, Franco and Willie Mammone, with Francesco Sanavio. When we went south, Sandro Ottaviano, a portly figure, came with us. A short man of very few words, Sandro's two most common phrases were 'I go eat' or 'I go cinema'. My interest in food most certainly stems from this period. I had been to Italy a couple of times before, on one occasion with my father to the 1960 Olympic Games in Rome, but for the first time I appreciated how amazing Italian food can be in Italy, where it is so dependent on fresh Mediterranean produce. The *Red Michelin Guide* soon became a passport to good eating.

There were some massive clubs in Italy, often outside towns, that hosted bands and also operated as dance or disco venues. One, L'Altro Mondo, near Rimini, was massive, accommodating well over three thousand people. We were always up and down the Adriatic coast at such venues, and we also played the western side of the country. On one occasion, we drove all the way from Rimini to Portofino in the Gulf of Genoa and back, for a gig at Covo di Nord Est – an 800-kilometre round trip. We suggested staying overnight but were told that all the hotels were full. While we were driven back the 400 kilometres, the roadies left after the gig with the truck and found rooms in the first hotel they came across. There had evidently been quite a party at the club: the son of the famous Italian motorbike manufacturer M. V. Augusta was there, off his yacht, throwing a New Year's party which eventually included us, in August. The year had not been good for business so he thought he should start it again!

Funnily enough, the only time we could be confident of properly organised concerts and of getting paid was when the gigs were promoted in conjunction with the Communist Party. The rest of the time it was always fun but we had so many disasters. I can vividly recall how once, at a Naples club, after we'd played, the audience stormed the stage for souvenirs; souvenirs like my saxophone and parts of the drum kit. One group had their hands on the legs of my electric piano before they were beaten back by the road crew. I did quite well out of this, though, since the promoters replaced my saxophone with a Selmer Mark VI that was far superior to the one that had been stolen. On the island of Elba, we turned up for rehearsal and there was a minor problem: they hadn't built the stage. It was lying there, just a load of planks and supports, in a heap on the ground, in a football stadium. Another stadium saw the stage facing the wrong way, towards the short end. What's more, we often had to suffer the 'free-music brigade': people who held the view that music belonged to everyone and therefore concerts should not cost them a penny to attend. They were all over Europe and the situation could become ugly, and even tragic on one occasion, when someone tried to climb in via the roof and fell to his death. In addition, it was not unusual to find people selling bootleg cassette copies of our concerts and recordings, outside the venue. Some were well organised, with, on occasion, their wares shamelessly and proudly displayed on a trestle table.

Every time we were on a percentage of the door, our promoters used to survey the assembled throng and, with much deliberation, prevarication and waving of the hands, finally announce: 'about-*a* eight-*a* hundred-*a*'. It was always 800, even when there were obviously a couple of thousand there. Money was left, on a shelf, in a bank in Milan by an employee who shall remain nameless, and who turned his back on it. It didn't help that the envelope was marked 'Money'. When he turned around, it had gone. We also lost our fee after some concerts in Tunisia. Flying back via Rome, there were strict currency regulations in those days of the lira, restricting the amount one could bring through Italy. The proceeds from our tour were confiscated at Rome airport. The glamour of life on the road! Tourism, in Tunisia, was in its infancy then. Hotels were being built, but very often essential elements such as the sewage system and air-conditioning simply didn't work. We really must have been an egalitarian outfit, since our roadie, Gerry Stevens, had a room that had no problems of this kind, while some of us 'artists' suffered – and suffer we did, with sickness and diarrhoea; and we didn't even move him out!

Gerry had joined the band not long before me, and I never saw such a transformation in anyone during the few years we were together. From a very staid, conventionally dressed young lad from Gloucester he morphed into a rock roadie: denim-clad and with extremely long hair, his huge, droopy moustache hung proudly from his chin and put mine to shame. Gerry also wore a wide-brimmed leather hat. This he used to take from his head and vehemently hurl to the floor when problematical situations arose. He once showed us a cutting from a local Gloucester paper that announced his joining Soft Machine. In what was clearly meant as a compliment, the band was 'known throughout the world for its cacophony'. He eventually left us to join the Police (the band, not the force).

While touching on the subject of moustaches, I've sported mine since I was at university. It came off only once, when I flew to California for a family holiday. My mother-in-law, May, who was looking after our dogs, was aghast when I shaved it off the morning of the flight. By the time I returned it was very much back on, and has been ever since. Later on, in my advertising days, I was in vision for an ad, conducting an orchestra performing 'O sole mio' for a Wall's Cornetto commercial, with the estimable tenor Dennis O'Neill. It was a 'period' shoot; as we were leaving for the day, 'make-up' came running after me demanding their moustache back!

But back to Gerry Stevens, and his far more superior facial hair. Although originally a roadie, Gerry later became tour manager, which meant he travelled with us and not with the truck. We had quite a few quirky experiences with Gerry driving us. On one occasion, in Brussels, we left the hotel in plenty of time to make the sound check. Both the hotel and the venue were on the ring road. Off we set. Nearly one hour later, we were passing the hotel again. Another time, the transit van transporting us ran out of fuel on the motorway en route to Calais and the boat home. Gerry went looking for petrol while one of our musicians disappeared across the fields of rural France, looking for cheese!

I don't know what it was with Gerry and vehicles. I was with him one day, driving around Leicester Square, at a time when one could, looking for somewhere to park; executing several laps of the square, Gerry driving his exotic Jenson Interceptor and sporting his wide-brimmed leather hat and drooping moustache, I suppose it did look somewhat suspicious. Suddenly the police arrived. We were ordered out of the car, hands placed on the roof while we were searched, the police thinking we were drug dealers.

We had some experiences in the air too: from a multi-band European tour called 'Star Trucking', with everyone and everything (musicians, instruments, road crew and gear) all together in one of those massive bulbous freight aircraft (with our tour logo on the side) to some dodgy moments in a light aircraft. Softs had a gig at a festival in Belgium, in the middle of a tour of the south of France. Good logistical planning! Leaving our wives behind in Nice, we had to make the trip by light aircraft with all the gear. The Lowry organ, which we had to clamber over to reach our seats, was in the aisle with other instruments strewn around. The plane was too heavy to take off so we had to jettison 'odds and ends' until we could. We eventually became airborne – but not by much, never making it above the cloud cover. Not a pleasant journey.

As the personnel changed, so sometimes did the instrumentation. The fact that I introduced the oboe to the band was quite novel. There were very few of us improvising oboists in captivity: Bob Cooper, predominately a tenor sax player in the Stan Kenton band who 'doubled', as did Yusef Lateef, a black American tenor player who had converted to Islam, as a few black American musicians did. Playing at a jazz festival one time, our band room was next door to that of Yusef Lateef. It sounded quite bizarre, both of us warming up on oboes. We also played a club in Cleveland, My Father's Moustache. The outgoing band was Ralph Towner's Oregon, featuring oboist Paul McCandless.

The year 1974 saw an important instrumental change in Soft Machine. For the first time since its inception, the band added a guitarist, Allan Holdsworth, who had come to London in 1969 with a Bradford-based band called 'Igginbottom. Allan was a phenomenal guitarist and was somewhat held in awe by more well-known players. Allan was also one of those musicians who didn't read music. Like many who had initially come through rock, he could read chord symbols but not the dots. There was a common fallacy prevalent in popular and rock music – not that Allan necessarily subscribed to it – and that was a fear that a musician would lose his 'feel' if he learned to read music. Where this nonsense came from I don't know, since although there were many outstanding players who did not read, it was not because they hadn't acquired this ability that they were good. No musical genre depends on 'feel' as much as jazz, and many of the great American jazz players came up through the big-band era where they *had* to read the ensemble charts.

Allan had played a few times with Nucleus in 1972, eventually joining Softs in January 1974 for an Italian and German tour. We then toured the eastern seaboard of North America, from Quebec down to Atlanta, playing, among other places, Harvard University and Howard Stein's Academy of Music in New York, where we took the opportunity to visit other iconic jazz haunts while in the city: the Village Vanguard and Slug's Saloon on the Lower East Side, for example. John had befriended Rashied Ali (a drummer who had played with John Coltrane) in London. I think John even bought some drums from him. Anyway, Rashied Ali was our chaperone for the evening. Slug's was the club where trumpeter Lee Morgan had been shot dead in an argument over a woman. The atmosphere was very heavy in there; we were the only Caucasians present. In Detroit, we played opposite a band whose bass player was hoisted up by wire during his solo. Allan told us that, knowing of his love of cycling, some fellow players in a previous band of his had suggested that he do some solos while balancing on a unicycle. Clearly, the music was never enough.

In July we recorded *Bundles*, at CBS Studios, London, the first album in Softs' history that had a name and not a number as a title. My compositions were: 'Hazard Profile', 'Bundles' and 'The Floating World'. The last was inspired by an exhibition of Japanese prints, but in the world of jazz it was quite common to take titles from anywhere, without the need for a specific source of inspiration. As in Nucleus, with 'We'll Talk About It Later', sources can be unexpected and frivolous. We were staying at a hotel, Punta Nord (North Point), near Rimini. It *was* a 'punter' hotel too. It was near a railway line and every time a train went by, one Englishman used to get up from his poolside sun-bed and wave at it. Hence, 'The Man Who Waved at Trains'. 'Peff' was named after me, a nickname coined by Allan Holdsworth. I had an irritating cough (I smoked heavily until I was thirty, then suddenly stopped out of fear of death) and apparently the word 'peff' was a colloquialism from Allan's original locality. Sometimes, Carol would conjure up titles for me and she would later invent one of huge significance.

The *Bundles* aggregation was a particularly strong one and an exciting creative future beckoned. There were, however, some dis-quieting whispers and murmurings to the effect that the American drummer Tony Williams wanted Allan to join his band in the States. Williams had joined Miles Davis aged just seventeen; the first time he played in a New York club with Miles, they had to close the bar because he was a minor. We could understand Allan going if the opportunity arose, but we pleaded with him to let us know in good time if he were going to take the job. Two days or so before a tour of Italy, he slipped a note under the band's office door to the effect that he had left for the US. Italy was cancelled. We then auditioned a few guitarists, in Richmond Rugby Club, with not much luck. We had heard of a man called John Etheridge who was playing somewhere out of town with the Global Village Trucking Company. We went to have a listen and he was hired, a terrific player and a lovely person. One of John's heroes was the French jazz gypsy guitarist, Django Reinhardt: an amazing musician who had two paralysed fingers on his left hand, burnt in a caravan fire, and who played with the jazz violinist Stéphane Grappelli in the 1930s. Happily, John Etheridge would later join Grappelli's band; this extraordinary violinist continued playing well into his eighties.

Not that it's relevant to playing music, but by this point we then had, from a time when university degrees meant something, four graduates in the band: Mike Ratledge had read PPE at Oxford; John Marshall, Psychology at Reading; John Etheridge, History of Art at Essex; and I had read Music at Cardiff. We recorded an album with the title *Softs*, the band's sobriquet, in 1977.

Our manager was Sean Murphy, whose organisational skills left a lot to be desired. For some reason, the record company WEA gave Sean a label to run called Raft Records, which foundered. We missed one day of a scheduled three days of recording our live and penultimate 1978 album, *Alive and Well: Recorded in Paris*, since the management had not renewed the Carnet (a customs document) and the truck was impounded in Calais. We were taking the cheaper option of recording live only since there were insufficient funds in the coffers to finance a studio recording, and we had a contractual obligation to deliver an album. That trip had further disasters when guitars were stolen from our transit van. Sean also confused Beirut in Lebanon with Bayreuth in Germany (where the Wagner theatre is situated), referred to Sicily as Cicely in a diary entry and once mentioned the 'leaning tower of pizza' during a conversation in Italy. He was unfortunately prone to such malapropisms, and he departed owing everyone money. The financial side of Soft Machine Ltd and

Soft Machine Publishing was chaos. We never saw statements and we really didn't know what was going on until a new and competent accountancy firm, that Sean, of all people, had appointed, unearthed a mess. We successfully brought legal action through the Musicians' Union only to discover there were far bigger fish ahead of us in the queue: the Inland Revenue and Customs and Excise. Sean was declared bankrupt.

When it came to the end of Soft Machine, there was no grand finale and no farewell tour. Quite simply, the band just petered out. John Marshall and I were the last official members and we made a final recording in 1981, *The Land of Cockayne*. The title refers to the fantastic land of plenty in medieval literature and not to the drug.

When it came to what I should do next, I didn't have any kind of plan in place – but very quickly, my musical journey would take an unexpected yet extremely welcome turn.

6

THE ADVERTISING YEARS

*L*ast year, I turned seventy. As with any milestone birthday, it offered a chance to look back over my life so far,
and to reflect on the path I've taken. Understandably, a
great many people took my big birthday as an excuse to ask me about
my career as a composer – and to politely enquire as to whether I
might be hanging up my pencil and manuscript paper any time soon.
To be honest, I know of no composer (or poet, painter, writer) who
has ever retired. Laid low by illness, yes, but never retired. It's not a
job; it's a way of life. I am defined by what I do.

For me, the idea of a 'career as a composer' has always been a
slightly unusual one. The reason: over the course of the last fifty years,
I feel as if I have had at least four different careers. All of them have
involved creating music, but the way in which this has manifested
itself has varied immensely. And never more so than in the late 1970s
and 1980s, when I became very closely associated with writing music
for advertising.

During the mid-1970s, I had already gained some experience
in composing for a music library. This is where recorded music,

in every style imaginable, is made available to the media for use in documentaries, films and adverts. I wrote for De Wolfe in Wardour Street, a family concern that was very successful in this field. They had started out as a sheet-music library for theatres. James De Wolfe managed the company, and Gordon Chambers was the producer who initially hired me. They had a small studio, called Red Light, on the third floor in a building that had no lift. It was a curious name for a studio in what was the 'red light' district of Soho. One wonders who else turned up there for a session. For larger sessions, De Wolfe hired outside facilities until they bought and converted a church in Islington into the Angel Recording Studios where, over the years, I have done most of my large-scale recording. In some ways, though, De Wolfe was somewhat cheapskate. I remember doing one session with brass and rhythm sections, too big for the studio – but the company was very reluctant to spend money by going to a large outside studio. The solution? The rhythm section sat in the studio with the brass in the stairwell, with someone posted downstairs to prevent people coming up when recording was in progress. On another occasion, the drummer, Clem Cattini, brought his kit up the stairs, did the session, then packed up and took it downstairs from the third floor – only to be recalled (for another fee!) since the engineer had erased the percussion from the tape.

De Wolfe produced the occasional specially commissioned commercial, and sometimes asked me to provide the music. I can't recall the product but, on one particular occasion, the song the client wanted arranged was about money and De Wolfe had sent me a tape of the original song. There were two songs that had some currency then (pun intended) that dealt with this topic: 'Money, Money, Money' by Abba and 'Money, Money' from the show *Cabaret*. Everyone assembled in the control room while the band struck up with the chosen song. I knew something was up when the producer came in, red as a beetroot and muttered under his breath, so that his voice would not travel down the mike and into the control room, 'It's the wrong song!' The client was sent to have a cup of tea while I endeavoured to effect an arrangement of the correct song, with what we had at our disposal.

The first commercial I ever composed was for Chanel No. 5, filmed by the American photographer Lester Bookbinder. Carol and I wrote this together, scored for 'prepared piano'. Invented by American composer John Cage, a 'prepared piano' involves placing objects such as coins, erasers, nails – anything, in fact – between the strings of the piano, thus creating a 'new' instrument of weird and different sounds. It was perhaps the most avant-garde piece to which I've ever lent my name, and although scored for only piano, since the project was deemed important we used a more upmarket studio just behind Marble Arch. Strangely, they had not hired a studio that had 'picture lock' where one could run the film while listening to the music being recorded. Understandably, it made it difficult for the client to tell how well music and film were working together; however, the whole project was completed and aired. We still have the handwritten score hanging on our wall.

After the end of the Soft Machine era, I unexpectedly found myself returning to the world of writing music for commercials – something that would occupy most of my time for the rest of the 1970s, and a great deal of the 1980s too. I soon met up with Mike Ratledge again: he had secured a recording deal with EMI but instead of the customary advance against royalties, the label helped facilitate a recording studio in his basement. Incidentally, with regard to recording deals, there is a huge misconception by the public as to how, in reality, such arrangements work. One often hears of an artist signing a five-album deal for a million pounds. What this invariably means is that the artist is advanced £200,000 per album to make the recording. The artist does not earn a penny until the label recoups this amount.

So, in effect, artists pay for their own recording. Furthermore, if extravagant sums are involved, it is rarely five albums per se but one plus one plus one plus one plus one, there being an option (but only on the record company's side) to make each successive album. If the first doesn't do well, then the label won't take up the option. It is also salutary to realise that an artist's royalty is usually, at best, around 15 per cent with 5 per cent or so going to the producer. The record label receives 75 per cent.

Mike's studio was in Richmond Road in Dalston, east London, where he now lived with his girlfriend, having moved from Westbourne Grove. We decided to work together again and were open to offers: production, music for TV commercials and film, orchestrations, or anything else a potential client thought we could set our hands to. Our venture was originally called Mooz. It seemed a short, snappy, zippy, memorable name and it was 'zoom' spelled backwards. The first logo a designer came up with was an image of a mooing cow; it made us look more like a dairy than a trendy London music company. For a while, we retained the name but changed the graphic to a diagonal angular slash, a little like fork lightning, in silver on black. People then started calling us Mooz Music which we hated, so, eventually, we settled on plain Jenkins–Ratledge with our signatures as the logo.

Mike Ratledge is, intellectually, one of the brightest people I have ever known. He developed a keen interest in computers when, commercially speaking, they were in their infancy, and built a sequencer music programme long before such a thing was commercially available. I often suggested to Mike that he patent the idea or take it to one of the major music instrument firms but, for whatever reason, he never did. At the time we were collaborating on our new venture, Mike's girlfriend, an American lady called Priscilla Scanio, had a rather unusual vocation: she was a model but by then specialising in feet and hands, working regularly with a very well-known stills photographer by the name of Mike Berkofsky. Many eminent stills photographers, particularly fashion photographers, shot commercials, including Brian Duffy, Terence Donovan, David Bailey and John Swannell. Soon after Jenkins–Ratledge was formed, Mike Berkofsky was shooting a Boots No. 7 commercial and, given his link with Priscilla, contact was made with us. The commercial was called 'Changing Faces' and it showed the head of a girl with no make-up, which was then applied – unseen, as it were – until completed. The music the advertising agency wanted to use was a version of the song 'The First Time Ever I Saw Your Face' by Ewan MacColl. We did a striking arrangement of it with just a saxophone, played by Dick Morrissey, triple-tracked (Dick overlaying himself so that there were three of him). This, combined with a repetitive chord backing that sounded unusual, made the arrangement very innovative for the period. This commercial won the coveted D&AD (Design and Art Direction) award for music. D&AD hands out the premier industry gongs in advertising, and the prize specifically awarded for music soundtracks is termed 'best use of music', so it covers everything from original music to arrangements. The actual award takes the form of a large ornamental yellow pencil; with this, we were very much up and running and in demand for supplying music to TV commercials.

At this point in the early 1980s, production values were extremely high in the field of advertising: it was said that more money was spent on film footage for commercials than for movies. Many directors, with some of whom we worked, would later become celebrated names in the film industry: Ridley and Tony Scott, Alan Parker, Hugh Hudson. Much was dire but the best adverts looked great and had good innovative ideas, with plenty of scope for fine soundtracks. Our reputation was one of writing classy, filmic scores that did not belong to the 'jingle' category – something that would stand us in very good stead for many years.

We soon came to the attention of Bartle Bogle Hegarty (BBH), the agency that was making waves within the industry, having just been formed in 1982. The creative force was (Sir) John Hegarty, the doyen of great thinkers in the world of advertising. In 1984 we scored the iconic 'Levi's Russia' ad. Shot in black and white, except for a red tag on the jeans seen at the end of the commercial (a forerunner of the movie *Schindler's List* and the girl in the red coat?), the film concerned a young man smuggling jeans into Russia through an airport, before reaching his bleak, depressing and austere apartment block (shot not in Moscow, but in the East End of London) and finally revealing the jeans in his suitcase. My music was very Russian, with a choir of low male voices and orchestra before a very Western denouement when a saxophone – played, again, by Dick Morrissey – came in. We won our second D&AD and another 'Pencil'. *Campaign*, the trade magazine, ran a series on music showreels and concluded that, having seen ours, they had better stop since they couldn't imagine there being a better one.

For the orchestral scores, I had started working with the London Philharmonic Orchestra, which was resident at the Royal Festival Hall. Carol's closest friend, Joan, was playing oboe and cor anglais in the LPO, so I asked her to hire the players for the sessions. The 1980s was a purple patch in the history of this orchestra, in part due to Klaus Tennstedt, its German conductor of genius. His performances, particularly of Mahler symphonies, were legendary and inspiring. The LPO recorded Mahler's Fifth Symphony at the Royal Festival Hall, the *Adagietto* from which I chose for my *Desert Island Discs* programme some years later.

Jenkins–Ratledge tended to record at Angel Recording Studios but on one occasion it was already booked, so we used the old CBS studios in Whitfield Street, which was next to a pub. Some of the musicians met there before the session, which was with members of the LPO. As we were about to start, one violinist had nowhere to sit. We thought we had overbooked the players. Much discussion followed until the question was asked: 'Who is the fellow sitting at the back?' It turned out to be a very inebriated Irishman, who had been in the pub, and thought it a good idea to tag along when all the musicians, with their instruments, left.

During the course of our ten years or so in ad music, Mike's domestic situation changed in that he and Priscilla parted. He sold the house and closed the studio but we made some positive changes that improved our modus operandi in a number of ways. We knew someone called Mark Cellier who ran a design company, Quick on the Draw. Mark had offices in central London so we enquired whether he had some space we could sublet from him. He did, and we then followed him when he moved. First of all we went to Greek Street in Soho, which was the hub of the film and advertising industries. We gradually collected quite a few Clios (US) and Lions (Cannes) for being associated with commercials that won awards, but for which there was no specific music category. Commercials that we scored include: C&G (the boy diving for pearls); the 'Nicole and Papa' Renault Clio campaign; many orchestrations of the 'Flower Duet' from *Lakmé* by Delibes for British Airways; Volvo, Audi, BMW, and the De Beers 'A Diamond Is Forever' campaign, which formed part of my extended concerto grosso, *Palladio*.

Along the way, Mike and I came across some pretty daft directors. The worst were those who conceptualised everything, like the one who asked the drummer to play on the drum case, rather than on the actual kit. He was living out some fantasy of bands, eager to participate in some impromptu jam session at every opportunity. There we were, in a state-of-the-art recording facility, with everything geared to a super sound, and he wanted to hear someone hitting leather. It sounded horrible and no potential viewer would be aware of the 'story' or concept since there was nothing in vision relevant to this. Another low point that comes to mind was the biscuit commercial where the director wanted to record someone eating the biscuits. Again, despite the drummer's best efforts (for it was he we nominated to do the munching), it sounded rubbish. The musician did well out of it, though, since he insisted on extra 'doubling' fees (for playing more than one instrument at a session). Along similar lines, a great jazz pianist friend, Gordon Beck, once demanded a double fee when he was asked to play badly.

It was always a problem trying to convey the fact that a set number of bars occupies a finite amount of time, and one cannot cram more in without playing the music more quickly. Nowadays, one hears ridiculous edits made to well-known songs where, to maximise the amount of lyrics that can be squeezed in, beats and bars are cut indiscriminately, making the end result ridiculous. One doesn't have to be a musician to recognise this; the song just feels uncomfortable or lopsided. Then the endings present a problem since, to my mind, there are only two options: fade it out or construct a pleasing and satisfying conclusion. Too often, tracks are not resolved and are simply cut off in mid-flight. I always tried to retain whatever integrity was relevant to any piece of music but once the tape left the studio it was the agency's to do with as it wished. We once recorded the opening of the Beethoven Violin Concerto, obviously a very well-known piece of music. It begins with four unaccompanied notes on the timpani; when I saw it on-air there were five! Part of this particular commercial was filmed at the Royal Albert Hall, with the orchestra in vision. I gave the film company an outline of how an orchestra is seated, a directive that was totally ignored. They had decided to rearrange the orchestra, which had sat, with one or two variations, in this time-honoured formation for hundreds of years. The director had clarinets and flutes mixed up with violins, timpani where they should not have been, and cellos where you would ordinarily expect to find a tuba. It was a total mess, and looked crass.

Sometimes agencies wanted to use an established piece of music, usually a recording that was still in copyright. Very often, the composition was quite readily acquired but the use of the recording was often problematic and could be refused. This gave rise to what was known as 'soundalikes'. The agency, having secured the song rights, would ask a music company to re-create the original recording. We did quite a few of these: perhaps the most well-known was a Levi's 501 commercial called 'Laundrette' where a young man – played by the actor Nick Kamen – undressed in a laundrette to wash his jeans, to the strains of 'I Heard It Through the Grapevine' by Marvin Gaye. Except it wasn't Marvin Gaye. We were asked to re-create the track: an interesting exercise, which meant transcribing the original orchestration and hiring people to sing – including a Barbadian by the name of Tony Jackson who, for the purposes of this project, 'was' Marvin Gaye. It was massively successful in relaunching the brand and led to the original single being re-released, becoming a hit in the process. Record labels were then queuing up to place a track on a Levi's ad. Other 'soundalikes' we produced were a Frank Sinatra impersonator (Ken Barry) singing 'Nice and Easy Does It' with the Nelson Riddle Orchestra for Audi, and Linda Taylor (whose voice bore an uncanny resemblance to that of Doris Day) singing for Pretty Polly tights, where the tights became an emergency fan belt for a Jaguar car. Eventually they came to an end – and rightly so. Bette Midler and Tom Waits successfully sued in the US for 'passing off' since that is what it was: duping the public into thinking the original artists were the soundtrack.

We were once close to being sued when we were asked to copy a track without infringing copyright. This was another common situation, where clients wanted the style and content of a track without paying for it. To my mind, the contentious passage was a clichéd rock 'n' roll figure. In retrospect, it was madness to get involved in this, but it was so easy at the time to be seduced into it. Our then lawyer was confident that it would be settled but this didn't prevent sleepless nights. If action were taken, three parties would be sued: the ad agency, the brand client and us, as the music company. Our lawyer's opinion was that the agency would have to protect its client and not expose them to a lawsuit. He rang a few days later saying he had been at a party, saw someone involved, and told us that all would be well. It was settled out of court and that was the last we heard of it.

Some projects provided us with the opportunity to bring in artists to re-create their own song, one of whom was the American blues singer and pianist, Champion Jack Dupree. The agency wanted an authentic sound (which he certainly had) but thought it prudent to have a jangly honky-tonk piano as well. These can be readily hired, so there we were, standing in the studio with two pianos side by side: one battered upright and one gleaming Steinway Grand. Jack was asked which he would prefer; he thought about it for a moment, looked at us as though we were mad, and declared in his gravelly voice, 'That's best for the blues', pointing at the Steinway! Another person I have very fond memories of working with is Jack Bruce, one of the great electric-bass players. Jack always used to refer to himself as a jazz musician – as indeed he was – but he was famous for being one third of the band Cream with Eric Clapton and Ginger Baker. Jack had 'depped' with Nucleus for one gig, and John Marshall had made some albums with him. We were called into a meeting to discuss a Renault car commercial and the agency wanted to use a Cream song of Jack's called 'I Feel Free'. Their collective jaws dropped when I said I could probably get him to play bass and sing, which he did.

I learned a huge amount from scoring for commercials, particularly by researching the rare and obscure instruments that were sometimes required, especially for ethnic-sounding scores. This is where I learned about ethnic percussion – something that would later become a feature of my composing. London, being so big and with a vibrant recording industry, was home to musicians who could play almost any instrument imaginable from any corner of the world.

There remains an absurd view, in some quarters, that it is somehow more honourable to drive a taxi, apparently as the American composer Philip Glass did, to make ends meet, rather than, as they see it, 'prostitute one's art'. To my mind it is more beneficial to work as a musician, in music of whatever kind (like Liz Lutyens and her Hammer Horror film scores), honing one's skills and learning. It was both enormous fun and an education, writing and recording music that spanned the spectrum from the blues to Elgar's Cello Concerto.

Eventually, the attraction of advertising music, creating a pithy, concise musical statement and the diversity of the musical styles required, wore off – and I yearned to stretch out again. I grew tired of always being at the mercy of film directors or advertising agencies that, inevitably, had the last word. They were the client, they were paying, and so it was their prerogative – but that didn't mean they were right, and very often they were not. It was time to move on, and to broaden my career. More importantly, though, it was also time to welcome a new Jenkins to the family.

7

BRIARWOOD

*F*amily has always been hugely important to me. My relationship with Carol has been a long and harmonious one, and I am immensely proud of my son's achievements, too. Jody was born on 24 January 1981 at Roehampton Hospital. His registered name was Joseph Karl Jenkins. Carol maintained that Jody was a moniker for Joseph but I, although endorsing the choice, wasn't convinced. The only male Jody I'd heard of was Jody Scheckter, the South African racing driver and the 1979 Formula One World Champion. With Jody's birth, we decided to look for a house and £50,000 was about our limit, so we had to search quite far out from anywhere that even faintly resembled central London. With two pounding pianos, we needed a detached house, therefore we moved into Briarwood, 224 Uxbridge Road, Hampton Hill, in October 1981, when Jody was nine months old. It was not all plain sailing. Having moved in, I didn't work for three months, not through illness or for any reason other than no work came in. We tried not to panic.

On a busy road, the A312, Briarwood was in a bad state and needed much renovation. I found a skeleton of a squirrel in the loft with its jaws still clamped around the electric cable through which it had gnawed. Hampton Hill is near both Twickenham and Hampton Court, south-west of central London. One of my first walks to explore the area was down the attractive high street: I noticed a gate, adjacent to a parade of shops, so I took a look. A vast expanse of greenery stretched out before me with ponds, roaming herds of deer and woodland. It turned out to be the second largest of the capital's eight Royal Parks, Bushy Park, a bonus of which I was unaware. We gradually made improvements at '224' and Jody started school in 1985 at The Mall, an independent boys' prep school, in Twickenham.

It was around this time that we got into a right old tangle with our names. Carol Jenkins continued to be known professionally as Carol Barratt. She had some problem before leaving for a lecture tour of Australia in that the name on the passport didn't match the promotional name. Again, at music conferences, taxis arriving for Jenkins would be turned away since no one knew her married name. This she solved by changing her name by deed poll to Barratt-Jenkins; the hyphen was deemed to be important so that the Barratt was unequivocally a surname, although Carol never liked the hyphen. She maintained it sounded too 'posh'. That should have been an end to it but I, stupidly, was unhappy with us having different names, so Jody and I also became Barratt-Jenkins. I had credit cards in both Jenkins and Barratt-Jenkins. It was not unknown for me to turn to Carol in a shop and enquire, 'Who am I?' to the disquiet of the shop assistant. Jody and I therefore changed back to Jenkins. While we were at it, the consensus was to change the Joseph to Jody as well since that, to all intents and purposes, was really his name.

Jody was doing well at school and showed excellent musical ability, not that this was necessarily seen or appreciated at The Mall until he started passing his Associated Board of the Royal Schools of Music examination grades with distinction. He began learning the flute, on which he produced a lovely sound, and he also took the lead part of Oliver in the school production of the Lionel Bart musical.

In winter we sometimes spent the New Year in the snow in Grindelwald, a village beneath the north face of the Eiger. It was here that I met Rod Temperton: a songwriter from Grimsby, he had gone to the US to work with the legendary musician and producer Quincy Jones and had written much of Michael Jackson's *Thriller* album. When younger, Rod had worked in the local fish industry. He told me of a local news cutting that read: 'Grimsby fish filleter reels in Wacko Jacko!' Rod once invited us to his birthday party. Apparently, every year in October, he invited six couples to join him and Kathy, his wife, to his birthday bash, which lasted a few days. 'Wonderful,' we said. 'Where is it?' The response: 'Fiji!' Off we went to Wakaya Island, which had been transformed into a luxury resort, mostly staffed by locals. There were a few individual bungalows (a modest name for the grand accommodation) dotted around the grounds. I felt at home when I saw the rugby pitch in the village and I met one local whose son was playing 'centre three-quarter' for Fiji at that time. It gives you some idea of the type of establishment it was in that the actor Nicolas Cage had just been there and Steve Jobs from Apple was next in.

The hotel in Switzerland had a pretty good resident trio and Jody, from the age of five, used to sit on the drummer's knee and play 'time' on the ride cymbal. He obviously had an aptitude for this, and it was something we were very keen to encourage. Carol taught Jody the piano at first, naturally using her own books, while at school he learned the recorder before later graduating to the flute. Carol established a Music Circle for some of her pupils to take part in charity concerts for Save the Children, and Jody, aged six, began playing at such events.

Carol found it a normal thing to arrange charity concerts, just as her mum had assumed it was a natural thing for her children,

Alan, Roy and Carol, to play in places such as chapels, churches, old people's homes and hospitals, once they could read music. Alan and Carol played piano duets (for example, the polka and fugue from *Schwanda the Bagpiper*), and Alan on the piano accompanied Roy on the violin. The rows before these events, Carol remembers to this day. Carol didn't have 'proper' piano lessons until she was eleven, but taught herself to read music with the help of the chimney sweep next door. Her mum's attitude was 'If you can read music, you can play for others.' She herself vamped on the piano – in a most comical fashion. She could 'do' tonic sol-fa, just like Aunty Ev, and similarly had a good ear, but couldn't read 'sheet music'. She was always buying songs of the day and plonking the sheet music in front of Carol, expecting her to sight read anything!

Much later in life, Carol wrote some animal songs and Jody was once asked a question as to what his parents did. He replied, 'Mum writes camel music and Dad writes loud music.' As he was growing, Jody was aware that Carol was writing music, some of which was for young beginners at the piano like him. He couldn't understand why, just as Carol edited or made changes to her music, she couldn't change Mozart, especially a passage that was proving difficult for him to play. Carol later asked Patsy Taylor, a pianist and teacher friend who had also studied at the Royal College of Music, to teach Jody. When he wasn't awarded a 'gold star' for excellence one week, Carol said, 'You can't get a gold star *every* week.' The response: 'I bet Mozart did.'

We were also active at the Piccolo Concerts in Twickenham where guests would come and play for children. Carol ran these for a time with Patsy. These Sunday afternoon concerts for children proved extremely popular. Eminent guests, such as the clarinettist Jack Brymer and the saxophonist John Harle, would play and talk to the young people, and the percussionist Tristan Fry was a 'big hit' since he brought along about fifty tubes of Smarties. He invited the children to eat a few to make some more space inside the container; the tubes of Smarties were transformed into maracas, which he soon had them playing.

Before long, Jody expressed an interest in learning percussion. Initial lessons at Kingston Association of Music Education with Dave Barry, a percussionist from Cardiff, who I had known from my time there, led to him playing in the National Children's Orchestra from 1991, travelling up to Ackworth in Yorkshire for their residential courses. Then, in 1992, Jody gained entry to the RCM Junior Department, where he studied with Jackie Kendall for six years. Every Saturday, the London music conservatoires held what were called 'junior academy' or 'junior college' for students of pre-conservatoire age. Jody absolutely loved it there, and made friends for life; it was wonderful to see him blossoming into not just a fine musician, but a happy and confident young man as well.

It's interesting how people come to play and shine on a particular instrument. My Dad chose the oboe for me, an idea that worked; the virtuoso harpist Catrin Finch knew from the moment she saw one being played, as a very young child, that it was to be her destiny; Jody was a decent flautist but became a brilliant percussionist having asked to make the switch. Lester Young, one of the great jazz tenor players from the mid-20th century, had a more prosaic reason for becoming a saxophonist. Originally a drummer, he found that by the time he'd packed up his drums after the gig, the rest of the band had gone off with the girls, and he'd had enough of it.

In 1993, Jody was offered a music scholarship to Hampton School. He had already gained a scholarship via the Common Entrance examination so this was an extra bonus. An independent school for boys, it had the traditions and heritage of a grammar school, which it once was, and although now totally 'private' there were many assisted places offered. Apart from academic excellence, it was well known for producing first-class rowers and the guitarist Brian May.

The piano we had at Briarwood was an upright Steinway, originally from Benson Cottage. My father had purchased the new instrument when I was in my early teens, replacing the Bell model we had. The Steinway had been delivered while I was at school so when I came home my father suggested I go and play the piano. I prevaricated for a while before going into the front 'music' room, having no reason to play at that particular moment. However, I was thrilled when I eventually capitulated and found the new instrument. This piano, which had been taken to Melina Court, was now at Briarwood, before we eventually part-exchanged it for a Steinway 'baby grand', 'baby' signifying a length of about 5 feet 6 inches, whereas a full concert grand can be up to 9 feet long.

The early 1990s were a predominantly very happy time for our family. Jody was excelling at school, I was enjoying a varied career, and, with every month that passed, Carol's work with Chester was winning her new legions of young fans and appreciative parents. I was still in very close contact with Aunty Ev and, in September 1994, she was admitted to hospital in Swansea. It was nothing really major, and she was in good spirits, but I arranged for my friend Tony Small to bring some players from Penclawdd Brass Band to come and play for her birthday. Aunty Ev always loved music, and Tony and his friends brought a twinkle to her eye when they performed for her in hospital. She used to call the trombone the 'step-and-fetch-it', a wonderfully apposite name for this instrument when used in marching bands. Not long after that, however, her health deteriorated quite quickly, both physically and mentally, in the form of dementia. We always thought of her as being indestructible. She was a great cook and her diet was very typical of her time – she ate full-fat dairy products, fried foods, hearty dinners, cakes and pastries – and she had no major illness except chronic arthritis. Aunty Ev had no family left, other than me, so she went into a care home near the village, where friends could visit. Sadly, she wasn't there for very long, and Aunty Ev died from pneumonia on 12 March 1995, aged ninety-one. She had been a mother to me and a grandmother to Jody. We all missed her enormously, and still do. We'd repeatedly invited her to come and live with us in London but she wouldn't leave Penclawdd. We still use her phrase 'when I do hear the sound of your voice, my spirits do rise' when phoning each other in the family.

Amid the sadness at this time, there was one positive thing to emerge. I had lost touch with Tony during my years on the road but this occasion rekindled our friendship and we are now very close. Coming from a family of trumpet players, his two sons Gareth and Ian also played. Ian went into IT as a career but Gareth is now Principal Trumpet of the Hallé Orchestra in Manchester. Tony was at the Royal Academy of Music with Graham Whiting, the husband of our friend Joan, the oboist. Graham died not long after I met Carol, and their daughter Becky is Carol's goddaughter. Joan later remarried a lovely and thoughtful man – Ken Graham, Transport Manager for the London Philharmonic Orchestra. Tony played in various orchestras before returning to Wales, and he had married Gillian, with whom I started at infants' school. He worked as a peripatetic brass teacher in the area, including our old school, Gowerton, which had become a mixed comprehensive, where all subjects were taught through the medium of the Welsh language.

In 1973, Tony established Penclawdd Brass Band and their logo was a cockle shell. In 1983 they became, at the Royal Albert Hall, National Brass Champions of Great Britain. Tony has made a huge contribution to music in the area and has been heavily involved in the National Youth Brass Band of Wales, while also transcribing much of my music for band. In 1999, I was delighted to accept an invitation to become the band's President, on their twenty-fifth anniversary, and write a piece for them, *Theme from an Unmade Movie*. He was awarded the British Empire Medal in 2015. We also share another passion, rugby, and we have debentures together at the National Stadium, Cardiff, for Welsh internationals.

Meanwhile, a major shift was looming in my professional life. Its genesis began quite innocuously, with a request to compose the music for a Delta Airlines commercial.

8

ADIEMUS

*I*n 1994, Mike Ratledge and I were approached by the London-based advertising agency Abbott Mead Vickers to compose the music for a campaign for Delta Airlines. This campaign had already been given the nickname 'Synchronised Flying' and the ad was to be shot by Hugh Hudson, director of the film *Chariots of Fire*. Frank Lieberman was Creative Director at AMV and the brief was one of the most vague that had come our way: 'something ethnic'. I sketched out a few themes and we eventually made a demo of one of the songs. I scored the harmonies for orchestra, played on a synthesiser at that stage, and Mike added the percussion, again mocked up electronically.

Around this time, I had been flirting with the idea of writing a work that, although based on the principles of classical music, possessed a vocal sound that was more akin to world music – and that had no obvious affinity with the Western European classical choral tradition. It's not always easy to rationalise where ideas come from. Often they appear as if floating down from the ether, or cyberspace, as one might say nowadays. All the ingredients were in place for

'Adiemus' to happen though: my classical roots and exposure to raw congregational hymn singing; my knowledge of jazz and 'nonsense' scat singing lyrics, as well as the use of percussion providing a regular pulse – and there was a singer on the horizon who would realise this concept. But more of that in a moment.

This sound would have two sides: one gentle and ecclesiastical, the other more aggressive and 'tribal', in part redolent of the singing I heard in church as a boy in Penclawdd. The missing element in this jigsaw was the text; that was when I thought of scat singers in jazz who make up words (of the *be-bop-ba-doo-da* variety) when they improvise on songs. Adopting this approach both resolved a dilemma and opened up other opportunities. It meant I could customise the text as I was writing each phrase, really treating the human voice as an instrument and not as a conveyor of text that had meaning or a narrative. It also meant that since I did not write lyrics or libretti, I did not have to source or commission text. Of course, unlike the jazz reference above, this text of the nonsense lyrics I was to compose was not improvised but written, organised and notated.

I should stress that although this as-yet-uncomposed music would go on to become perhaps one of my most famous works, at this stage it was simply the proposed soundtrack to a commercial. But regardless of where it would end up, a crucial part of the process was to have the right person singing it, and we knew someone in London who would be ideal. Mike and I had already worked with Miriam Stockley on a couple of commercials, and I asked her to be involved. Miriam was a white South African who had been working in London for a couple of years; she possessed a voice of rare beauty and was very much a studio animal, knowing how to work that environment to her best advantage. Miriam suggested that we employ Mary Carewe as well for the louder, 'tribal' sections.

Mary was, and is, a singer with a wide range of skills, ranging from classical and cabaret to music theatre. To create the tribal sound, the vocalists have to sing *fortissimo* (very loudly) and with no vibrato. It is not unlike the singing of younger children. It is, however, very taxing on the voice. To create the choral effect meant overlaying each melodic line three times. This was found to be the optimum number to produce a smooth rendition. There weren't any exponential gains by recording more tracks and one had to be careful that phasing did not creep in, whereby the vocals began to sound 'electronic'. For the gentler passages Miriam would be the only voice employed, but for the more strident moments she would be joined by Mary. The vocal range of this new work was, in the main, kept between C above middle C in the top part, and down to E below middle C in the bottom. The music was generally written in three parts; therefore on the quiet reflective passages, we had nine Miriams (three per line) and on the tribal passages, which they recorded together, eighteen tracked voices as well as embellishments. Miriam thought the lower vocals could do with some enhancing so we brought in the session singer Bob Saker. He lent some weight to the 'choir' but it was a very subtle contribution and you cannot really hear a male voice in the mix. I recall the agency requesting one change but I can neither remember what it was nor whether I acquiesced.

One further element needed addressing: the ethnic flute. We knew a man called Mike Taylor quite well: he was in a duo with Tony Hinnigan called Incantation and they contributed the 'ethnic' wood-wind parts to films such as *The Mission* and *Braveheart*. Mike, an affable Irishman, had trained as a classical flautist. He brought a selection of instruments along, an array of primitive wooden flutes. These instruments did not have metal keys like an orchestral flute, and by sliding his fingers across the holes Mike was able to bend notes in a very 'non-classical' way. We eventually settled on the *quena,* the traditional flute of the Andes in South America. Although technically a flute – with air being blown across a hole rather than directly into the instrument – the player plays it straight on like a recorder and not sideways like a flute. It was a no brainer to record again with the London Philharmonic Orchestra, the orchestra with which I had been working a great deal. We recorded at Angel Studios, with the engineer Steve Price.

Once aired, the track pretty much hit the mark with everyone who heard it, and the advert reached many people in numerous countries. Very soon after, record companies began to approach us. The first bite came from an independent producer from Germany, Ully Jonas, who flew over to see us. He had a deal with EMI GAS (Germany, Austria and Switzerland). There was soon a great deal of interest from labels in the UK as well. I was more than keen to develop this track into a collection of similarly styled pieces that could occupy a whole album. We eventually signed with Ully Jonas and EMI for GAS, and Virgin for the rest of the world. The actual Virgin label was Virgin Venture, a small subsidiary within Virgin itself whose Managing Director, Paul Conroy, gave the project his full backing. Venture, run by Declan Coughlan, another engaging Irishman, was created to handle modern classical and New Age music, although I never did understand what that term meant.

I wrote the album fairly quickly, using some of the ideas I had been stockpiling, together with some that were newly composed. I don't want to give the impression that I rushed the work. Sometimes it just happens that certain pieces are composed relatively effortlessly. Shostakovich wrote his celebrated String Quartet No. 8 in three days, not that I'm comparing myself with him. People often ask me how long a particular work took to compose. Some of my larger pieces took well over a year but when something takes a relatively short period of time, and I answer accordingly, I am met with a look of incredulity. I then usually add, 'and forty years', meaning the time spent learning, maturing, experiencing and living.

In practical terms, we just continued where we had left off with the commercial track. That had to be extended, of course, the original slot being 60 seconds long, I believe, with a cut-down of 30 seconds. The recording process for the album was exactly the same as for the ad, and our modus operandi was as it has generally been ever since. Because of Mike's computer skills, it was possible to construct a 'click' or metronome track that could fluctuate, slow down and speed up as well as keep a steady tempo. By such means we could programme a musical click; this facility is common practice now but it wasn't then, and we used it daily in music for commercials. For our new project, to this click track we added percussion and then a guide keyboard track that simulated a string orchestra. After this, the master vocals were recorded and, finally, we added the layers of the 'real' orchestra. We recorded the album at Studio 1, Angel Studios, again with Steve Price – an outstanding sound engineer with whom I have collaborated on most of my recorded output. In fact, I had known his late father, Ronnie, who was a kind of house pianist at the BBC and was often seen (and heard) in various TV shows. I love the way Steve, who has won two Grammys, records orchestras, which, to a degree, is different from the traditional classical approach. The sound is more filmic, 'in your face' and to my mind more exciting, maximising the resources of a modern recording studio, whereas the time-honoured classical route is more basic: straight to stereo and generally 'miked' at a distance to use the natural acoustic with a more nebulous sound.

There was one major change, though. This time, we brought in Pamela Thorby on recorder, instead of Mike Taylor, although we retained the latter's solo from the commercial audio track of 'Adiemus' for the album. A renowned virtuoso performer who then played with the Palladian Ensemble, Pamela brought another dimension to the flute role while at the same time having the flexibility to 'bend' notes. We also engaged Frank Ricotti for some additional live drumming.

Up to this point, of course, the project had no name. One wasn't necessary for a TV and cinema commercial. We had a meeting in the boardroom at Virgin to discuss this, and someone suggested we take a look at the 'text', the written representation of my vocal sounds. I read some extracts and the word *adiemus* (a–dee–ay–moos) seemed to spark a eureka moment with the record company executives present, so that was that. Although I had taken Latin in school for O level, I had not borne the language in mind when composing, unless it was subconsciously. It was pointed out to me later that *adiemus* is the future tense of the verb *adire* which means 'to approach'. Similar-sounding words are *audiemus* (we shall hear) and *audiamus* (let us hear) from the verb *audire* (to listen or to hear). It therefore transpired that, by chance, I had been on safe ground with a Latin word that at least resonated with what we were about. It could have been a lot worse.

A couple of years later, when I was working with the future Finnish *Adiemus* singers, I noticed that they were highly amused by something or other. Apparently in one section, 'Song of the Plains', the text 'doo ma-ra ma-la doo' could be interpreted as 'Tuu Mara maalaa, tuu', which in Finnish slang means 'Come, Mara, come and paint!' Martti 'Mara' Ahtisaari was the then Finnish president, hence the laughter. In 'Song of the Spirit', meanwhile, 'shama kama, shama kama; kamasha kamasha va' apparently sounds like someone, with a strong lisp, saying in Helsinki slang, 'Same junk! Same junk! We're high!'

For some strange reason I gave some of the movements Latin titles, probably to lend an air of gravitas to the proceedings. Also, once we were underway with the first realisation (which was the commercial spot), there was always an aura of the spiritual about *Adiemus*, and the Latin language, more so than any other, was apposite and helped promote the feeling and ambience of this quality. It also, more poetically, described the characteristics certain songs possessed: 'Cantus Iteratus' (repetitive song) was just that, while 'Cantus Inaequalis' translates as 'uneven song', since the beat was lopsided in 5/4 time. Other titles came from my invented text: 'Amaté Adea', 'Kayama' and 'Adiemus', although we now know that the last has a meaning in Latin. My wife Carol came up with the perfect name for the album: *Songs of Sanctuary.* It quickly became a hit in numerous territories, including two of the biggest three record-buying countries: Germany and Japan. It helped, of course, if Delta flew to a particular territory because that meant the ad would be shown, giving the project massive promotion, but, interestingly enough, we had no such exposure in Japan since Delta didn't fly there, yet it still proved to be one of our biggest markets. The Japanese loved the spiritual ambience of the music and the CD was filed under 'Healing Music', for which they had a special category. Someone said of me at the time, with reference to *Adiemus*, that I 'wrote spiritual music for secular people'. I always felt that this was a most apt description for what it was, since the sound often conveyed an 'other worldliness'. However, this was never contrived but simply what the listener heard in it. This spirit could only come out of the music, of course, since there was no religious text at all. Much of my later choral music employed standard Latin sacred text but, as I will come to later, this was often accompanied by forays into other cultures as well.

The one country where *Songs of Sanctuary* escaped the net, but where the 'Adiemus' track did not, was the US. In one of the most idiotic decisions made by a record company – and they make many – some executive at Virgin decided to place 'Adiemus' on a compilation album before the album proper was released. This meant that for the many thousands of people who wanted to buy what they knew as the 'Delta Airline Music' in the US, they had but one source, this compilation. Once they had the jewel in this particular crown, they were oblivious to the existence of the album, a classic case of a record label undermining its own product.

First out of the blocks was Germany, where we had a top-three single with 'Adiemus', with the full work similarly placed in the album charts. It was hugely popular in France, Spain, Finland, Taiwan, Portugal, the Netherlands, Israel and Poland and the album gained 'gold' or 'platinum' status in seventeen countries in all. Different territories saw it as belonging to a different genre but whatever it was, it certainly was addictive and it connected with people. It wasn't long before Paul Conroy presented me with an award, at a London recording studio, marking the sale of a million units in Virgin territories – and that didn't include Germany, Austria or Switzerland.

Adiemus proved a phenomenon in the UK and created a bit of a fuss, which I enjoyed immensely. Too many people were concerned with what it was, and what box it should it be in. Does it really matter, anyway? *Adiemus* has been a favourite on Classic FM since 1996 and, nearly twenty years later, it is still being sung in schools, in singing festivals and in competitions. It has also been set by various education boards for GCSE examinations. It seems it was the catalyst for the creation of alternative charts that included anything and everything that could be loosely termed 'classical' but wasn't what was perceived as being 'core classical'.

Despite the success of *Adiemus*, I had serious reservations about performing it live. The main problem, as I saw it, was that we had 'one' Miriam who embodied the sound of the piece, and it was very hard to replicate this sound away from the recording studio. We overcame this challenge by combining pre-recorded vocals with live singers. To form the live choir we held auditions: some who applied were already known to Miriam and Mary, so eventually we had a good team of six vocalists in place, besides Miriam. Come the performance, which I conducted, the pre-recorded element, including a click track, was played into everyone's 'in-ear' headphones, and all the performers sang or played along. There was no miming, just two merged sources emanating from the stage, that from the album and the live sound.

A sound company was required to handle the many and various issues involved in presenting this kind of music live. Pamela's recorder could never compete with multiple drummers, so the level of her instrument had to be raised accordingly. This basic principle applies across the board – and R. J. Jones, in Wimbledon, an eminent firm in the area of producing live concerts, was hired to look after the sound. Bob Capel was the project manager, Simon Hodgkinson the front-of-house engineer (balancing what the audience hears) and Simon Hodge was the offstage monitor engineer (balancing what those on stage hear), who must have done a particularly good job with Pamela, since he ended up marrying her. The *Songs of Sanctuary* premiere, promoted by Raymond Gubbay, took place at the Royal Albert Hall in 1996 and was a great success. It was a massive relief that we had made this project work. Logistically and technically it was more akin to a 'rock/pop' concert than a classical one but the effect was electric and memorable. It was my first Royal Albert Hall concert and one to be cherished. To see my name on the dressing room door, and 'up in lights', certainly gave me a frisson of excitement. In addition, since the percussion tracks had been overlaid on the album, I had to score this element for the players. We ended up with eleven drummers at the premiere, one of whom was Jody.

In the same year, Mike Ratledge left our partnership and essentially left music altogether. He wanted to pursue other areas, such as writing words, as opposed to music, and he had a developing interest in computer programming.

In the meantime, I had been writing the second *Adiemus* album, which was given a Latin title: *Cantata Mundi*. A cantata is a musical work for one or more voices with orchestral accompaniment, and *Mundi* means 'of the world'. The actual word 'cantata' means 'sung' in Italian and, like other Italian words such as 'opera' and 'oratorio', has come into universal usage. The cantata began in the early 17th century and developed on two fronts: the secular *cantata da camera* (chamber cantata) and the sacred *cantata da chiesa* (church cantata). German Protestantism developed the latter on its own lines, an important part of which was the chorale hymn, which is a feature of *Cantata Mundi*.

By this time, Jody had started working with me, both as a percussionist and a programmer, and he provided all the ethnic percussion on the recording. Sequencers were now readily available, so the world had caught up with Mike Ratledge. The other protagonists on the album were as before but I increased the orchestration to include woodwind and brass, making the overall sound more symphonic in its texture. We recorded at CTS, Wembley, with another fine engineer, Dick Lewsey. CTS was one of the largest studios in the capital and, by this point, we had a pretty large London Philharmonic Orchestra to contend with, too big for the room at Angel. Many film soundtracks were recorded at CTS, including numerous James Bond scores. The studio stood underneath the 'twin towers' of Wembley Stadium but CTS's existence was short lived since it was demolished in 2004 to make way for the new Wembley Stadium.

Cantata Mundi was released in 1997 and I was asked to play two concerts at the Helsinki Festival at Huvila-teltta in the August of that year. The orchestra would be the Tapiola Sinfonietta. There was no budget to bring singers from the UK apart from Miriam. I recoiled from the idea of using local singers but the deal was: have the Finnish singers or don't have a concert. How wrong could I have been. They were incredible. I have already written about the way the outstanding education system in Finland embraces music; the six female singers were products of that. They each worked in different fields as individuals – jazz, classical, theatre, pop – but they were all excellent readers of music and a couple taught at the Sibelius Academy. They are credited in the acknowledgements but my main contact has been Säde Barling who was the nominal musical leader of the ensemble. Säde is incredible. A composer herself and possessing perfect pitch, she has usually hired the singers for me and directed rehearsals before we meet up. She also performed with the EMO ensemble when they later sang on my *Stabat Mater*, a standard Christian Latin text set by many composers. I see her very much as a kindred spirit in that her ability and appreciation also crosses many genres.

We took the same technical team over and replicated what we had done at the Royal Albert Hall. The acoustic wasn't flattering, since we were playing in a massive marquee, but the experience was nevertheless a very memorable and special one.

Away from the concerts and albums I was busy recording three pieces – *Elegia*, *Cantilena* and *Beyond the Century* – that later appeared on various compilations or albums as 'bonus tracks', much beloved of record companies. *Beyond the Century* was written for the Japanese broadcasting corporation NHK, while *Cantilena* had been composed for a Cheltenham and Gloucester commercial, showing a young Indian boy diving for pearls, shot by Mike Portelli. Mike had two careers, as a dental surgeon and as a commercials director specialising in underwater shoots. I had worked with him before on a commercial for BBH for Speedo swimwear: this brilliant film was quite disturbing to watch since it showed athletes and cyclists, breathing underwater, exhaling air bubbles and struggling to perform, while the swimmer in her Speedo gear ('made to cut through water') came gliding by.

The year 1997 was very busy, because it also included a surprise but very welcome commission from W11 Opera, who asked Carol and me to compose an opera for young people. I was to write the music and Carol the libretto. We collaborated very happily together, although Carol might say 'most of the time', and created a 65-minute work, *Eloise*, scored for a small chamber group.

Carol based the libretto on a Nordic fairy tale of Princess Eloise. Some of the required proper nouns were invented by her (runs in the family, *à la Adiemus*?) but based on Norwegian (witch = *heks*; hence witches became Volheks). The world premiere took place on 12 June 1997 at St James's Church, Holland Park, conducted by Dominic McGonigal. Elaine Kidd was the director brought in to stage the production and also deal with dramaturgical issues that needed addressing. She was brilliant but it all sounded somewhat 'middle class' and polite, which was not *her* fault. A further performance, in Wales, at the Taliesin Theatre in Swansea had far more bite and raw emotion.

Having since been translated into German by Hanna Francesconi, *Eloise* has had some success in Germany, where I believe the witches have morphed into vampires.

Carol, by now, was increasingly contributing lyrics or libretti to my work, when English was required. Not long after, I was looking for text for a commission when she came up with the idea of using collective nouns as the basis for a narrative. *A Parliament of Owls* was composed for the Yoxford Festival, and scored for choir, four hands at the piano, percussion and improvising saxophone, the last played by Nigel Hitchcock. A 'knot of toads' croaks on tenor sax as a 'piteousness of doves' (a trilling soprano sax) 'discusses how to trill'. As Carol remarked, 'I'm handy and I'm cheap!' She later dispensed with music altogether on one project, a delightful illustrated children's book, *Idwal: A Tall Tree and Some Tall Stories*.

Around this time, I was also writing the next album: *Adiemus III: Dances of Time*. This was to be a celebration of dance forms such as the courante, bolero, rumba, pavane, minuet, tango, sarabande, waltz, square dance and ländler. It was the first *Adiemus* album to include the Finnish singers as well as Miriam. We recorded at CTS with the same team, both musical and technical. While scoring, I discussed with Jody the percussion instruments required. He then arranged and played the ethnic percussion parts, generally nine on each track. I wrote at the time:

The impulse to move to musical sound is universal. Historically, dance has found expression in an infinite variety of styles or forms, ranging from the solemnity of a religious rite to that of the obscene. The unique feature of dance however is that, as an art, it needs the crutch of another, namely music, to func-tion, even if the dancers themselves provide that sound. The ancient Greeks in fact had a single term – 'art of the muse' – for dance, music and poetry. Historically, dance had been orally transmitted but the 15th century saw the appearance of instruction books from Italy. Dance gained in popularity and was to have a profound influence on the new musical forms such as the suite. From 1630, French influence grew greater, culminating in the *opéra-ballet*. The 18th century saw the minuet, the social dance of the century, which also saw its introduction as a movement of the symphony. There fol-lowed the ländler (with couples embracing for the first time) and then the waltz. Dance was then listened to in concert format for the first time thanks to the likes of Johann Strauss. The 19th century saw the rise of romantic, classical and then later, modern ballet. In the 20th century, the influences of social dancing came from North and Latin America: ragtime, Charleston, foxtrot, rumba, bossa nova, rock 'n' roll, salsa, etc.

I have entitled this piece *Dances of Time*. We know mankind has always danced, so this is a celebration of dance through the centuries, through 'time'. The first notated evidence we have of what the music sounded like dates from the 15th century and one of the earliest dances available to me with an identifiable personality was the 'pavane'. Therefore, in practical terms my dances span six centuries, although spiritually they are timeless. The word time also refers to time signature (the number of beats in a bar) so the title also alludes to that.

Looking back, 1997 might well have been the busiest year of my career to date. A multitude of different projects all presented themselves to me, underpinned by the unprecedented success of *Adiemus*. I could have been tempted to pull back a little, and to opt for an easier ride the following year but, to be honest, I was having far too much fun even to contemplate that for a moment. The year 1998 was therefore similarly busy: it included broadcasts of my music from the Plan International Gala in Helsinki in February and the UNESCO Gala in Palma. 'Zarabanda' (the sarabande) from *Dances of Time* was used as an UNESCO anthem for a time, and the London Philharmonic Orchestra was flown out to Majorca for this particular concert in the April of that year.

By this point, I had rationalised the percussion parts to involve fewer players, and I was slowly assembling a regular team. Two had come out of jazz but were outstanding players of ethnic percussion: Paul Clarvis and Dave Hassell. They were also among the 'specialist' visiting professors at the Royal Academy of Music and we had met at Jody's first Shell LSO Scholarship competition a couple of years before. Jody was on board as well, on merit I hasten to add. The fourth was Gary Kettel, who was something of a legend. In the early 1970s he had been Co-principal Percussionist of the BBC Symphony Orchestra at the age of twenty and had a good relationship with the resident conductor (and composer) Pierre Boulez. By this time, Gary was a freelance musician. The fifth player was Neil Percy, Principal in the London Symphony Orchestra; he sometimes worked with us

when a concert did not clash with one of the LSO's. These players would complement the contracted percussionists of whichever
orchestra we were working with. There was quite a bit of partying
after the UNESCO concert in Palma: Gary went AWOL and missed
the flight back to the UK but he eventually turned up, safe and well.

In June and July, we recorded *Dances of Time*, which was released
that year, and we also performed at the Henley-on-Thames Festival.
Our next *Adiemus* outing was to be in 2000 but, unknown to me,
The Armed Man: A Mass for Peace was looming. And if the success of
Adiemus had surprised me, the life-changing nature of this next piece
of music was about to take things to a whole new level.

9

THE ARMED MAN:
A MASS FOR PEACE

*A*llow me to take a moment to wind back a little in my story, to 1993. There are two reasons why I want to take this brief pause. In part, it is to contextualise the developments in my career at the time, and to highlight a few other opportunities that had fortunately come my way during the early part of the decade. But I also want to focus in on 1993, in particular, to acknowledge a significant development in music technology, which would go on to have a major effect on my work. For it was in that year that a now-famous music notation software programme called Sibelius was launched. I assume that the programme was called Sibelius after the Finnish composer, since the surname of the British twins who wrote the programme, both music students at Cambridge, was Finn. I had always been accustomed to writing in the traditional, time-honoured way, with manuscript paper with its 'five lines' of the musical stave, and with a pencil. At home, we were always searching for, borrowing from, or arguing over, pencils. They had to be 2B, a soft lead that was ideal for music and that could be easily erased. An electric pencil sharpener was also indispensable and we had two, to save someone commandeering the use of a single gadget.

I was about to start work on a blank score one day, when dear Bridie Beck entered the room. She was a lovely Irish lady, well over eighty, who helped us with a bit of ironing, babysitting and much else besides. No one was sure of her exact age, even she, since, when she had come over from Ireland, she had given the authorities erroneous information concerning her date of birth in order to gain entry to the UK. Her records had been destroyed in some fire or other at government offices, Bridie always maintaining that Michael Collins the Irish revolutionary leader had something to do with it. Anyway, Bridie looked at this large blank sheet of score paper with its many staves and enquired, 'Do you have to fill it all in?'

There were other music-notating programmes available, such as Finale and Score, but these were off-putting since I was then computer illiterate and, to operate these programmes, one apparently needed good computing skills. Sibelius was, reputedly, more user friendly so I took the plunge and embarked on dual concurrent learning processes: how to use a computer in tandem with the Sibelius music programme. The first Sibelius programmes (I came on board around Sibelius 3) were compatible only with the Acorn computer but that gradually changed and I eventually upgraded to Apple Mac, since that was the tool of the media, music and recording industries. Learning the two skills took some time but I had help to hand with my computer-literate and musical son.

Our Roland electric piano was MIDI-compatible so I could combine this with the Mac and Sibelius to compose music. An amazing tool, Sibelius is fast and neat and can do things that computers do that would take an age by other means: cut and paste, transpose music into another key, lay out a score, play back the instruments if so desired, and much more besides. The possibilities were endless. One thing that came to an end with the advent of such technology was the composer's sketches and false starts of old, unless one was archivally minded enough to save each version for posterity. One could also extract from the full score, and then print individual parts – trumpet, viola, oboe, etc. – not that I needed this facility since by this point I had a publisher to deal with this. Boosey & Hawkes is one of the premier names worldwide in the publishing of classical music, and they have published my music since *Adiemus*. Founded in 1930, their catalogue includes works by Bartók, Britten, Copland, Kodály, Prokofiev, Richard Strauss, Rachmaninov, Stravinsky – and Carol.

Back to the early 1990s and, to house both my burgeoning para-phernalia and me, we decided to build a small wooden chalet in the garden. We hired an expert carpenter to do the job; he was good, but as an ex-trombonist he wanted to talk music the whole while. In retrospect, perhaps he wasn't that good since on one occasion he turned up having severed the tops of two fingers on another job. The 'Sibelius House', as it was henceforth called, complete with a photo of the Finnish master on the wall, was somewhere in which I was cosily ensconced, and it became a creative refuge for me. I ventured all of the ten yards to this haven quite early each morning to work, scantily clad in summer and in a dressing-gown with wellingtons in winter. The dogs often accompanied me. Sam had passed away to be succeeded by two other Westies: Jamie first then, shortly after, Meg. By this time we had created a kind of Italianate garden with gravel and paving stones, exotic shrubs, a small pond with a fountain and a couple of statues; my vista as I composed.

Our garden took a couple of hits from the weather over the years: first there was the Great Storm of 1987 that caused havoc over Greater London (many trees were decimated in Bushy Park) and beyond, and then, a couple of years later, a tornado hit Hampton Hill. We had, by now, quite an elegant and sprawling mature conifer. I looked on aghast, through the kitchen window, as the tornado just ripped it out of the ground, destroying a stone boundary wall in the process.

Living in Hampton Hill also made it easy for me to feed another passion: rugby. London Welsh, the club against which my father had broken his collarbone, was nearby, in Richmond, as were a number of others. London Welsh had been one of the great teams in the 1970s and had provided seven players for the 1971 British Lions tour of New Zealand, including J. P. R. Williams and Gerald Davies. I was 'on the road' then, which made it difficult to go to matches, but having settled in the area I joined the club. Other Welsh musicians used to congregate there: Drac, my LSO horn-playing friend; conductor Owain Arwel Hughes; and the music copyist and trumpet player Brian Vaughan. My old Cardiff University contemporary Neil Kinnock was also a London Welsh supporter when time permitted.

At home, meanwhile, Jody's array of percussion instruments was also growing, necessitating even greater space, so we decided to extend the house, in effect converting the garage that ran down the side into a music studio, while still retaining the 'Sibelius House'. Jody had started improvising on vibraphone and often asked, having returned from school, 'Can we play the jazz tonight, Dad?' We teamed up as a duo, with me on piano and Jody on either vibes or drums. He was becoming very interested in music technology and asked if we would subscribe to the magazine *Sound on Sound*, which he devoured avidly. A side effect of his developing interest in this element of the music industry meant that Jody was to prove to be of massive benefit to me in the coming years. He was once even hauled out of a class in school to help me with a technical matter of some importance. I was always something of a Luddite and have still not totally embraced technology.

In 1995, I was approached by Work Music, a subsidiary of Sony, to record an album for strings. It was to include *Palladio*, which was a development of the theme I had composed for the De Beers 'A Diamond is Forever' commercial; 'Passacaglia' (a passacaglia is a piece where the melody is always present somewhere in the orchestration), dedicated to my Aunty Ev; *The Adiemus Variations*; and my String Quartet No. 2. The first two pieces were played by the London Philharmonic Orchestra, and the last two by the Smith Quartet. This album appeared twice, first as *Palladio* and later re-released as *Diamond Music*.

It was Work's idea to take the motif I had written for the De Beers ad and develop it into my long concerto grosso. During my many trips to Venice, I had been inspired by the buildings of the 16th-century Venetian architect Andrea Palladio, such as the church of San Giorgio Maggiore. Palladio is widely considered the most influential individual in the history of Western architecture. Since my piece was to be written in a retro style, loosely reflecting that period of history, I decided to name it after him.

Then, in 1997, a second one-off project (a stand-alone release not part of a deal or series) was proposed by Work. From the time of the earliest civilisations, the moon has fascinated man. In the 1st century, the Roman writer Plutarch described it as being inhabited 'by the greatest living creatures and fairest plants', and by the 17th century it was believed by European astronomers that the large dark areas of the moon, visible from Earth, were oceans, seas and lakes. Science, with sophisticated telescopes and Apollo space missions, has shown these shadows to be craters or the general land relief of the moon's surface but, paradoxically, and coinciding with the making of this recording, a space probe found some evidence of water at the moon's poles. *Imagined Oceans* is a musical interpretation of thirteen of these features. Early astronomers gave evocative Latin names to these supposed 'water features'. By incorporating various instrumental and compositional techniques – ranging from the relentless repetitive rhythm of 'Lacus

Pereverantiae' ('Lake of Perseverance') to the pizzicato strings evoking raindrops in 'Mare Imbrium' ('Sea of Showers') – I endeavoured to create a world of aquatic fantasy, a world of *Imagined Oceans*.

For text, I adopted a variation of the *Adiemus* approach by 'de-structuring' the movement titles and using only such derivatives of the song title as text. For example the word *lacus* meaning lake was intoned thus: *la-la-la-lacus*. This enabled me to indulge, to a degree, in 'word painting' to enhance the programmatic or visual element of the music. I brought Pamela Thorby in on recorders; meanwhile, Nic Pendlebury (viola player with the Smith Quartet, who had earlier recorded my string quartet) put together a select group of string players and conducted the sessions. I didn't want the *Adiemus* sound for this project and so asked Micaela Haslam to come on board. I had heard her sing *Tehillim*, very impressively, with the composer Steve Reich, so she joined us with Sarah Eyden and Heather Cairncross, two colleagues with whom she regularly worked in the vocal groups Synergy and the Swingle Singers. Between the three of them, they possessed a four-octave range. *Imagined Oceans* was premiered at the Royal Festival Hall in London, on 29 May 1998.

In what was rapidly becoming a happy habit as far as I was concerned, Jody had worked on the percussion parts for *Imagined Oceans* and had, by now, joined the National Youth Orchestra of Great Britain, becoming Principal Percussionist in 1998 and playing under conductors such as Mstislav Rostropovich, Sir Colin Davis and Sir John Eliot Gardiner at major venues throughout Europe. After receiving the Gerald McDonald Award for the young player displaying outstanding potential at the Shell LSO Music Scholarship of 1996, when he was fifteen, Jody won the Silver Medal at the subsequent event in 2000. He studied with Neil Percy (percussion) and Kurt-Hans Goedicke (timpani), before being awarded a scholarship to my old stomping ground: the Royal Academy of Music.

It was in the NYO that Jody met Rosie Hillier, an oboist from Teesside. Rosie had studied at Chetham's School of Music in Manchester – known to all as 'Chets', and the largest music school in the UK – at sixth-form level for two years. Like Jody, Rosie was destined to go to the Academy. Jody brought her down to Briarwood and, as Carol said, 'It was as if the sun had come into the room!' A lovely, lovely girl, she and Jody became an item at this time and it is remarkable how much the oboe has featured in the lives of family and friends. It being my father's favourite instrument led to my playing it. Carol's elder brother Alan Barratt had played it in the RAF band when stationed in Germany, while his elder daughter, the fine inno-vative jazz composer Issie Barratt, played oboe before switching to saxophone. The aforementioned oboist Joan Graham, Carol's closest friend since school, played in the London Philharmonic Orchestra for many years and Rosie, similarly, was to reach the top of her profession as an orchestral oboist. In another life, my friend Cerys Matthews played the oboe, in the 'West Glam'. Both Carol and Jody have written pieces for Rosie – Jody a *Sonata* and Carol a *Prelude and Jig*. An ardent fan once approached me with all sorts of embarrassing, fallacious and exaggerated compliments, along the lines of 'You are the best composer in the world.' I replied, 'I am not even the best composer in my family,' an absolutely genuine and heartfelt response.

As the 20th century was drawing to a close, I was about to com-pose one of my very few commissions for the BBC, *Dewi Sant* or 'St David', inspired by the patron saint of Wales. His exact dates are unknown but he is thought to have died *c.* AD 600. Three sayings, in Welsh and taken from his last sermon, provide the text for three of the seven movements: 'Byddwch Lawen' ('Be Joyful'), 'Cadwch y Ffydd' ('Keep the Faith') and 'Gwnewch y Pethau Bychain' ('Do the Small Things'). The four remaining movements are a mix of Welsh, English and Latin, and comprise three Psalms: No. 22 – a psalm of conflict and desolation; No. 2 – a psalm of trust and confidence; and No. 150 – a psalm of praise and rejoicing. Completing the text was a setting of 'Good Night, House of Dewi', adapted from Dafydd Johnston's translation by Canon A. M. Allchin of Waldo Williams's poem 'Ty Ddewi'. The premiere took place on St David's Day (1 March) 2000 at St David's Hall in Cardiff, and was given by the BBC National Orchestra of Wales. The choir was comprised of massed youth choirs from different parts of the principality, and there later followed a televised performance, by BBC Wales, from the beautiful cathedral at St David's in Pembrokeshire, the smallest city in the world. My skirmish with the establishment was apparent even then. Radio 3 refused to air the recording.

By the time this piece received its premiere, Jody was taking his A levels. At Hampton School, he had managed to involve music in all three of his A-level subjects (apart from General Studies): Music itself, Music Technology (which he had studied on a self-taught basis, since the school had no teacher) and Theatre Studies, for which he adapted a traditional tale, *The Bridge*, into a play that he produced while also composing the incidental music. He did well, gaining A★ (for Music), A A (and a B in General Studies) – something that really was the icing on the cake for an already very proud mum and dad.

Jody was a prolific prize-winner at the Academy, including the BMI Principal's Prize and the Zildjian Prize, which, much to his delight, meant a trip to Boston to collect some cymbals from the factory and eating lobster as street food. Halfway through his course he made the major decision to change from percussion to composition and graduated with a first-class honours degree in 2003, winning the Edwin Samuel Dove Prize for 'special merit during studentship'. In what was a very special occasion at St Marylebone Parish Church, Jody was awarded his degree and prize at the same ceremony where I was awarded the FRAM (Fellow of the Royal Academy of Music) following the ARAM (Associate) I had been presented with a few years previously.

Around the time that Jody began playing with the National Youth Orchestra, I was approached, by the Royal Armouries and Classic FM, to compose a piece of music to commemorate the millennium. I, of course, was not party to the history of the commission, so that tale is better told by Guy Wilson, the then Master of the Royal Armouries:

> The Royal Armouries is Britain's oldest national museum. It grew out of the arsenal of the medieval monarchs of England housed in the Tower of London. From an organisation that equipped this country's armed forces has developed a museum that has as one of its main purposes the display of the hardware of war and through this the encouragement of an understanding of what war really is, and what it means and does to the people involved in it. We were looking for an appropriate way for the Royal Armouries to commemorate the millennium. We had decided that as we were moving into a new century we should be doing something new, something of lasting value that we could continue to use and something that should somehow reflect this country's Christian tradition.
>
> I began to consider the possibility of a musical commission – something that we could use in our continuing educational work and something through which, by involvement and performance, could deal with some of the historical and moral issues raised by our subject. Then Bob Smith, our Head of Collection Care and a great enthusiast for early music, came to see me. He had an idea to celebrate the millennium by putting on a series of concerts featuring some of the *L'Homme armé*

masses of the late-15th and 16th centuries. This we decided to do, but it gave me another idea.

L'Homme armé is a song written at the Court of Charles the Bold of Burgundy between 1450 and 1463. Soon afterwards, a cycle of masses was written, five using parts of the melody of the song, the sixth including the whole tune. Thereafter, until the end of the 16th century, over thirty more masses were written using the tune of the song in some way.

The theme that 'the armed man must be feared', which is the message of the song, seemed to me to be painfully relevant to the 20th century and so, the idea was born to commission a modern Armed Man Mass. What better way than within the framework of a Christian and liturgical form, both as we leave behind the most war-torn and destructive century in human history, and we look ahead and commit ourselves to a new and peaceful millennium.

And so the idea developed to combine with the basic mass form a variety of poetry and prose, and a wide range of musical styles that reflect the multi-cultural society in which we live, to attempt to create a work that dealt in an inclusive way with a theme of universal interest and relevance. The challenge then was to create a work that tells a story, makes people think, and tugs at the heartstrings. The next step was to see if I could produce an outline that really appealed to someone who really knew about these things. I put pen to paper and, two years ago (1998), took the result to Michael Bukht of Classic FM. He liked it and so began the association with Classic FM and their Masterclass Music Charitable Trust that has resulted in this work.

Between us we established a little group to choose a composer to work with us and we managed to persuade Karl Jenkins to take up the challenge. And how fortunate we have been to work with him. It has proved to be an exciting and constructive partnership. He has responded to the commission by composing the most marvellous, varied, accessible, appropriate and 'sing-able' music that embraces the whole world and the full range of emotions that the subjects of war and peace evoke. In addition, he has taken an active part in developing the form and content of the work and has greatly improved my first crude and overlong selections of text. He has, I believe, created something of raw power. It certainly moves me and I am sure it will move you, too.

From my perspective, it was a privilege to set such inspiring text as that chosen by Guy, who supplied more material than we used; it was the frame over which to drape the music. It took me about twelve months to complete the composition. In my case, it is not always a matter of starting at the beginning and working through to the end of the score, especially with such clearly defined sections as here. Very often, a musical idea comes readily to mind for a section later on in the work. With *The Armed Man*, the 'cantus firmus' (the *L'Homme armé* tune) was there anyway, as a motif for structural cohesion, to be used with all kinds of techniques if needed.

The premiere took place on 25 April 2000 at the Royal Albert Hall with the National Youth Choir of Great Britain alongside the National Musicians Symphony Orchestra conducted by Grant Llewellyn, with Julian Lloyd Webber as the cello soloist in the 'Benedictus'.

Guy of course researched and collated the wonderful text that was mine to set. Once this was established, it was a question of my getting on with it, in isolation almost, since it was what it was – it didn't have the characteristics of a dedicated libretto that could be changed, edited or developed. It simply told the story that Guy, as the 'writer', now relates:

The Mass begins with a marching army and the beat of military drums, the orchestra gradually building to the choir's entrance, singing the 15th-century theme tune – 'The Armed Man'. After the scene is set, the style and pace changes and we are prepared for reflection by first the Moslem Call to Prayer (*Adhaan*) and then the 'Kyrie', which pays homage to the past by quoting (in the 'Christe Eleison') from Palestrina's setting of *L'Homme armé*. Next, to a plainsong setting, we hear words from the Psalms asking for God's help against our enemies. The 'Sanctus' that follows is full of menace, and has a primeval, tribal character that adds to its power. The menace grows in the next movement as Kipling's 'Hymn Before Action' builds to its final devastating line: 'Lord grant us strength to die.'

War is now inevitable. 'Charge!' opens with a seductive paean to martial glory that is followed by the inevitable consequence – war in all its uncontrolled cacophony of destruction, then the eerie silence of the battlefield after the battle and, finally, the burial of the dead. Surely nothing can be worse than this? But think again. At the very centre of the work is 'Angry Flames', an excerpt from a poem about the horrors of the atom bomb attack on Hiroshima written by a poet who was there at the time and died in 1953 of leukaemia brought on by exposure to radiation. But if we think that the obscenity of this mass destruction is new to our consciousness, we must reconsider as we listen to the eerily similar passage from the ancient Indian epic, the *Mahabharata*.

From the horror of mass destruction the work turns to remember that one death is one too many, that each human life is sacred and unique. First the 'Agnus Dei', with its lyrical chorale theme, reminds us of Christ's ultimate sacrifice, and this is followed by an elegiac setting of some lines I wrote (to accompany one of the dramatic interpretations we use in the museum) about the feelings of loss and guilt that so many of the survivors of the First World War felt when they came home but their friends did not.

Even the survivors can be hurt to destruction by war. The 'Benedictus' heals those wounds in its slow and stately affirmation of faith and leads us to the final, positive, climax of the work. This begins back where we started in the 15th century with Lancelot's and Guinevere's declaration, born of bitter experience, that peace is better than war. The menace of the 'Armed Man' theme returns and vies for a time with Malory's desire for peace. But time moves on and we come to our moment of commitment. Do we want the new millennium to be like the last? Or do we join with Tennyson when he tells us to 'Ring out the thousand wars of old, Ring in the thousand years of peace'? It may seem an impossible dream, we may not have begun too well, but the *Mass* ends with the affirmation from Revelation that change is possible, that sorrow, pain and death can be overcome. 'Dona Nobis Pacem'.

The text is taken from the Ordinary of the Mass, the Bible, the *Adhaan*, and the *Mahabharata*. Obviously the flavour of the text affected aspects of the music as it went through; word painting, instrumentation, mood and so on, but this is no different to any work that one composes when setting words. Writers quoted are Kipling, Dryden, Swift, Malory, Tennyson, Sankichi Tōge and Guy Wilson himself. Guy's haunting contribution, 'Now the Guns Have Stopped', came rather later in the proceedings. I recall that these moving words were written only because we could not secure copyright clearance on some selected text, by Maurice Baring. In the event, at the last minute we did secure clearance but I was more than happy to stay with Guy's memorable words.

During the composition process, the tragedy of Kosovo was unfolding. I was thus reminded daily of the horror of such conflict and so I dedicated this work to the victims of the war there. A few years later I visited an orphanage in Priština, the capital city of Kosovo, with a children's charity that was working with some of the most vulnerable children in that country. This was in conjunction with a performance of *The Armed Man* in the UK. It is the one and only time that I have been to what had recently been a war zone; it was still occupied by UN forces. I also visited some families living in abject poverty and dreading the coming winter. It was a deeply emotional experience. I was reminded, once again and at first hand, of the futility and resulting devastation of armed conflict.

The CD recording of *The Armed Man* was made at Air Studios during the summer of that same year. Another one of London's large studios, Air, housed in a converted church in Hampstead, was founded by Beatles producer George Martin in 1969. The soloists came from within the National Youth Choir, and Duncan Riddell led the London Philharmonic Orchestra with Paul Beniston as principal trumpet. Mohammed Gad was the Muezzin, and Guy Johnston, who had recently won the BBC Young Musician of the Year competition, played the cello solo in the 'Benedictus'. I can't properly recall the situation with the cello solo but due to some misunderstanding or lack of communication I was told that Julian was unable to make the recording. There was no intention to slight anyone.

The album was released on 10 September 2001, and I then forgot about it for a while. For the first couple of years after release, *The Armed Man* lay pretty dormant, and I've no idea what initially caused the explosion in the popularity of the piece on a global scale. There was no massive publicity drive by the publisher or the record company but, as far as the UK was concerned, there *was* Classic FM, a station that has been enormously supportive of me over the years, since

Adiemus. Perhaps, in part, because, as *Classic FM Magazine* wrote of me, 'As a composer, he recognises no boundaries – musical, commercial, geographical or cultural. His is a way of thinking and composing that is perfectly in tune with the spirit of the times.'

The 'Benedictus', with its cello solo, was perhaps the catalyst that drew people towards it. This solo lies, in part, towards the top of the range for the instrument and is tricky to keep in tune 'up there', but it is eminently playable by good performers, as anyone who has heard the recording can testify. On one occasion, when I conducted the work with the Leicester Philharmonic Choir and the BBC Philharmonic Orchestra, the principal cellist on that date, who obviously had neither heard the piece nor really bothered to look at his part beforehand, came up to me at the commencement of the rehearsal and said, 'Of course, you mean this to be played down the octave.' A look of dread and incredulity crossed his face when I said I most definitely did not. It is always best to have players on your side, but I was slightly annoyed since the implication was that, as a composer, I didn't know the range of the instrument. I politely replied that it had been performed, and recorded quite beautifully (and in tune) by both Julian Lloyd Webber and Guy Johnston respectively, among many others. On another occasion, a player told a mutual acquaintance that he thought he 'got away with it', when palpably he hadn't. He 'ghosted' each entry, ever so quietly, to find the note before he played it. It's been known for some beginners, when learning the cello and double-bass, to draw chalk on the fingerboard to mark the notes. I knew one eminent woodwind principal in a London orchestra who, when subjected to out-of-tune string playing, used to surreptitiously murmur, 'Chalk, chalk!'

Apparently, the 'Benedictus' is often played at funerals. Carol's mother, May, said on her deathbed, 'I've got to have that there "Benedictus" by Karl at my funeral.' Since the millennium premiere, at the time of writing this book, *The Armed Man* has been performed

1,820 times (averaging more than two per week around the world), in 43 countries and more than half the American states. It has sold 123,000 vocal scores, and the recording has been in the UK classical charts continuously for 579 weeks.

The only contentious issue, over what is now a period of performances spanning fifteen years, has been the inclusion of the Islamic 'Call to Prayers' – and this issue has probably surfaced on no more than five occasions. Invariably, the objections come when the piece is to be performed in a church or cathedral from church authorities or elders who demand or request that the 'Call to Prayers' be omitted from the performance. One of the most publicised was a scheduled performance at the Berliner Dom (Berlin Cathedral) given by the Berliner Domkantorei. Permission to perform the work was withdrawn so the performance, which I attended as a guest, was moved to the Konzerthaus (concert hall). Its exclusion caused a brouhaha and one German journalist wrote, 'This is the church that, sixty or so years ago, was happy to have the swastika draped over the altar.' There was also a backlash in that most liberal of countries, the Netherlands, after Theo van Gogh, the Dutch filmmaker, was targeted and shot by a terrorist. Following a couple of instances in the Bible Belt of the US where the work was banned from the churches in question, it surfaced once again in Sweden where some choir members resigned in protest over its exclusion, although the decision was overturned and it was included in the end. It's even occurred in the UK, too, at Chester Cathedral and recently (in 2015) in Bangor, North Wales. One group even asked whether they could slip in an alternative piece of music by another composer, an extraordinary suggestion! However, the work has been performed in numerous British cathedrals, including Salisbury, Wells, Truro and Exeter, as well as at the Queen's Chapel, St George's, at Windsor Castle, so I'm happy to say that not all church authorities have taken such a narrow view.

In order to deal with such objections, which, historically, have arisen at very short notice (no doubt when the church authorities learned of its inclusion, which could be weeks into rehearsals), we have a prepared mission statement:

> Karl Jenkins composed *The Armed Man: A Mass for Peace* as a meditation on the destructive nature of divisions between different cultures and nations. The reason for including the Islamic Call to Prayer, as well as texts and musical quotes from Western Christian sources, Hindu sources and from a Hiroshima survivor, is that the composer believes that tolerance will heal and prevent such divisions. It is therefore Jenkins's explicit wish that any performance of *The Armed Man: A Mass for Peace* includes the *adhaan*, either recited live by a muezzin or played on loudspeakers from the EMI CD recording. If the 'Call to Prayers' must be omitted, the composer reluctantly allows this, but stipulates that a period of silence must replace it, with the programme notes making it clear that, at this point, the Muslim Call to Prayer would normally be heard.

I once had an enquiry about the possibility of a performance in Russia to mark the fiftieth anniversary of the brutal Battle of Stalingrad, one of the bloodiest of the Second World War. A perusal score of this *Mass for Peace* was sent, only for the message to come back eventually that the work was not suitable for the occasion. Something that marked and celebrated the glorious victory of the Russian Army over the German invaders was apparently required.

Over the years, I have collaborated many times with the filmmaker and musician Hefin Owen – and at this point, I hand over to him to offer his reflections on the film he made that was inspired by what is, I suppose, my most famous and most celebrated work to date:

Following the filming of the *Celtic Adiemus IV* concert in St David's Hall, I received a copy of the *Armed Man* CD in the post from Karl. I sat in the office on a work day and listened through to it from beginning to end, and was very moved. Later that afternoon I took it to J. Mervyn Williams (who had been my boss at the BBC but now we were partners in Opus Television) who also listened to it in his office. I told him how I thought it was a very visual piece of music with a strong narrative – something that we were always looking for when proposing something for television.

I noted that Karl's sixtieth birthday was on the horizon; therefore I proposed an S4C special from St David's Hall when we would use some of Wales's finest choirs and solo-ists, but more importantly have the story of the work told in film behind the performance. The aim was to enhance the audience's experience of the music but not dominate to the extent that the music became subservient to the film. It would be important that the film followed the performance, as opposed to the tempo of the performance being dictated by the film.

Karl gave me contact details for Guy Wilson, as I was keen that my interpretation would echo – wherever possible – his vision when choosing the text for the work. I went and met Guy, who showed me around the Royal Armouries museum in Leeds, and over an evening meal we talked through what might be possible as appropriate archive footage.

A researcher in Opus – Luned Phillips – set about find-ing what footage might be available to an independent TV company. Such material can be very expensive to incorporate in a TV programme, which is why it is often used sparingly. Derek Blades from Images of War came to the rescue, and his terms were very reasonable. However, his material effectively ran out in the 1950s and we wanted the footage to be as all-encompassing as possible, especially with the Afghanistan/Iraq hostilities that were occurring at the time.

I managed to obtain the services of the film editor Chris Lawrence for three weeks; Chris was a very experienced editor who used to work in BBC Wales, but was now freelance and who had edited countless dramas, documentaries and films in his time. His credits included the legendary drama *Grand Slam* and the Oscar-nominated *Hedd Wyn*. I cannot emphasise enough how much the film's effectiveness is due to his craft, vision and humanity. On several occasions we both needed to retreat to our own little corners to recover emotionally as we were dealing with such horrendous material.

I knew we had something special when I saw for the first time the planes crashing into the Twin Towers. The eight timpani beats leading to the 'choir scream' fitted so perfectly with the plane crashing into the tower and the subsequent explosion. At the time the footage we had was very poor quality, and we had to argue very strongly to be allowed to incorporate TV-quality footage as there was a restriction as to how often such footage was given a licence to be shown. The rough cut was shown to Guy and Karl before it was shown in the concert as I was keen to obtain their blessing. Surprisingly and reassuringly, their reservations were few and they were very supportive and enthusiastic.

Gratifyingly, on the night of the original showing, I didn't receive any criticism for attempting to put on such a performance, but there seemed to be two main points of discussion. The first was about the positioning of pictures of Blair and Bush among the other war leaders at the end of 'Save Me from Bloody Men'. At the time, this seemed rather brave and controversial, and apparently was even discussed at the Welsh Assembly government's cabinet meeting the following morning. The second was the celebratory footage during 'Better is Peace'. It is very difficult to convey the relief that war is over without seeming to join in with the celebrations of those that won, and therefore there's a danger that it is seen only through the eyes of the victor.

Generally, there was tremendous enthusiasm for the concept of the film and, following some tweaks forced on us by financial considerations due to the cost of some of the original footage, a DVD was made available for hire, so that other performances can be made with the film as a background. I have received some very moving comments as to how powerful performances with the film have been and I feel very proud to have been associated with such an amazing work.

The film echoes and traces the story as told in the text of the work: the build-up to conflict, conflict itself; and the aftermath, finally looking forward to a better future. It has been seen as a backdrop to performances innumerable times all over the world – from Carnegie Hall to the Royal Festival Hall, from Johannesburg to Shanghai. Its presence greatly enhances the musical performances and inevitably leaves the audience emotionally drained, often in tears.

Of all the performances of *The Armed Man*, in my estimation I have conducted fewer than one per cent of them, but some were certainly memorable. Perhaps not the best musically, but certainly emotionally, was the one on the very day of the tenth anniversary of 9/11 at Carnegie Hall, New York. The programme included *For the Fallen*, which I wrote for the Royal British Legion Festival of Remembrance at London's Royal Albert Hall on 13 November 2010, and which I later recorded with soprano Hayley Westenra, narrator Bernard Cribbins (actor but also ex-paratrooper), the National Youth Choir and the London Symphony Orchestra. In New York we were fortunate to have, as narrator, the legendary soprano and New Yorker Jessye Norman, who also read out a letter from Mayor Bloomberg.

For the Fallen is a setting of Laurence Binyon's famous ode honouring the war dead which includes the lines, 'At the going down of the sun and in the morning, We will remember them.' The 'Last Post' is incorporated into the score, for unison trumpets. It is dedicated to my uncle, Alfryn Jenkins, who lost his life as captain of a Lancaster bomber over Berlin in 1944. He was also a viola player so, in homage, the piece opens with solo viola.

Alfryn came home on leave and met me after my birth on 17 February 1944. He was killed just over a month later. On the fateful night – 24 March 1944, the 'Night of the Strong Winds' – Lancaster ND642 and its crew were lost. They were on a mission targeting Berlin, and the winds were incredible that night, the velocity of which none had experienced before. One George Saunders, a navigator, had a specialist role: he was one of 100 Squadron's 'windfinders', responsible for checking wind speeds and reporting them back to base at thirty-minute intervals. These readings were sent on to Bomber Command Headquarters where meteorological staff, the 'Met Men', averaged out the found wind velocities and rebroadcast revised strengths to all the navigators on mission, so necessary course adjustments could be made. But this system was ineffective that night. The Met Men thought there were errors in the readings and wouldn't believe the high speeds being transmitted to them.

STILL WITH THE MUSIC

The Lancasters were flying in the jet stream where the wind velocity was 70 mph faster than had been forecast, giving the bombers a speed relative to the ground of 360 mph. The Met staff apparently did not believe such a significant discrepancy and, accordingly, broadcast wrongly adjusted winds back to the bomber stream. Those crews who trusted the wrongly broadcasted winds drifted south of track on the return leg, taking many towards the flak hotspots of Magdeburg, Leipzig, Kassel and the Ruhr.

As ND642 left the skies over Berlin, homeward bound, they followed a south-westerly track towards Leipzig with a planned turn over Treuenbrietzen. Wind information was radioed back to RAF Waltham at 21.58 and 22.16. Nothing was heard from ND642 after 22.16. German fighters were now on station. Of the 811 aircraft that had begun the mission, 72 were lost, Bomber Command's heaviest reverses to date. Lancaster ND642 was hit by one of the fighters and crashed just north of the German town of Eilenburg, north-east of Leipzig. It was the aircraft's first sortie and it had taken off less than four hours earlier at 18.57. Although I never knew him, my Uncle Alfryn was often spoken about by both my grandmother and his widow, Aunty Gwen, who lived to a good age and had, of course, taught me in primary school. I now possess his 'wings' and the telegram from the War Office, stating that he was lost in action.

It is somehow a double tragedy when loss of life happens in a perilous situation that might have been avoided but for fate. Despite flying many bombing missions, on this occasion Alfryn might have returned if the crew had had correct information from the Met Office. When, in 2014, I was preparing my piece marking the fiftieth anniversary of the Aberfan tragedy, I was haunted by the story of one young girl. She was ill and didn't go to school that day and instead went to stay in her grandparents' house. If she had gone to school, she would have been in one of the classrooms that escaped the catastrophe.

As fate would have it, her grandparents' house was one of those, near the school, that was crushed. She perished.

The Armed Man occasionally took me to places I perhaps, otherwise, would not have visited. One such occasion was when I was asked to conduct a performance in Johannesburg. Rita van den Heever, who was the Head of Arts at the city's university, initiated the performances as artistic director and producer, assisted by Chris Avant Smith as production manager. The first concerts were on 26 and 27 September 2007 in the Johannesburg City Hall. The building, standing in a depressed part of the city, had fallen somewhat into a state of disrepair and it was a mission for those involved to revive and rejuvenate the place as a concert venue.

It was a memorable occasion and I was uplifted by the fact that performers were very much multi-racial, with some of the string players coming from the Soweto String Project, a spin-off of Buskaid. Buskaid is a charitable trust, registered in both the UK and South Africa, that was founded in 1992 by the British viola player Rosemary Nalden when she learned of the difficulties experienced by a group of string players in Diepkloof, Soweto. Rosemary enlisted the support of 120 of her professional colleagues, who took part in a simultaneous 'busk' in March 1992 at sixteen British railway stations. In two hours, they raised £6,000 for the benefit of the young township musicians. Since then, several hundred distinguished musicians have participated in a further four 'busks'. Funding now comes from corporate sponsorship, various South African and UK trusts, the South African National Lottery Distribution Trust Fund, individual donations, and CD sales and performances by the Buskaid students.

Rosemary Nalden established the Buskaid Soweto String Project in January 1997 in response to requests from the local Diepkloof community. Initially, the BSSP consisted of fifteen members of the original Diepkloof Project, and a few new beginners. Since then, it has more than quadrupled in size, and currently comprises approximately a hundred students ranging in age from four to thirty, all of whom are drawn from the less privileged local community. Sadly, however, hundreds of children have been turned away since Buskaid's inception, owing to lack of resources. On the positive side, some have made the grade, coming to the UK to study at music colleges, particularly at the Royal Northern College of Music in Manchester.

After a rehearsal for *The Armed Man*, it was suggested that I drop into a concert given by the Soweto Strings at the Linder Auditorium. I was moved to hear these young black performers play so expertly and was humbled when I was personally welcomed before they played *Palladio* for me – a memorable occasion on many fronts. I have been privileged to have since been associated with Soweto Strings, and I conducted my piece for them, *Soweto Suite for Strings*, at the Queen Elizabeth Hall in London during my (and Rosemary's) seventieth birthday year, 2014. The work and dedication of Rosemary, who has devoted her life to Buskaid, is absolutely remarkable.

Sometimes, when undertaking such engagements, I am happy to be 'paid in kind' rather than command a fee – and this trip was one such occasion. Someone on the university board had a connection with the Sabi Sands Game Reserve, adjacent to Kruger, so Carol and I went on safari, staying a few days at Lukimbi Safari Lodge and then Idube Private Game Reserve. We flew from 'Joburg' in a light aircraft and were driven to the reserve in a taxi. We rounded a corner to be confronted by an elephant in the middle of the road. Carol, of course, wanted to get out and reason with the elephant. 'What do we do now?' asked the local driver of us Europeans. Brilliant. Blowing the car horn didn't work. I suggested he phone ahead, to the lodge, and ask for help, which is what he then did, having taken an age to source the number. A ranger came out in a jeep, jumped out, clapped his hands and the elephant ran off. Carol is a great nature lover and it had always been her wish to go on safari and see the 'big five' and more. I was more ambivalent about it but once there it was absolutely amazing. When we left the camp on our first drive she hoped, at least, to see a giraffe. We had only just left the camp perimeter when we saw one happily strolling down the dirt track in front of us. A bad reaction to some malaria tablets meant I was ill one day, so Carol cheerfully went off with a ranger to examine elephant dung. Dinner at the lodge was at the BOMA: a large, circular communal table around the fire. I assumed this to be some native African word but it is simply an acronym for British Officers' Mess Arena.

There are eleven official languages in South Africa, apart from English and Afrikaans, spoken by various tribes: among them, Zulu, Xhosa (with that amazing clicking sound), Tsonga, Swati and Venda. We visited a kind of theme or culture park where many tribes had examples of their visual art and craftwork, and performances of their musical culture. A Zulu dance troupe performance was accompanied by some amazing drumming; the drummers were behind a low screen so the actual drums were hidden. I was fascinated by what I had heard so, after the performance, I went over and peered into the percussion area. What I saw was mainly a collection of Western drums. Such is progress.

We met the architect who designed the Apartheid Museum in Johannesburg, who arranged a visit. His wife, in fact, was a Holocaust survivor at the age of thirteen. There's a novel and imaginative method of entry: one is randomly given a disc, either black or white, which determines the door by which one enters. Carol, with her white disc, was inside in a matter of seconds. I, with my black disc, had to jump through so many metaphorical hoops and over so many hurdles, taking several minutes to gain access, a simple yet effective means of symbolising the abhorrent and degrading system that had existed. We heard of one bizarre test that was used to determine race: a comb was put in a person's hair; if it fell out you were deemed to be white, if it stayed in place you were deemed to be black.

I returned to Johannesburg in September 2010 to conduct my *Stabat Mater* – the story of which I shall tell a little later – with essentially the same cast as with *The Armed Man*, and at the same venue. *The Armed Man* was also responsible for establishing my relationship with DCINY (Distinguished Concerts International New York). In 2004, in London, I met Jonathan Griffith, an American choral director who at the time was working for MidAmerica Productions. Their novel business model was that they invite choirs to come to NYC and, for a participation fee, rehearse for a couple of days prior to giving a concert at Carnegie Hall or the Lincoln Center. An interest was expressed in them giving the US premiere of *The Armed Man* and this came to pass in June 2005 at Carnegie Hall, with a repeat performance in 2007. In 2008, Jonathan left Mid-America and established his own venture with co-founder Iris Derke: DCINY, with him as Artistic Director and Principal Conductor, and Iris as General Director. I was appointed to the advisory board and named 'composer in residence'. Since January 2008, a tradition has developed that a concert of my music takes place annually on Martin Luther King Day, which is the third Monday in January, usually at Carnegie Hall, sometimes at Lincoln Center. DCINY has programmed every one of my large choral works as well as a collection of my concertos.

10

CELTS, BALLET AND THE EAST

aving composed *The Armed Man* well in advance of the premiere (this is normal since the choristers have to learn the piece), I had turned my attention back to *Adiemus* and the fourth album.

Before that, though, I had a strange commission called *Composer's Challenge*. It was one of my few forays into the BBC and was part of a series. The idea was that, on camera, one was given an envelope containing a challenge to compose a piece of music and have it performed the next day. All the logistics regarding the venue and musicians would have been arranged and ready to go; that was a given. I can't recall what the other challenges were, save that one composer had to go into Wormwood Scrubs jail for his event. My envelope contained instructions to compose a piece of music to celebrate the Chinese New Year, 'The Year of the Dragon', and direct a performance of it in Manchester's Chinatown the very next day, 5 February 2000. The orchestration consisted of Chinese instruments, a choir and a small string ensemble, and the text was 'Spring Dawn' by Meng Hao-jan:

Asleep in spring I did not hear the dawn,
Till the birds broke out singing everywhere.
Last night, in the clamour of wind and rain,
How many flowers have fallen do you suppose?

It was quite a challenge but being used to deadlines and the use of ethnic instruments, I quite looked forward to it in a perverse way. A car was on hand to drive me home, with a delightful lady from the UK Chinese Ensemble. This turned out to be the internationally renowned academic, scholar and musician Dr Cheng Yu who had translated the poem for my text and who was also going to play the *pipa*, a fretted four-string lute. Her colleague would play the *sheng*, a wind instrument. Some atmospheric Chinese percussion was added so, following some instruction and plenty of welcomed advice, I 'pieced a piece' together, and rushed up to Manchester – where the choir and string players were based – to premiere it. It was an open-air performance and the Anglo-Chinese audience seemed to enjoy it, as did I.

In future years I was to have two more flirtations with China, composing two pieces: *Zhi Jiangnan (On Visiting Jiangnan Province)* and *Qing Zhu (Celebration)*. The first was commissioned by the Shanghai Spring International Music Festival, in conjunction with the 2010 World Expo. I was invited out to Shanghai, a city with an evocative past and intriguing areas such as the Bund and the French Concession, to soak up the atmosphere, in readiness for starting work. Two rather trivial memories, in particular, stand out from that rather special trip. The first was eating a dish (called 'Drunken Shrimp' apparently). Seconds earlier, the prawns had been swimming around in the dish before me, only then to be stunned by the alcohol present in the liquid. The second was reading *A History of Modern Britain* by Andrew Marr on the flight, and realising that the author was, by sheer coincidence, sitting next to me. He was kind enough to chat to me a little about the book. I couldn't fly back for the premiere a few weeks later since many flights were grounded due to the volcanic ash cloud eruption in Iceland – the only first performance I ever missed.

In a roundabout way, my next trip to China came via south London, of all places. In Dulwich, there is well-known public school that has international satellite schools around the globe, including one in Beijing where all subjects are taught in English. In January 2012, the music department, run by Sean O'Shea, invited me out for a week to mark an anniversary. I was to hear some new music of mine, commissioned by the International Schools Choral Music Society and performed in the Forbidden City concert hall, alongside a performance of my *Gloria*. Apparently, all foreign text (of which Latin qualifies) has to be translated into Chinese for the censor, and religious text is not allowed (I was told they even tampered with Mozart's *Requiem*). A 'friendly' translator was hired to gloss over references to God. It did not really cause me any concern since it was only a bureaucratic censorship issue, perhaps only seen by one person. The work was performed, as was that of Mozart, as written of course, with no change of text. In both Chinese works, each of which was scored for chorus and orchestra, I incorporated the beautiful indigenous string instrument, the *erhu*.

Soon after my Chinese experience in Manchester, I was commissioned by Hefin Owen to compose the music for a TV documentary series called *The Celts*, with which he was about to go into production. Two thousand years ago, northern Europe was occupied by groups of people who shared traditions of language, art and culture. Back then, they were known as Galatae, Keltoi or Celae – but today, we now refer to them as the Celts and I, save for my Swedish quarter, am one of them. Unlike the organised hierarchical societies of the Greeks and Romans, the Celts lived more as an association of separate tribes who threw their energies not into architecture or edifices, but into mythology and visual, decorative art. Celtic myths have never lost their potency, inspiring people for generations. It seemed a good idea to combine this with the making of the next *Adiemus* project album, effectively composing the same music for both projects. In 2013, the documentary soundtrack won a BAFTA Cymru.

All the movements were inspired by Celtic tales or characters, with deliberately evocative titles including 'King of the Sacred Grove', 'Ceridwen's Curse' and 'Isle of the Mystic Lake'. These separate pieces all combined to create an album entitled *The Eternal Knot*. For the vocalists, I returned to the original concept of using just Miriam Stockley and Mary Carewe with an extra high voice, that of the Welsh singer Caryl Ebenezer. While retaining all the *Adiemus* signature elements, the album returns to the greater intimacy and smaller orchestration of *Songs of Sanctuary* – but with a Celtic twist. Apart from the ever present Pamela Thorby, I used quite a number of Celtic soloists, or soloists that had settled in a Celtic country: Davy Spillane, the fabulous Uilleann pipe player from Dublin; the accordionist David Farmer; Martin Taylor, one of the world's finest jazz guitarists who then lived in Scotland; and my very good friend, the Welsh harpist Catrin Finch.

Back in August 2000, I was invited to lead a performance of music from *Adiemus* in Linz, Austria, and we were back with the Finnish singers once again. I had decided to increase the singing strength from six to nine and so we added three more vocalists. This particular concert took place in a massive space, a steel mill, before a few thousand people, with the audience on three sides. The orchestra was the Bruckner Orchestra Linz, and the Vienna Ballet performed a ballet choreographed to the music by Renato Zanella. Both the singers and dancers were on stage, with the orchestra in a kind of pit. The concert was sponsored by the mill owners, with the workers, about three thousand of them, gaining free entry, with a similar number of paying customers. It proved a big success.

We took the opportunity to visit Prague, by car with driver, for the first time: Carol, Jody and I, with Rosie flying out to join us. There was some drama about Austria closing its borders in protest over a nuclear reactor being built in Bratislava, which was now in Slovakia. It was like being in some spy movie, in that we had only so much time to make the border crossing. When we arrived at the frontier, that specific checkpoint had closed so it meant a detour, at speed, to another, eventually getting through just in time. Despite the journey and arriving feeling like nervous wrecks, Prague proved to be fascinating and we visited the residence of the Czech composer Antonín Dvořák.

A year or so later, I had another ballet performed, in a vast, old and disused industrial site – Kraftwerk Vokerode – about 125 kilometres from Berlin, by the Gregor Seyffert Dance Company of the Dessau Theatre. The ballet was *Marquis de Sade* and they used the recording of my *Requiem* for most of the music – which seems, on the face of it, to be an insensitive and contradictory use of this work, one being the antithesis of the other, but it worked amazingly well. The performance was on an even bigger scale than the one in Linz: the ballet was in three acts but instead of the set being changed, the audience moved to a different area of this enormous industrial plant. Access to some of the seating was along gangways, across gantries, up and down spiral staircases, even the occasional ladder. The run was for quite a few days. I'm sure the production would not pass muster here with the UK health and safety regulations, and the dancers were in no less a dangerous position either, sometimes with a drop of several metres separating audience and dancers. It was crazy, but mightily effective. Gregor Seyffert choreographed several other ballets using my music at that time.

Another noted choreographer who has used my work is Nacho Duato of the Spanish National Ballet Company. The beautiful abstract ballet he made, 'White Darkness', has since been performed by many companies around the world, including this year, by the Berlin Staatsballett. I've always found the ballet world odd, though, in that it seems to relegate the composer to a role subservient to that of the choreographer. A billing would be, for example, 'Kenneth MacMillan's *Romeo and Juliet*'. So much for Prokofiev's contribution. I was once commissioned to write bespoke music for the touring arm of the Royal Ballet, for a production called *Love's Fool*, written and choreographed by the excellent William Tuckett. I went to a performance in High Wycombe. There was an interval drinks reception for 'the great and the good'; I wasn't admitted. There they were, all cosy behind a cordon sipping bubbly, while I was queuing, with the paying customers, at the bar for a drink.

I sometimes think that dancers, and singers for that matter, of the *prima donna* (or the male equivalent, *primo uomo*) variety should adopt the aphorism 'Without composers we'd have no career; without composers we'd have no career; without composers we'd have no career', and chant it thus, like a mantra. All that said, I am grateful for the fact that the strong rhythmic elements to much of my music have meant it has been used regularly by ballet companies over the years, and some wonderful choreographies have resulted, even though I remain frustrated that whenever I query the dismissive attitude to composers, the response is always an irritating 'That's the way it is.'

In September 2000 we premiered *The Eternal Knot* at the Royal Albert Hall. After that, I continued to explore *Adiemus*-related opportunities around the world, including a trip to Japan that was planned for the autumn of 2001. I had been to the country a couple of times previously, with Miriam, to undertake promotion. It seemed strange to me but Toshiba–EMI, our record company, had initially been very keen, insistent even, to present *Adiemus* as a project shrouded in mystery with no promotion or acknowledgement of the people behind the music. This went on for years. The promotion events we started doing later were rather bizarre occasions, such as Miriam and I opening a branch of the perfume shop Sephora in Tokyo and performing a short concert outside on the street to a backing track and a couple of string players. We were then approached by the promoter Satoshi Fukuoka of Conversations with an invitation to come out and play four consecutive concerts at the Bunkamura Orchard Hall in Tokyo. Some of us had flown out a few days early and we were in a bar one evening, the night before the recording of *The Armed Man: A Mass for Peace* was released in the UK. A waiter approached us, possibly thinking we were American, and drew, on a serviette, a building with a plane stuck in the side of it. We didn't understand what he was on about, laughed, and carried on drinking. When Carol and I returned to the hotel we turned on the TV: 9/11 had happened.

Apart from the shock, horror and dismay, putting all else into perspective, we still had a scheduled concert to address and we therefore had to make some decisions. Initially, all international flights were grounded. When this ban was eventually lifted we had to decide what to do since some of our performers were still in the UK. Pamela Thorby was pregnant and so, understandably, she refused to travel. We were extremely fortunate in that we found an excellent recorder player in Tokyo who had studied in Italy and even knew my music: a delightful young lady called Mitsuko Ota. Then we had issues with the three drummers who were due to fly out: Gary Kettel, Paul Clarvis and Dave Hassell. One of the wives didn't want her husband to travel. Then Gary hit on the idea that they would go down to Heathrow and see what it was like (shades of guitarist Ray Russell and the train from Wiesbaden in the 1970s) before deciding and taking a vote, though quite what a cursory glance at Heathrow would reveal I don't know. In any case, they flew. The singers and Jody were already out in Tokyo with us so we went ahead and I dedicated the concert to the victims of this monumental catastrophe.

Above: My parents, David and Lily.

Below: Me as a baby.

Above: Penclawdd and the Bury Estuary taken from The Graig, with Tabernacle Chapel visible in the distance.

Below: With Mam, my paternal grandmother.

Above: Benson Cottage, the house I grew up in from 1950.

Below (left): My mother with Morfar at New Inn, Penclawdd.

Below (right): With my parents, aged three.

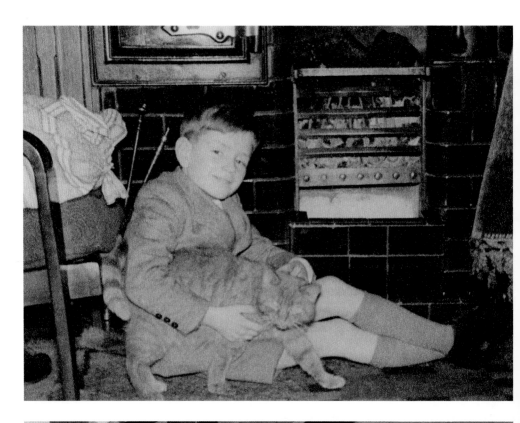

Opposite (top): At the hearth in Benson Cottage, aged seven, with my cat Sparky.

Opposite (bottom): At the piano, aged nine.

Above: Sketched in Sweden, aged nine.

Left: A young oboist, aged twelve.

Left: Cardiff University Jazz Club,
1964.

Above: At Ronnie Scott's 'The Old Place' with Graham Collier, 1967.

Opposite: At Ronnie's, Frith Street, in the 1970s with Nucleus.

Above: Soft Machine, mid-1970s. Right to left: Karl Jenkins, John Marshall, John Etheridge, Mike Ratledge and Roy Babbington.

Left: On stage with Soft Machine, 1977.

Above: *Adiemus*: Anna-Mari Kähärä, Rika Timonen, Miriam Stockley (soloist), Nina Tapio, Mervi Hiltunen, Säde Barling and Mia Simanainen (standing); Pamela Thorby and me (seated).

Below: On the podium, 2011.

Above: With war victims in Kosovo, 2004.

Below: With Dame Kiri Te Kanawa, 2006.

Above: *The Armed Man* rehearsal, with Hefin Owen's film, in Johannesburg, 2007.

Below: At our *mustache* studio with my son Jody, 2007.

Above: Aunty Ev with our first Westie, Sam.

Below: Jamie and Meg.

Left: My wife Carol, c. 1995.

Below: Jody, me, Carol and my daughter-in-law Rosie at Windsor Castle for the CBE in 2010.

Above: Portrait by June Mendoza.

Above: At the piano, Angel Studios, 2013.

Left: My grandchildren, Astrid (aged four) and Minty (aged one), in 2015.

11

THE STUDIO

When the 21st century began, I was in the fortunate position of having become established, to a certain extent, as a mainstream composer. As you know by now, I've always recoiled from the idea of being categorised; nevertheless, with the commercial success of *Adiemus* and the increasing appreciation I received for *The Armed Man*, my music was now widely enjoyed – and life was good. In many ways, however, things remained the same (in a very fulfilling way, I might add). Carol wrote and composed, as did I; and I continued to need the use of a studio in central London. In the late 1990s, once my partner Mike Ratledge had retired, I established myself in Foubert's Place, just off Carnaby Street. Also at this time, I formed a new company: Karl Jenkins Music Limited.

In 2002, my good friend Mark Cellier was looking to acquire a building in Poland Street, just down the road from Foubert's Place. Mark had sold his company and was putting together a consortium of people to invest in the project. He invited Carol and me to come on board. Including the basement, there were five floors, and the plan was to renovate the building and then let it. Of the consortium, only

Mark and I ran a business, so we became tenants, renting from the consortium (which included ourselves) at the market rate. By then, Mark had established a video company and a casting agency. Initially, I rented the top three floors.

For many years, Yamaha had been developing and selling acoustic grand pianos that were excellent instruments in their own right and in 1992 they added as an option an ingenious invention known as the 'silent piano'. By throwing a switch, the piano became 'silent' but could still be heard by listening through headphones. Technically, this worked by suspending the action whereby the 'felt hammers' hit the strings, the piano becoming a digital instrument, using a sampled dig-itised piano sound. Perhaps the selling point was that the instrument could be played in any circumstances – but it had a more important benefit for musicians such as me. It made the piano MIDI-compatible, so it could communicate with my Mac and Sibelius music-notation programme, while also being able to perform admirably as a grand piano. I needed both: one as a compositional tool and one for meet-ings or rehearsals. Although I could have used two instruments, the Yamaha represented the best of both worlds. I contacted Coach House Pianos in Swansea, the best piano retailer in the UK, and ordered a Yamaha C2 'Silent' (5'8"). Then the drama started.

The piano was to go on the top floor of the building, and further investigation showed that it could not be negotiated up the stairs. The problem was the half-landings, where there was insufficient space to manage the turn. The only option was lifting the piano with a crane and manoeuvring it through a window. The windows on the street side had too small an aperture to allow entry but to the rear was a balcony, to which access from the room was gained through a pair of large sliding glass doors. Not only did the piano therefore have to be hoisted to the top floor; it also had to go over the roof at the back. It meant closing the road, and Westminster Council would allow this to take place only on a Sunday. Poland Street is pretty deserted on Sunday mornings anyway, but for the privilege of closing the street, Westminster Council charged £1,000. Much later, when we decamped to Wales, the process was reversed, incurring further expense. We couldn't really house two grand pianos, so, with great regret, our Steinway had to go. Coach House Pianos facilitated the sale, placing a note on the instrument to the effect that 'Karl Jenkins composed on this piano', and sold it to someone in Newport (Wales, this time, not Rhode Island!).

The issue of composing at the piano occasionally comes up, often with the inference that it is somehow cheating or that it betrays a lack of ability. I don't think Stravinsky or Ravel lacked ability. Many composed at their desk, including Richard Strauss and my tutor Alun Hoddinott (apart from piano music, so he said, since he needed to be mindful of hand positions), and some, a combination of both. Berlioz played the guitar. Only one thing matters: the end result, and not how one gets there.

By 2003 I was spending so much on recording costs that I was slowly coming round to the idea that we should have such a facility at Poland Street. Jody was beginning to work as well, as a media composer, in addition to assisting me on my projects, so it made commercial sense since he could now engineer and operate such a space. Building a soundproof room was a pretty complicated project and the job of designing the facility was farmed out to Recording Architecture, experts in this field, before being constructed by a building firm. To help with soundproofing, we had to create a room within a room, a bit like the vacuum-flask principle, while dividing the space into two: a live recording room and, separated by a glass partition, a control room.

Naturally, we still had to hire large studios for the recording of orchestras and choirs but our studio, called *mustache* when I used it and *Jenkins Music* when Jody did, paid its way by facilitating most of what both of us required: recording anything that didn't require many

people nor vast amounts of gear – so, solo vocalists and instrumentalists, the layering of click tracks, percussion, sampled and programmed
tracks, overdubbing all manner of things, and mixing. From that point
onwards, all my percussion for albums was done there, by Jody for the
greater part, and all the solo voices or instrumentalists. Many illustri-
ous names were to record in that studio, from Dame Kiri Te Kanawa
to Bryn Terfel, and Sacha Distel to Cerys Matthews, as well as jazz
greats such as sax player Nigel Hitchcock, guitarist Martin Taylor and
bassist Laurence Cottle. Nigel, a prodigy, is one of the most phenomenal musicians I have ever known and, although not formally educated
(he left school as soon as he could to play the saxophone), he is a man
of remarkable intelligence: Mensa territory, total recall and perfect
pitch are just three of his many accomplishments. As an improviser,
Nigel always plays what I want to hear – not that it is predictable,
anything but – but it is always 'right'. In my varied musical life, I have
worked with all kinds of musicians in different genres: classical, rock,
folk, and plenty more besides, and I know one cannot generalise, but
the best of the best in terms of imagination, good time, instrumental
facility and aural ability have always been jazz players.

By now, 'recording tape' was a thing of the past, and had given
way to digital recording on hard drive. We filled the room with a
range of kit, the names of which would have been completely foreign to music students in the mid-20th century: Mac-based ProTools
HD3 recording system with Control 24 control surface, Logic Pro
running on a further Mac with MOTU interfaces, various analogue
outboards, Neve and Focusrite preamps, a box of classic microphones
and an ATC 5.1 surround monitoring system. My very first project
in this new studio was an exciting one – but before I share the story
of how it came about, allow me to tell you a little about the musician
who christened the facility.

Catrin Finch is a rare being: a harpist who plays with fantastic rhythm and sense of time, performing in anything but the 'wishy-washy' manner one sees, and hears, all too often. I had heard of this prodigy from Wales and I was introduced to her a year or so later when Rosie, a good friend of Catrin, strongly recommended her to me. They, and Jody, were students together at the Royal Academy of Music and had all been in the National Youth Orchestra at around the same time. In 2000, Catrin was appointed Royal Harpist to HRH The Prince of Wales, reviving this ancient position, last held by John Thomas, who was appointed by Queen Victoria in 1871. In 2006, the Italian harp manufacturer Salvi presented the Prince of Wales with a £150,000 gold-leaf harp, the instrument that the official harpist now plays.

In 2001, I was commissioned to compose a double harp concerto, at the behest of the Prince of Wales with the generous support of the Peter Moores Foundation, for Catrin and her mentor, teacher and future mother-in-law, Elinor Bennett. It was premiered in Cardiff on 1 March 2002, St David's Day, by the BBC National Orchestra of Wales in the presence of the Prince. Titled *Over the Stone*, the work is in six movements and the written cadenza contains, at the suggestion of the Prince, a quote from *Mae hen wlad fy nhadau*, the Welsh national anthem.

The first major piece of work I undertook in the new studio was an album with Catrin. In 2002, a situation arose whereby I was in a position to introduce her to the international record label Sony Classical, run by Peter Gelb, who later became General Manager of the Metropolitan Opera in New York. He was interested in signing Catrin, so she was summoned to play for him in his suite at the Savoy Hotel. Catrin had to transport a concert harp from the Academy, across London and all that entails, all the way to the hotel when all Peter had to do was transport himself in the other direction. Nevertheless, he loved her playing and they agreed to do something together.

The album, which I was to produce and orchestrate as well as contributing some material, was to be pretty broad in concept. Titled *Crossing the Stone (Tros y Garreg)* after the Welsh folk tune I had used in the concerto I had written for her, it also alluded to 'crossing barriers' musically. We recorded three movements from the concerto, three 'jazz fusion' classics, 'Mountain Dance' by Dave Grusin, 'Spain' by Chick Corea and 'James' by Pat Metheny, for whom Steve Reich had composed 'Electric Counterpoint' – which we also recorded, overdubbing eight harps. We later heard, via our shared publisher, that Reich was much taken by this version. From the classical repertoire, we took a Bach prelude and also the Bach–Gounod *Ave Maria*, *Arrival of the Queen of Sheba* by Handel and *Clair de lune* by Debussy. In addition, we selected a tango by Ástor Piazzolla, while I contributed 'Palladio', 'Harpers Bizarre' (a multi-harp piece where minimalism meets the blues), 'Thingamujig' (a jig that also featured Rosie on penny whistle) and an arrangement of mine of the Welsh folk song 'Suo Gân'.

Most of the recording was done at *mustache* but we went to Prague to record the orchestra. There were budgetary restraints on the funding, so Prague was a cheaper option and, in fact, many film soundtracks are recorded there. An Englishman, James Fitzpatrick, set up business in Prague, acting as a go-between for clients in the UK and the US on the one hand, and the studio facility on the other, so that one phone call to him guaranteed the studio and the necessary musicians. He frequently used UK engineers as well and John Timperley, who had been at Angel, was a regular visitor. (I had worked there once before when I conducted and part-arranged an album of classic rock songs sung by someone else from my home town of Swansea: Bonnie Tyler.) With regard to *Crossing the Stone*, an idiot of a critic wrote something along the lines of: 'How can one hope to have good performances when the music is recorded in different places?' Perhaps he should have dusted off the mothballs and joined the real world. The strings were excellent, with many from the Czech Philharmonic playing on these sessions. Jody and I produced the album.

The year 2001 was one of those where, very fortunately, a variety of different projects was coming my way from all sorts of directions. One of the most memorable came about when I was invited to conduct extracts from *Adiemus* at an event in Europe, where classical and pop combine on the same bill. The brainchild of Jan Vereecke in Antwerp, it is called 'Night of the Proms' and has nothing to do with the Royal Albert Hall version. The only constant is the format: everyone, including pop artists, performs with orchestra – and often with choir as well. Orchestral numbers are usually repertoire favourites but with one classical guest. Among my predecessors had been Andrea Bocelli, and, immediately after me, the German-American violinist David Garrett, who later went on to record his own celebrated version of my piece *Palladio*.

All 'shows' were in enormous sports halls, often playing to ten thousand people a night, sometimes even more. Although based in Antwerp, the cavalcade moved into the Netherlands and Germany as well. We would play for a few days at each venue and it was quite a schlep: forty-nine concerts in fifty-four days, as I recall. A few of us Europeans darted off home for the odd forty-eight hours that we had free. This particular tour, an annual event leading up to Christmas, had an assortment of artists well known in mainland Europe and from the UK: Bonnie Tyler, Martin Fry from ABC and Chris de Burgh. Heading the bill was the American rock musician Meat Loaf. He certainly gave his all; when he came off stage there was an oxygen cylinder at the ready to aid his recovery.

This experience was certainly a fun one; but there were numerous projects awaiting my return to London – not least, the next stage of the now career-defining *Adiemus* project.

12

VOCALISE

*T*he next recording in the new studio was *Adiemus V: Vocalise*, in 2003. It was somewhat cramped in there but we managed to squeeze in the nine Finnish singers. By now, Miriam Stockley had semi-retired and had moved to Florida. *Vocalise* (a French word pronounced 'vocal-eeze') refers to a composition featuring the voice with accompaniment, but without words, usually sung to one vowel and using the voice purely as a musical instrument. This concept has been at the core of the *Adiemus* project, with its use of my invented 'language', which has no literal meaning.

This particular album incorporated two of the most famous such compositions from the 20th century: *Vocalise* (1915) by the Russian composer Sergei Rachmaninov and *Aria* (1938) by the Brazilian composer Heitor Villa-Lobos. However, the latter includes a section in Portuguese, an innovation on an *Adiemus* recording: the use of words that *do* have a literal meaning. Another obvious departure was the inclusion of material not composed by me, but taken from the classical repertoire and reworked within the *Adiemus* style.

Apart from Miriam, the rest of the cast was pretty much as usual:

the nine *Adiemus* singers from Finland, Pamela Thorby on recorder, and the London Philharmonic Orchestra with the percussion played by Jody and Paul Clarvis. I was also privileged to have been able to feature three of the greatest improvisers in world jazz: once again, I worked with saxophonist Nigel Hitchcock and guitarist Martin Taylor, joined on this occasion by the trumpet player Ken Wheeler. A New York-based counter-tenor – a male alto by another name – called Terry Barber featured in some movements along with blues har-monica player Mark Feltham, cellist Richard Harwood and vocalists Belinda Sykes, Mary Carewe and bass Gavin Horsley. I endeavoured to integrate the seemingly disparate strands into a cohesive whole that hopefully defied categorisation. As Meat Loaf once enthusiastically questioned me about *Adiemus*, 'What vibe is that?'

Pieces from the classical canon I included were: *Rondo* (the Beethoven Violin Concerto), *Allegrettango* (Beethoven's Symphony No. 7 and a 'natural' tango), *Akruzam* ('mazurka', a Polish dance, spelled backwards and borrowed from Chopin), *Schwanda the Bagpiper* by Weinberger (suggested by Carol's brother, Alan), *Schubert's Dance* (taken from a piano duet with the German word for dance, *tanze*, making an incursion into the *Adiemus* text), *Aria* from *Bachianas bra-sileiras No. 5* by Villa-Lobos (the title alluding to Bach the composer and Brazil the country) and *Vocalise* by Rachmaninov. Originals of mine were 'The Protector', 'Dona Nobis Pacem', 'Bendegedig' ('Blessed' in Welsh and dedicated to Carol), 'Berceuse Pour un Enfant Solitaire' ('Lullaby for a lonely child', a tune that Nucleus and the Ronnie Scott Sextet had played some years before), 'Mysterious Are Your Ways', 'Boogie Woogie Llanoogie' and 'Mi Contra Fa: Diabolus in Musica'. The last was a reworking of 'Down the Road' that I had written for Graham Collier thirty years earlier, in part because it opens with an interesting interval: the note B to the note F. Between the 14th and 16th centuries, this interval, called a tritone, was banned in church music because it was considered unstable, even dissonant. How times have changed, or else singers were not very good then. It was called, in Latin, *diabolus in musica* ('The Devil in Music'). For the academically minded, and to save correspondence, they jumped modes in those days, so the *mi* comes from the G (Mixolydian) mode and the *fa* comes from the C (Ionian) mode. Once again, I co-produced the album with Jody.

We played a concert in Madrid in April 2003 with the *Adiemus* ensemble and Il Novecento Orchestra. A charity concert in aid of the worthy cause of supporting abused women, it was played to a packed house, but we didn't get paid by the promoters and I was seriously out of pocket, having already paid my 'suppliers': orchestra, singers and tech crew, flown from Belgium, Finland and the UK. The eventual outcome was my suing them and going to a Madrid court for a hearing a year or so later. The judge declared in my favour. I still haven't been paid, twelve years on.

We launched *Adiemus V* at EMI Wrights Lane in London in September. Soon after, preparations were complete for two concerts in Japan at the Tokyo International Forum on 15 and 16 February 2004, the latter of which was Carol's birthday. With my sixtieth the following day, we made a family trip, with Jody and Rosie, for a couple of days to the Hakone National Park near Mount Fuji. On these concerts, I was reunited with Dave Nolan again, former leader of the London Philharmonic Orchestra and now leading in Tokyo. He had met a Japanese violinist in the Philharmonia Orchestra in London, married her and so moved to Tokyo. This trip was also memorable because it saw my one and only visit to a karaoke bar. The whole troupe went and it didn't surprise me that those who sang were stage crew and 'management', frustrated artists all! They gave out hand percussion instruments (well, they did at this place) and some of the locals were suitably impressed by the playing of our drummers, not knowing who they were!

Our trip to Japan was a relatively short one, because on 1 May we performed a sixtieth birthday concert at the Royal Festival Hall. This was the one that was running late when the London Philharmonic Orchestra decided to play 'Happy Birthday' for me. This meant the show ran over by an insignificant margin, for which the orchestral management charged me overtime! It was a wonderful occasion, though – and more recently, I have been fortunate enough to celebrate my seventieth birthday in a multitude of musical ways, of which more later.

But back to my sixtieth for a moment. By this point, *The Armed Man* had been recorded for Virgin Venture, an EMI company that was run by Declan Coughlan – the man who had 'signed' *Adiemus*. EMI, mindful of my drift towards music that was perceived, perhaps, as being more classical at its core, called a meeting with Tony Wadsworth, CEO of EMI UK – and the decision was taken, with my blessing, to move me to EMI Classics. It was here that I met The Hon. Richard Lyttelton, President of EMI Classics, for the first time. He is a true gentleman with a love of music, and we would have a rewarding relationship over the coming years. Having a committed recording deal for five albums, but not worth the £1 million I alluded to earlier, I was now in a position to plan accordingly. My works over the next few years were funded by one of two ways: either by a commission or by being composed for specific recordings, funded by the record company. Sometimes I would be in a position to combine both, as with *The Armed Man*.

Having put this particular work to bed, I cast round for other texts for my next work and recording. I was immediately drawn to that of the Requiem. Three of my favourite pieces are the Requiems of Mozart, Verdi and Fauré. I had never had the opportunity to dedicate a work to my father, and a Requiem, being a Mass for the souls of the dead, seemed a fitting vehicle for this, especially since he did not live to see this period of my life where I returned to a style that had the classical tradition at its heart. I set the established Latin text but, in keeping with my usual trait of drawing from other cultures, I also set five Japanese haiku poems (sung in Japanese) written by Gozan, Issho, Hokusai, Kaga-no-Chiyo and Banzan. They dealt with life, death and rebirth in an allegorical way: for example, the cycle of precipitation and melting snow, or the blooming of cherry blossom only for it to eventually wither. A haiku has a single idea, and consists of 17 syllables divided 5–7–5 over three lines. I combined Western and Eastern texts in two of the haiku movements, which incorporate the Latin mass texts of the 'Benedictus' and the 'Agnus Dei' respectively. Both are intoned by male voices in a monastic style as a counterpoint to the Japanese text sung by women.

Another oddity in this piece is the use of a hip-hop dance rhythm in the driving, relentless 'Dies Irae': another piece of mine that was adopted for a television commercial, this time for a Lynx product. At the time of writing, I was told that this ad has had, apparently, nearly 60 million hits on YouTube! The instrumentation of these haiku settings included the ancient Japanese flute-like instrument, the *shakuhachi*, just one note of which cries out 'Japan', so idiosyncratic is it of that country. Elsewhere, as usual, I used some ethnic drums – the Arabic *darbuka*, the Japanese *daiko* – to create what I hope is a unique and beguiling sound world.

This is where Marat Bisengaliev comes into the story. A virtuoso violinist from Almaty in Kazakhstan, Marat came up through the Soviet system, when his country was part of the Soviet Union. Making his debut aged nine, he went on to study at the Tchaikovsky Conservatoire in Moscow, eventually settling in England, in 1991, for a time. A fabulous player and to my mind very Russian, with a passionate approach and a huge 'heart-on-the-sleeve' type of playing, Marat had heard some of my music and made contact. This led to his orchestra, the West Kazakhstan Philharmonic, playing on both the *Requiem* recording and at the premiere at Southwark Cathedral on 6 February 2005. Clive Bell, from London, played the *shakuhachi*, and Sam Landman was the treble voice. Tim Rhys-Evans trained the three Welsh choirs: Serendipity, Cor Caerdydd (choral director Gwawr Owen) and Cytgan. The soprano soloist was Nicole Tibbels, who had sung many times for me in the past. She performed all nine female voice parts on the haiku movements, which made for a wonderfully homogenous sound.

All the small-scale recording, including the soloists and the over-laying of single instruments, was done at *mustache*. The orchestra and choir, meanwhile, were recorded at Angel with Steve Price, and Catrin Finch recorded the harp at her own facility near Cardiff called Acapela. *Capel* is the Welsh word for chapel and the studio and con-cert facility is housed in a converted Welsh Nonconformist chapel. Catrin was 'engineered' by her husband Hywel Wigley, son of harpist Elinor Bennett and Lord Wigley, one-time leader of the Plaid Cymru party and MP for Caernarvon.

Marat later became Music Director of the National Centre of the Performing Arts in Mumbai and established the Symphony Orchestra of India there. I went over there to conduct an intriguing concert of *Adiemus* music. The choir comprised excellent young singers who, not understanding Western notation, had learned the music by rote under the guidance of a choral trainer who did. Two *tabla* players cov-ered the percussion while the 'flute' solos were played by the Indian *bansuri*. We even played *Dos a Dos*, an American square dance from *Vocalise*; multi-culturalism in music that worked a treat. The whole performance was accompanied by Indian shadow dancing behind a screen. Carol said to me at the time, looking at this Bollywood choir, 'It is certainly the most beautiful choir you've ever conducted.' The concert was on Valentine's Day (a very big occasion in India) and I was showered with kisses and heart-shaped gifts.

Marat and I often worked together on various concerts and projects including one charity performance at Buckingham Palace for HRH The Prince of Wales, and The Prince's Foundation for Children and the Arts. I conducted the Philharmonia Orchestra, first with tenor Alfie Boe singing my 'Ave Verum' and then Marat playing the last movement of the Violin Concerto, *Sarikiz*, I had written for him. It was a mixed-media event with readings by Rowan Atkinson and Jeremy Irons.

A few months prior to the premiere of the *Requiem*, I had been commissioned to write a work for the opening of the Wales Millennium Centre on 28 November 2004, with a Royal Gala concert in the presence of Her Majesty The Queen. Three very eminent Welsh poets, Grahame Davies, Menna Elfyn and Gwyneth Lewis, contributed the text, a mixture of English and Welsh. Gwyneth's poem included an extract that formed the six-foot-high words, 'In These Stones Horizons Sing', over the entrance to the WMC, the text I set for the main anthem-like movement and from which the piece takes its name.

This was also the first time I had worked with Bryn Terfel. Although I wasn't present, I had first heard of him from his visit to Penclawdd as a young oratorio soloist, many years before, when he was known as Bryn Terfel Jones – and I had naturally followed his career. I was also thrilled when Bryn, one of the undisputed great voices of the age, had included *Adiemus* on his *Desert Island Discs* for BBC Radio 4. Later that year, Bryn asked me to compose something for his upcoming album, entitled *Simple Gifts*, which was to be recorded with the London Symphony Orchestra and released on the prestigious Deutsche Grammophon label. I set the text *Ave Verum Corpus*, which I was to later include in my *Stabat Mater*. I sent Bryn two scores, one for solo baritone and one a duet for two baritones. He selected the latter and recorded the piece with another Brit: Simon Keenlyside.

Apart from Bryn, *In These Stones Horizons Sing* features, as soloists, Catrin Finch on harp and Nigel Hitchcock on soprano saxophone. The work is in four main movements with the first in two parts. CDs accommodate around eighty minutes of recording time and, since there was space to include this work on the *Requiem* recording, we did exactly that. The CD was recorded about two weeks before the *Requiem* premiere; the *Requiem* has had several hundred performances since and is, apparently, my second most popular work after *The Armed Man*.

As I look back over my career, I'm reminded of the handful of people who have worked for me along the way. I inherited Tracy Hazell from Mark Cellier, and she is still, I am very pleased to say, my accounts administrator.

Jenkins–Ratledge also had a succession of PAs who assisted with the running of the company. They were many and varied, coming and going, one at a time. The last one I employed was Helen Connolly. When she joined Jenkins–Ratledge, she was Helen Hodkinson and married to Richard Hodkinson – who 'was' Work Music, the composer-led independent record label that had a distribution deal with Sony. It was for Work Music that I recorded *Palladio* and *Imagined Oceans*. This particular relationship, with Work, foundered due to a dispute regarding the payment of royalties. Richard and Helen Hodkinson eventually divorced, she reverting to her maiden name, Helen Connolly. Having joined Jenkins–Ratledge as a PA, she effectively became my manager. For a time, when we were very busy, we hired a second person: Marie Jarman. Carol and I later decided to move back to Wales, still composing, but no longer running a business with a London office, manager and occasional staff. I had already relinquished one floor at Poland Street and the intention now was to just retain the studio on a single floor, to be used for both my and Jody's projects.

We were now looking forward to a new chapter of our lives: composing on the Gower Peninsula and returning to London for recordings. As ever, concerts would be wherever they took us.

13

STEMBRIDGE MILL

*I*n early 2004, Carol and I returned to Wales. I had asked a builder friend of mine, Elwyn Davies (also an Old Gowertonian), to keep his eye out for a property on the Gower Peninsula. Stembridge Mill was situated in the Cheriton valley on the banks of a stream called the Bury Pill, which ran from central Gower out into the Bury estuary at Cheriton, to the north. There were quite a few mills on this stream and the one at Stembridge was mentioned in the Cheriton parish records of 1720. Though it ceased grinding corn around 1890, Stembridge received a new lease of life as a woollen mill, with the addition of a factory building in 1899 by Isaac Tanner. It was very much in use for this purpose through until 1925.

Gower runs from east to west for about twenty miles and a few miles north to south. I have always thought that what gives it its special character is that, like all peninsulas, it is three-quarters of the way to being an island. It boasts seventeen churches (many going back eight hundred years) and several castles. Gower is a land of beautiful beaches, with cliffs and caves along the southern stretch. In 1823 in one such cave was found the Red Lady of Paviland, one of the oldest human skeletons to have been discovered anywhere in the world, with carbon dating placing the remains at over 30,000 BC, while Parc Le Breos, a burial chamber, was built around 6000 BC. Atop Cefn Bryn stands King Arthur's stone, a Bronze Age standing stone. Local legend has it that it was a stone in Arthur's shoe that he threw, from Camelot, over the Bristol Channel to Gower.

Stembridge Mill sat in twenty-two acres and consisted of two dwellings: the mill itself and a farmhouse, both pretty much in the centre of the property. The owner wanted to sell off the mill and the land west of it, comprising thirteen acres in all. The mill had not long been renovated and had been let as holiday accommodation. We sold Briarwood in Hampton, as well as Benson Cottage in Penclawdd, which was about five miles east of Cheriton valley, and moved into Stembridge Mill. Since the one property had become two, we needed a name to differentiate between them so we added the prefix 'Noddfa', which is Welsh for 'sanctuary', before Stembridge Mill.

Carol's mother, May, loved the Mill. In many ways May was a fine woman: principled, generous, honourable, hard-working and kind, but there was an embarrassment when it came to emotional matters, and she found it impossible to praise her daughter. When May had passed the 11+, the family still could not afford to send her to the grammar school and she probably felt she was ill equipped to comment on Carol's career. Carol's father Tom was a quiet man and had been a plumber. When Carol said she was going to the Royal College of Music he warned her 'not to get above her station'. What would he have made of Lady Jenkins now? I don't think he saw much point in further education, especially for girls. However, to their credit, both Carol's brothers, Alan and Roy, gained degrees in later life, not, for various reasons, having taken examinations at the usual time. Tom died in 1998 and May later, at seventy-six, married an old family friend, outliving him until she died at ninety-two. She had never told Carol that she loved her, and Carol yearned to hear these words. On her deathbed, Carol said to her, 'I love you, Mum.' May replied with 'I love you too, you chump!' She had often come to the mill and her wish was that her ashes would be scattered in the stream that ran through the property. She left Carol a little money when she died, and we used it to buy a gypsy caravan. May was known as Nanna to her grandchildren, so we named the caravan 'Nanna May'.

Carol and I needed another space for composing and soon erected a building – of sorts. Being an area of outstanding natural beauty, Gower has quite stringent planning regulations, so we built what was, to all intents and purposes, a stable block, comprising four stable doors with, ostensibly, four stables within. Inside it was like a Tardis: a time warp with one long, fifty-foot space, which enabled both of us to compose there. It was open plan but there were dividers that segregated different areas. We already had the Roland Digital piano, and the Yamaha MIDI Grand made the return journey, over the roof in Soho and down to Gower. Of the four stable doors, one was the actual working door while the others, when opened, exposed large picture windows that afforded us glorious views over to Ryer's Down across the valley.

For the necessary trips to London, we stayed at Le Meridien Hotel in Piccadilly, perhaps one week in every five or so. Some would see it as a somewhat corporate establishment but we got to know the staff well and had excellent service there, and often we were very fortunate to be upgraded to a suite. We used to store our 'office suitcase' (printer, paper and various paraphernalia) and also a portable electric piano in the luggage room, which the porters would bring up on our arrival. As well as being a very happy place to stay, Le Meridien also had the advantage of being a stone's throw from my Poland Street studio.

When in London or abroad, we left Noddfa in the more than capable hands of Lorna and Johnny Francis. They became special friends over the years. My father had taught Johnny at school and Lorna had been at Gowerton Girls' Grammar, but I had not known her in those days. They both came from the village of Llanmorlais, only a mile or so from Penclawdd – but back then, it could well have been a different planet. We were introduced by Elwyn the builder, who had been one year behind me in Gowerton, for whom Johnny worked and who had found Noddfa for us. It was a running joke that they were our 'estate managers' but they were fantastic and we couldn't have coped without them. They have also been loyal followers of my music, attending every Welsh or London concert I have done post-*Adiemus* – Johnny, invariably with tears in his eyes, saying, 'I wish your father could have heard this.'

Elwyn used to organise coach trips up to the Royal Albert Hall, unfurling the Welsh Dragon in the stalls. On one occasion, this busful of people sang 'We'll Keep a Welcome in the Hillside' to me at the side of a busy London road. It felt very special – and still does now – to have people back home in Wales supporting my music and waving a flag for what I do, both literally and metaphorically. I found my return to Wales to be a very inspirational time – and, before long, I had a whole bunch of new musical ideas in my head, just waiting to come to fruition. And one of these was my first and last film score.

River Queen was directed by Vincent Ward, and starred Kiefer Sutherland and Samantha Morton. Set in New Zealand in 1868, it follows Irishwoman Sarah O'Brien as Maori tribes resist the British occupation. She has a child, named Boy, by her Maori lover who dies. Seven years later, his grandfather, a Maori chief, captures the child. Sarah's mission is to search for her son, with only the disillusioned Irish soldier, Doyle – played by Kiefer Sutherland – to help her. When she finds Boy, she must decide to which culture she belongs, torn between the attachment she has to the Western world and her love for her son and his uncle, Wiremu, with whom she is now in love.

I had as an assistant Rupert Christie, who, like me, had also gone to the Royal Academy of Music. His father had been in a trio, Instant Sunshine, a comedy musical cabaret group formed in 1966 that broadcast and made recordings. For their day jobs they were medical doctors. There is a whole plethora of technical skills that is required when composing a soundtrack for a movie that go way beyond the purely musical, and Rupert filled this responsible role admirably. As far as the actual composing goes, writing music for a film is exactly the same as writing music for a television commercial, save that everything is magnified tenfold and then some: the cues (length of sequence), the time frame, the arguments, the problems, the egos, the plain unreasonableness. It was always a battle and felt relentless, day after day, for weeks on end. At the end of the scheduled post-production period we had recording sessions booked at Angel, and the London Symphony Orchestra confirmed.

As I started writing each cue, it was clear that Vincent didn't particularly like orchestras. He preferred more homespun sounds, in particular the harmonium. Many of the potential luscious orchestral episodes were to be substituted by a harmonium, again a dubious conceptual idea based on the fact that the harmonium could have been an instrument that might have featured in the daily lives of the Europeans portrayed in the movie. Another fixation Vincent had was the lambeg drum, a large Irish instrument played primarily by Unionists in Ulster. Considering the size of the thing, to my mind it has a very thin, 'cheap' sound; but every time Vincent came along to hear a cue he would ask about it. He had never seen one, let alone heard one; but the connection with Ireland apparently made it a must-have ingredient in the score. We never actually sourced one and instead said it was in the mix with the other percussion. He seemed happy.

For the title sequence, I composed a folk-type Celtic song, with lovely words by Carol. The song was called 'To Still My Mind' and it was beautifully performed by the Scottish singer Mae McKenna, who had taken part in the first ever *Adiemus* concert at the Royal Albert Hall. The orchestral sessions went really well and Vincent was as good as gold, deferring to the composer. I had expected something far worse: a session of fraying tempers and a heavy atmosphere. I was never approached to score another film, nor actively sought one, but I must have done something right since it won the Golden Goblet Best Music Award at the Shanghai International Film Festival in 2006.

Rupert also later worked with me on another project. Mike Oldfield, of *Tubular Bells* fame, was writing an orchestral album called *Music of the Spheres*. I had played in a televised performance of *Tubular Bells* many years previously so we vaguely knew each other. Mike contacted me to orchestrate the work and co-produce the album. Rupert was responsible for transferring Mike's Logic files to Sibelius so that I could formulate scores for an orchestra to play. It was taxing work and meant many trips with Rupert to Mike's 'rock mansion', near the Severn Bridge on the English side, to talk through sections, retrieve files and then depart to orchestrate at home, and that process was repeated several times over. We recorded at Abbey Road and Lang Lang overdubbed some piano from wherever he was – the US I think, but I was not party to that session. I believe the album had some success.

The year 2006 was also when I appeared on *Desert Island Discs*, the BBC Radio 4 programme where one is cast away on a desert island and allowed to take eight recordings, one luxury, and one book, except for the Bible and the complete works of Shakespeare, which are already there. The show had its seventieth anniversary in 2012 and was the brainchild of Roy Plomley, who first presented it. Since 2006, Kirsty Young has been the presenter. A brilliant and sympathetic interviewer, she drew revelations from me regarding my parents' deaths that I wasn't expecting. My choices, in playlist order, were:

> 'The Prize Song' from Wagner's opera *The Mastersingers of Nuremberg*. For those who recoil from the very name Wagner, this opera is essentially a comedy and extremely funny, with fantastic music. The plot concerns a song contest, and on my chosen recording, Plácido Domingo is the tenor soloist, singing the role of the winner, Walther von Stolzing, a young knight from Franconia.

> Concerto in C minor for violin, oboe and strings by J. S. Bach. I simply had to have some oboe playing and something by Bach, so this choice covered both.

> 'Blue in Green' from *Kind of Blue* by Miles Davis. My favourite jazz ensemble of all time, featuring, apart from Miles: John Coltrane, Cannonball Adderley and Bill Evans – one of the greatest jazz recordings ever made.

> 'The Goodbye Look' from *Nightfly* by Donald Fagen. This album was the first solo recording released by Steely Dan co-founder Donald Fagen, and it was remarkably inventive, both in terms of song writing but also with regard to the orchestration.

> The *Adagietto* from Mahler's Symphony No. 5. I was present at the actual recording, made at the Royal Festival Hall with the London Philharmonic Orchestra (with Joan on oboe) conducted by its genius of a Principal Conductor from 1983 to 1987, Klaus Tennstedt. I simply had to include it in my list.

> 'Birdland' from *Heavy Weather* by Weather Report. Joe Zawinul was one of jazz's finest composers and a very rare breed: someone

who created a distinctive, individual and recognisable voice when playing a synthesiser.

♪: 'Benedictus' from *The Armed Man: A Mass for Peace*. When the great soprano Elisabeth Schwarzkopf was the 'castaway' in 1958, I remember her choosing seven of her own recordings. What arrogance, I thought, as a fourteen-year-old boy. Well, I, unashamedly, did something similar in selecting the original recording of my own 'Benedictus', not because I want to wallow narcissistically in my own music, but simply because of the memories it invoked of a life as a musician.

♪: *Der Rosenkavalier* (*The Knight of the Rose*), an opera by Richard Strauss. I picked the trio from the last act, in a version featuring the soprano Elisabeth Schwarzkopf. It is, quite simply, among the most sublime pieces of music ever written, and I chose it as the answer to the customary 'if you could take only one' question. Part of the story line involves the presenting of a ceremonial silver rose, as I did to Carol on our twenty-fifth wedding anniversary. It is invariably a tearjerker in the Jenkins household.

When it came to choosing a book to take to the desert island my selection was, unfortunately, pathetic. I somehow thought it funny to have the *Michelin Guide to France*. Not *that* funny, and a stupid idea really. If I could turn the clock back I would have the complete works of either Dickens or Dylan Thomas. At least the Bible and Shakespeare were there. My luxury was a piano, under which I could sleep. It was a difficult task: no Mozart, no *Rite of Spring*, no French music. However, I'd probably make the same choice today.

Around the time of the *Desert Island Discs* interview in 2006, I was approached by Richard Lyttelton, President of EMI Classics, who was very soon to retire. But before he did so, Richard made me an offer I simply couldn't refuse: he suggested I work with Dame Kiri Te Kanawa on an album, subject to us meeting, getting along and agreeing to work together. It was an audition for both of us. I'd met Kiri previously, very briefly, when we gained Fellowships at the Royal Academy of Music and where she was presenting awards. She was an icon, of course, and I'd seen and heard her sing in some of my favourite operas by Richard Strauss, at Covent Garden and at Glyndebourne. I went to a dress rehearsal of one such opera at Glyndebourne; it was either *Arabella* or *Capriccio*, I can't recall which. Some phone or paging device went off in the audience and Kiri stopped the rehearsal until the devastated culprit was exposed. She seemed quite fearsome and I felt some trepidation about seeing her but when we met at EMI in London, we got along so well and shared a vision of what the album should be. She was amazing and very down to earth but, like many of us, Kiri doesn't suffer fools gladly.

There were sixteen tracks on the album, *Kiri Sings Karl*, which I produced, and I orchestrated those pieces not composed by me. I contributed 'Antema Africana', 'The Mystics' (with words by Carol), 'In Paradisum' from the *Requiem*, 'Capriccio d'Amore' and 'Paya Paya', while Kiri suggested seven pieces by Argentine composers Carlos Guastavino and Ariel Ramírez. The album features a vast array of unusual South American percussion instruments, as well as the great jazz guitarist Martin Taylor on a couple of tracks. In addition, there is the playing of virtuoso Pamela Thorby, bringing to bear once again her ability to bend notes in a way that makes the recorder sound more like an ethnic instrument. The recorder plays a prominent part, in lieu of the original harp, in a new version of 'In Paradisum'. On 'Antema Africana', Kiri sings nine overlaid tracks. ('Nine versions of me,' as she said at the time. 'We call it the Kiri Chorus!') We recorded the

London Symphony Orchestra at Abbey Road and overlaid Kiri's voice at our *mustache* studio, where Jody engineered her voice.

The eminent fashion photographer John Swannell, whom I knew from another life when he had been shooting commercials with me writing some music for him, took the photos for the album. Kiri, who is invariably very well groomed, thought my moustache somewhat unkempt for the occasion so she had her 'dresser' trim it. Who was I to argue? The next day Carol asked Kiri if she had tried kissing me as my moustache was now very prickly! We performed a couple of pieces from the collection at the Hampton Court Festival and then at a José Carreras televised charity gala concert in Leipzig. One of the pieces on the album had Italian text by one Carlo Cinque. We invariably take our summer holidays in Italy and we had discovered an incredible hotel just outside Positano on the Amalfi coast and constructed into the cliff face: Il San Pietro di Positano. The hotel is family owned (one of the few 5-star establishments that is) by Victoria Cinque and her sons Vito (manager) and Carlo. We came to know them over the years and had soon discovered that Carlo had a gift for writing lyrics. Needing something Italianate for the album, Carlo penned the text for 'Capriccio d'Amore'.

In 2004, the Cinque family kindly facilitated Jody's and Rosie's wedding reception on the beach of the San Pietro, just a group of twelve or so friends and family. They had been married, earlier that day, by the mayor, in the Municipio (municipal offices) situated on the cliff top, the process itself not without its problems, involving months of red tape. Even then, they were on the verge of being thwarted at the last minute when the precious documents were blown by a gust of wind over the parapet of the courtyard, where the ceremony was taking place, to the depths below. Luckily, they landed in the police station and were so retrieved, concluding a story that sounds more like an opera plot than a real-life event.

I have another, more sombre memory of the Amalfi coast. The commercials director Roger Lyons, with whom I worked on the famous Levi's 'Laundrette' ad, was shooting there. Walking backwards while directing, he fell from a cliff top to his death. When I heard about this I was saddened, but not totally surprised. The coastline is staggeringly beautiful but can be dangerous with steep precipices abounding. The hotel we stay at does not allow children under ten for this reason.

For our Italian holidays, we often put our car on the motorail train and thus travel overnight to either Milan or the south of France. For some reason SNCF, the French rail company, stopped this service. No doubt it was not a paying concern but every time we travelled it seemed very busy. An alternative service eventually started operating from 's-Hertogenbosch in the Netherlands to Livorno, near Pisa, in Italy so we tried this on one occasion. Initially, the journey went to plan. We drove to the Netherlands, stayed over one night and then boarded the train the next afternoon to be transported, with our car, to Italy, followed by a drive down to Positano. A couple of hours or so later we arrived at Venlo on the Dutch–German border, where there was to be a change of engine. There was an announcement that we could leave the train to stretch our legs, which I did and to check my car, on the transporter wagon to the rear. However, there was no announcement to reboard. The train set off for Italy with Carol and car on board; I, meanwhile, was left on a station platform in Venlo. I had my phone but that's all: no money to speak of bar a few euros, and no passport. I rang Carol and rather sheepishly said, 'I'm not on the train.' Very quickly, she went from being stunned to being far from amused. I could not possibly see any satisfactory conclusion coming out of this. Carol would arrive in Livorno next morning with a Porsche she wouldn't drive on the road, let alone off the train, while I remained in the Netherlands. Then what? Once the panic had subsided I approached the station staff; it transpired that there was hope of some sort, at least. The motorail train apparently took a slower route than standard passenger services; the station master wrote out a note, in German, no doubt along the lines of 'This British idiot got off the train with no passport and no money, didn't get back on and so is trying to catch up with his wife.' The plan, which seemed pretty ambitious to me, was to catch three trains, the last being the Cologne–Basel express, which would arrive at Basel on the German–Swiss border, one hour before the motorail service, which was scheduled to stop there. It seemed unlikely, but off I went. The first train went only three stops before I was told to get off and wait for the service to Mönchengladbach. I was still there an interminable thirty minutes later. This seemed hopeless but the train came, and the driver's cabin formed part of the first passenger coach. Handing my note of passage over, he read it and beckoned me to sit with him. He even gave me a bagel and a copy of *National Geographic* to read.

On arrival at Mönchengladbach, where this service terminated, he escorted me over to the platform where the express for Basel would shortly be arriving. When it did, he handed the note over to the guard and explained what had happened. I was in periodic communication with Carol so at least she knew there was a plan, but my phone battery was running very low. I clambered on board and found a seat. A German, who spoke English, was sitting opposite me with a Mac powered by the train electricity supply so I asked him whether he had a phone power lead, and whether I could charge my iPhone via his Mac. Having explained my predicament, he kindly agreed. For the first time I could anticipate a satisfactory outcome, so I celebrated by spending my few euros on a beer in the restaurant car. Meanwhile, Carol was having the dinner previously booked in the restaurant car on the other train, receiving much sympathy from the many who now knew the details of this saga.

I reached Basel as planned late that evening, at about 11 p.m., one hour before the motorail. Even then it involved more panic and running since I was at the wrong end of the extraordinarily long motorail train for boarding. I'm a belt-and-braces type of traveller and nothing remotely like this has happened before or since. At least Carol and I could keep in touch with one another; my main worry was for her. Goodness knows what would have happened if I had not got back, literally, on track.

14

THE CONCERTOS

*B*etween 2002 and 2009 I composed a series of concertos for various people, each remarkable in their own way (the people, not the concertos). My musical persona usually changes when I write instrumental music, with the style being quirky, whimsical or 'off the wall'. The first was *Crossing the Stone*, written, at the behest of Prince Charles, for the then Royal Harpist, Catrin Finch, and discussed in Chapter 11.

La Folia ('The Leaf'), for marimba and strings, dates from 2004 and was commissioned by IMG Artists for Dame Evelyn Glennie, who premiered it during her UK tour that same year. It is based on a violin sonata by Arcangelo Corelli and is in one extended movement. Corelli, an Italian Baroque composer, was born on the same day as me, 17 February, but much further back – in 1653. What makes this work unusual is that the marimba had not really been invented until two centuries later – it is a relatively modern instrument consisting of wooden bars arranged like piano keys; a bigger and lower-pitched xylophone would be another way of describing it. Its origins lie in central Africa as a diatonic instrument (imagine a piano with just the 'white notes'). The first chromatic instruments, with all the 'black notes' as well, were built by African slaves in Central America. Apparently, the name 'marimba' stems from the African Bantu dialect: *ma*, meaning 'many' and *rimba*, a single-bar instrument. It is quite common nowadays, as in *La Folia*, for the player to employ four mallets, with two held in each hand. I well remember Jody's excitement when I collected him from Junior College one Saturday: 'Dad, I'm on four mallets!'

The next concerto I wrote, entitled *Quirk*, is a concertante – a concerto-type piece with more than one soloist – for flute, keyboard, percussion and orchestra. It was commissioned by the London Symphony Orchestra in celebration of its centenary year in 2005, through the support of the late Eddie Waters. What made the commission more meaningful was that the LSO had four such pieces commissioned and, unusually, to mark the occasion, the chosen composers were selected by the principals in the orchestra. My featured soloists were: Gareth Davies (piccolo, flute, alto flute and bass flute); John Alley (piano, harmonium, celesta, honky-tonk piano); and Neil Percy (xylophone, vibraphone, marimba, whistle, bamboo chimes, rainstick, temple blocks, and various drums and cymbals).

Quirk was premiered at London's Barbican in 2005 under the baton of Sir Colin Davis and is in three, intentionally quirky, movements. The first, 'Snap', suddenly snaps between two ideas, one redolent of American film music, and the other almost minimalist. The second movement, 'Raga Religioso', is a juxtaposition of church-like harmonies and harmonium against a raga-like scale, with the sound of an Indian sitar simulated by the pianist plucking the strings inside the piano. And the finale, called 'Chasing the Goose', is slightly manic, and was written when we had three geese on our land in Gower that were continually chasing each other. I conducted a further performance of *Quirk* at the Swansea Festival, again with the LSO, when Sir Colin conducted Beethoven's Symphony No. 3 ('Eroica') and *The Lark Ascending* by Vaughan Williams. At a post-concert function, the Mayor of Swansea congratulated Sir Colin on his wonderful new composition, *Quirk*. Afterwards, Sir Colin wryly apologised for my work being misappropriated!

In 2006, Marat Bisengaliev approached me on behalf of the Kazakh philanthropist, patron of the arts and businessman Sapar Iskakov, who wanted to commission a choral work called *Tlep*. The piece takes its name from Iskakov's ancestor, Tlep Aspantaiuly, who was a celebrated composer and player of the *kobyz*: a two-stringed, violin-like instrument with no sound box, played in an upright fashion on the knee. This hour-long work was scored for female chorus, orchestra and four percussionists, who play both Kazakh and 'world' percussion instruments. There were five featured soloists, an improvising saxophonist (the ubiquitous Nigel Hitchcock) and four Kazakh folk musicians playing *kobyz*, the *saz sýrmay* (a Kazakh ocarina), the *dombra* (a two-string balalaika) and a Jew's harp (the player doubling bass-voice drone). The last was Yedil Khussainov, who has mastered the split-voice technique, or 'throat singing', so that two pitches or overtones are produced. The project resulted in a world premiere at the Royal Albert Hall on Easter Monday, 17 April 2006, and an album for Sony/BMG. My *Adiemus* singers from Helsinki learned the Kazakh text, coming over to London to perform. Marat's niece Camilla, also a musician, helped with the language coaching, while his daughter Aruhan, a soprano, contributed some solos. The orchestra was again Marat's ensemble, the West Kazakhstan Philharmonic Orchestra.

Tlep offered scope for further world music explorations and as I wrote at the time:

In all my works I tend to look outside the purely Western European for inspiration and freshness, so here was a

heaven-sent opportunity to marry what I do to Kazakh culture. Within my piece I have referred to two indigenous
Kazakh melodies [in 'Dudarai' and 'My Eyes'] and also
included text by the ancient philosopher, Abai.

A year or so later, Sapar Iskakov surfaced again and requested yet
another piece dedicated to the memory of Tlep Aspantaiuly: the
Violin Concerto, *Sarikiz*, to be performed by Marat Bisengaliev. It
is in three movements and, apart from the occasional use of Kazakh
themes, I used two Kazakh indigenous percussion instruments: the
dabel (hand drum) and *kepshek* (tambourine).

When Kazakhstan became independent from Russia in 1991,
the city where Iskakov lived was renamed Akmola, literally meaning
'white temple'. The word *astana* in Kazakh is translated as 'capital'
and the city was so named in 1998 when it gained this status. Set in
the vast plains or prairies known as the steppes, in winter it is one
of the coldest cities on earth, and very dry. It is now home to many
futuristic buildings, hotels and skyscrapers but at one time, during the
Stalinist era, one of the worst of the gulag labour camps sat just outside
the city, a camp for 'Wives of Traitors of the Motherland'. I visited
Kazakhstan on three or so occasions and once went to the home of
Sapar Iskakov. He had made his money in construction, building this
new, glistening and shiny city.

My trip there coincided with a TV programme that the ITV
South Bank Show was shooting about me. Melvyn Bragg came down
to Stembridge Mill to interview me, and the crew shot various scenes
around Gower. Previously, they had filmed some of the *Requiem* premiere at Southwark Cathedral in London. Part of the plan was to
come out to Astana, Kazakhstan, with me, which they did, minus
Melvyn. When we arrived after a long and tiring journey, we went
immediately to a kind of indoor theme park, conceived by Sapar

Iskakov, where replicas of such edifices as the Eiffel Tower and the Pyramids stood. Next up was a huge outdoor water fountain complex, where a blaring version of my recorded *Palladio* was used to choreograph the water jets. The louder the musical passage, the higher the water shot.

Later, I was guest of honour at Sapar Iskakov's house, where we had dinner. A sheep's head was brought out and placed in front of me, from which I was then told I had to remove the eyes. Thankfully, that was my duty done since I didn't fancy tucking in to the creature's head. The head was then removed while we waited for the next delicacy: three different cuts of horsemeat, a slight improvement but not by much. I'll eat anything (including those live prawns once swimming in my dish in Shanghai) but I found horsemeat very grey, in both look and taste. The most treasured cut of the three were slabs of white fat that apparently came from the head. The horse features quite large in Kazakh culture: they ride them, drink the mares' milk (something else I don't recommend), eat them, and no doubt they wore the hide in earlier times. The meal was followed by everyone having to make a speech and down copious shots of vodka. Subsequent occasions told me that this was very much common practice. When one has done something of note, either in or for Kazakhstan, one is presented with a velvet cloak and a wizard's pointy hat. I now have three of these, presented to me after concerts. Much later I saw a photo in the UK press of three American astronauts that had come down in Kazakhstan. They, too, were similarly attired.

When I had completed the Violin Concerto, EMI suggested I combine all the concertos composed to date in one album. The release was titled *Quirk* and included all four concertos plus a re-recording of the first movement of *Palladio*. The orchestra for all the works was the LSO. Their version of *Palladio* is more together than that of the LPO but I put that down to my ineptitude, at the time, as a conductor. Strange to relate, but the first orchestra I ever conducted in my life was the LPO on recording sessions. Nothing like starting at the top. It was also the first time I realised that string players play late in relation to the beat and one has to pre-empt them, and keep doing so, otherwise everything grinds to a halt. Someone once told me that this tendency stemmed from the great German conductor Wilhelm Furtwängler, but I'm not so sure.

I neither trained nor studied to be a conductor and, when I do take to the podium, I see myself as a director of my own music. I never conduct anyone else's works and I am often asked how I find other people's interpretations of my pieces. I have to be present, of course, to have an opinion – and that does not happen all that often. When I am, naturally performances are variable, but the main area where I sometimes feel unease is with tempo, which is often too fast. My scores are clearly labelled with metronome markings and in one sense I am very fortunate, in that my music is usually recorded before it is made available for performance by others. When a tempo or performance query comes my way, I always refer the questioner to the recording, since that never fails to be my ideal template.

The euphonium has, for many years, been associated with the world of brass and traditional marching bands, rather than that of the symphony orchestra or the concert hall. Within brass bands it plays a central role, often being referred to as the cello of the band, on account of its similarity in register to its stringed counterpart. In the last five years or so, these perceptions of the instrument have begun to change, largely due to the vision of one man: David Childs, who has done much to develop it as a solo instrument. The Childs family, originally from Wales, is an institution in the brass band world. David's father Robert, having been bandmaster with the Cory Band for many years, is now with the Grimethorpe Colliery Band, while his uncle Nicholas is bandmaster with the Black Dyke Band. David won the brass section of the BBC Young Musician of the Year in 2000; he is a phenomenal soloist and – of this I have no doubt – would be a household name if he had played a more commonplace instrument. A major part of his campaign to win the euphonium new audiences has been to commission new pieces. I wrote my Euphonium Concerto for David in 2009; it is in four movements, lasting around twenty-five minutes.

David recorded this work with the BBC National Orchestra of Wales and the booklet notes read:

> The first movement, 'The Juggler', immediately establishes a sense of fun, graphically bringing to mind both the ease of movement and lolloping suspense of the juggler's art. The second movement, 'Romanza', is an unashamedly lyrical outpouring for the soloist, initially accompanied by strings and, later, the full orchestra. The third movement, 'It Takes Two . . .', is a sultry tango-like melody with an unusual ending, where the soloist sings and plays the euphonium sim-ultaneously. The work ends with a section called 'A Troika. Tidy!' – a traditional Russian dance that imitates the prancing of horses. The *Tidy!* part of the title is a 'Welsh-ism' that, as any fan of the TV comedy *Gavin and Stacey* will know, means something fantastic or terrific. (Q: 'Enjoy the trip last week?' A: 'Tidy!'). A slow romantic episode briefly interrupts the music's joie de vivre, out of which the soloist emerges with a cadenza of great brilliance accompanied by two sleigh bells, leading to the concerto's rousing conclusion.

David's father, Bob, transcribed the score for brass band accompaniment and David has performed the piece, in both guises, on over fifty occasions around the world. The band version was recorded in 2010 with Cory, conducted by Bob, on the Doyen label; the orchestral version in 2014, with the BBC National Orchestra of Wales conducted by Bramwell Tovey, on the Chandos label. The premiere was in July 2009 at the Welsh Proms in Cardiff, given by David with the BBC Concert Orchestra conducted by Owain Arwel Hughes. The Euphonium Concerto was commissioned by Euphonium Foundation UK, an organisation set up by David Childs devoted to developing an understanding of this wonderfully lyrical yet often neglected instrument.

15

BEYOND THE CONCERTOS

I will always be very humbled by the success of *Adiemus* and *The Armed Man*, both of which stand out as the best-known works I have composed. Indeed, by the end of the first decade of the 21st century, some were suggesting that I might even consider wanting to quit while I was ahead, and hang up my pencil and manuscript paper (or, rather, computer keyboard and Sibelius software) for good. This is a bizarre suggestion to a composer: it is like proposing that someone stops breathing. I therefore continued to write all manner of different works, three of which I shall turn to now.

My *Stabat Mater* was composed for Liverpool, when the city was designated by the European Union as European Capital of Culture in 2008. 'Stabat Mater' is a 13th-century Roman Catholic poem attributed to Jacopone da Todi; its title is an abbreviation of the first line, '*Stabat Mater dolorosa*' ('The sorrowful mother was standing'). This text, one of the most powerful and immediate of medieval poems, meditates on the suffering of the Virgin Mary during Christ's crucifixion. It has been set to music by many composers, among them Haydn, Dvořák, Vivaldi, Rossini, Pergolesi, Gounod, Penderecki, Poulenc, Szymanowski, Alessandro Scarlatti, Domenico Scarlatti and Verdi.

In addition to the standard Christian Latin text, I set six texts that lie outside the original poem. These were made up of a choral arrangement of the 'Ave Verum' that I composed originally for Bryn Terfel; 'And the Mother Did Weep', comprising this single line of mine but sung, apart from the English, in Hebrew, Latin, Greek and Aramaic (the lingua franca of the period in the Middle East); 'Incantation', semi-improvised in nature and sung partly in early Arabic; then two settings of ancient texts, revised into the original 'Stabat Mater' rhyming scheme by the poet Grahame Davies, which is sung in both English and Aramaic; and 'Lament', with text by Carol, written especially for this work. This movement was dedicated to Christine Brown, a close friend of Carol, who was dying in a hospice in Leeds. She was a piano teacher and an expert on the music of the Hungarian composer Béla Bartók. We gave her an advance cassette recording of this movement which, her doctors told us, she listened to in her final days.

Of the two ancient texts, 'Are you lost out in darkness?' comes from the Epic of Gilgamesh, which is the world's oldest written story, recorded on clay tablets in the 7th century BC and based on material from the third millennium BC. It is from the ancient Babylonian civilisation, which means that it has come from what is now Iraq, so it has real resonance for our current time. It tells the story of the hero Gilgamesh and his exploits. The central point is the cursing and subsequent death of Gilgamesh's friend and companion, Enkidu. Gilgamesh laments him bitterly and, stricken with the fear of death, goes in search of immortality, ultimately without success. The extract I set is from the passage in which Gilgamesh laments his friend. 'Now my life is only weeping' is by Jalāl al-Dīn Rūmī, the 13th-century

Persian mystic poet, for whom grief was a central fact of his personal history. He had an intense relationship with a spiritual mentor called Shams-i Tabrīzī, whose apparent murder turned Rūmī into a poet and mystic who sought consolation in the Divine.

The scoring of *Stabat Mater* features ancient instruments and modes from the Middle East/Holy Land: percussion such as the *darabuca*, *def*, *doholla* and *riq*; the double-reed woodwind instrument the *mey*; and, alongside Western harmony, scales or modes such as Hijaz and Bayati. The project was in two parts, since I recorded the work for EMI in 2007, in readiness for the premiere. As usual, I layered the recording, which gave me control over the disparate strands but also enabled me to record in different places. The orchestra, the Royal Liverpool Philharmonic, was recorded at the city's Philharmonic Hall by engineer Simon Rhodes and the Abbey Road mobile recording facility, as was the Royal Liverpool Philharmonic Chorus (chorusmaster Ian Tracey) – heard on three of the movements. Joining them was a professional choir, the EMO Ensemble, from Helsinki, which we recorded in Finland. Jurgita Adamonyté, who was at the Wales International Academy of Voice and was recommended to me by Dennis O'Neill, was the mezzo-soprano soloist, and Belinda Sykes the 'ethnic' vocalist. Belinda, who has a master's degree in Ethnomusicology and Arabic Music from London University, sang, among other passages, the 'Incantation of Mary at the Cross'. She also played the *mey*: an ancient Middle Eastern instrument, not dissimilar to the oboe. The same artists performed at the premiere, except for the Finnish choir.

That premiere, at Liverpool Anglican Cathedral, was an exciting event within a massive space: the largest cathedral in Britain and the fifth largest in the world, packed to capacity. The back of the nave, by the west door, is at a lower level than the remainder and has no sight lines to the choir. It was decided to place seating here and relay what was happening further down by video link. There were over two and a half thousand people present, and the reception was fantastic. All were on their feet come the end; well, all but one. A music critic. Still, he knows best.

In 2009, I started working on the *Gloria*; commissioned by the Really Big Chorus, the premiere was to take place at the Royal Albert Hall, conducted by Brian Kay. Then run by the late Don Monro, the RBC get together a couple of times a year and present major works, sometimes at the Royal Albert Hall, where the choir, occasionally numbering up to three thousand, has been known to outnumber the audience.

Gloria in excelsis Deo ('Glory to God in the highest') is the title and opening line of the text that begins with the words the angels sang when the birth of Christ was announced to shepherds (Luke 2:14). In addition to its inclusion in innumerable mass settings, the Gloria has been set, in isolation, by many composers, including Handel, Vivaldi and Poulenc. I was drawn to setting the Gloria because, aside from utilising such an iconic text that has been used by composers for generations, it gave me an opportunity to include references to how other religions perceive the Divine. In my setting of the Gloria the traditional Latin text is used in the first, second and fifth movements, entitled respectively 'The Proclamation', 'The Prayer' and 'The Exaltation'. Further to this I have extended the parameters by incorporating additional text in two further movements: the third movement, 'The Psalm', sets Psalm 150 in Hebrew (although it may alternatively be performed in Latin), and the fourth movement, 'The Song', is my own adaptation in English of Deuteronomy 32:2, Psalm 144:9 and 1 Chronicles 13:8.

In addition, between the movements, I have selected readings from various ancient religions, performed in chronological order, each expressing their own concept of the Divine or the Ultimate Reality. All world religions acknowledge an Ultimate Reality that is eternal and unchanging. This is usually defined as a personal and loving God or as an eternal truth that governs the universe. Someone who has experienced Ultimate Reality is one who has fulfilled the meaning of life. The Hindu reading, in Sanskrit, is from the *Bhagavad Gita* (Song of the Divine), the classic Hindu scripture. Buddhism is represented through Buddhist Hybrid Sanskrit, the very end of the Diamond Sutra, the world's oldest dated printed book. I also used the opening lines of the main Taoist scripture, the *Tao Te Ching* (The Classic of the Way and Virtue). And for Islam, I chose an extract, in Arabic, from the beginning of the Qur'an – the section known as 'Al Fatiha' ('The Opening'), which is recited in Muslim daily prayers. The work is scored for choir and orchestra with the addition, common to my work, of using percussion instruments indigenous to the referenced cultures.

My EMI recording of 2010 was completed by my setting of the *Te Deum*, an early Christian Latin text praising God. The title is taken from the opening line, '*Te Deum laudamus*', which translates as 'We praise you, O God'. This text has been set to music by many composers, among them Haydn, Mozart, Berlioz, Verdi, Bruckner, Dvořák, Britten, Byrd, Tallis, Purcell, Handel and Elgar. I am quite fond of this piece and it is quite unusual for me in that there is no ethnic influence or instrumentation. It is also relatively short, with no text other than the Latin. It is scored for choir, two trumpets, percussion and strings. Like the *Stabat Mater* it was composed for Liverpool as the European Capital of Culture in 2008, having been commissioned by the Liverpool Welsh Choral Union.

In 2009, a glossy brochure arrived on my desk, from Hungary, the contents of which concerned a new work for chorus and orchestra called *The Bards of Wales*, composed by Karl Jenkins. I thought this somewhat premature since this was the first I had heard of it. Further reading unveiled the mystery of the title.

During the Middle Ages, Hungary was a great power, a country very much bigger than its modern dimensions. It was also a flourishing centre of Renaissance culture and trade, but was ruined in the 16th century by repeated Turkish invasions and by the subjection of much of the country to direct Turkish rule. When the Turks were finally expelled in 1699, Hungary fell under the domination of the Austrian Habsburg dynasty, in whose empire all individual nationalist expression was discouraged. In the years following the Napoleonic wars, Austria became a police state; oppression mounted until, in 1848, the various nations in the empire rebelled in the name of both liberal and national freedoms, as they did elsewhere in Europe. Under the leadership of Lajos Kossuth, Hungary deposed the Habsburgs and declared independence, raising an army that kept the Austrians and their Russian allies at bay until final defeat in 1849. As the Austrians reoccupied Hungary, they took savage reprisals against rebel soldiers and the civilian population alike and instituted a harsh regime aimed at eliminating all future demonstrations of Hungarian nationalism.

In 1857, the Emperor of Austria, Franz Josef I, made a tour of Hungary and it was suggested that his visit should be commemorated in verse. János Arany (1817–82), a well-known poet, essayist and translator, refused to compose verses in praise of the head of a murderous regime. Instead, he wrote the epic ballad *A Walesi Bárdok*, which translates as 'The Bards of Wales', for private circulation, publishing it only in 1863 in the guise of a translation of an old English ballad, a necessary stratagem to bypass the Austrian censor. Arany's foreword to the published version is quite specific. The ballad retells a legend that Edward I of England executed Welsh bards for failing to sing his praises at a banquet in Montgomery Castle in 1277, thus placing the episode at the time of the Treaty of Aberconwy when, following a series of defeats, Llywelyn II of Wales agreed to accept the overlordship of Edward I of England. It seems that Arany apparently discovered a reference to the execution of the bards in a work by Dickens. It is said that he was well read in English literature, translating several of Shakespeare's plays into Hungarian, while also displaying great interest in the literature and folklore of the Celtic lands.

But it is in Hungary that his *Bards of Wales* had its greatest effect. From 1867, the Austrian Empire was transformed into Austria-Hungary with the Hungarians as a partner nation, rather than a subject people, and there was freedom to publish and to read national works of literature. When Hungary emerged from the First World War as a completely independent state, *A Walesi Bárdok* found its place in the national education system and is learned by heart by all children at the age of thirteen or fourteen. I've since put this to the test: whenever I meet Hungarians, I invariably ask them about the poem and, indeed, they do know it.

Its meaning for Hungarians today derives both from the fact that all Hungarians have knowledge of the poem in common, and also because it is such a powerful statement of the national will. The Hungarians are a unique nation in Central Europe, a Magyar island surrounded by German, Romanian and Slav neighbours with whose languages theirs has nothing in common. Yet the Hungarian language and culture have survived and even flourished despite this isolation. Time and again the nation has been at the brink of destruction – by the Mongols in 1241, the Turks in 1526, through long years of Austrian rule and lastly by the tribulations of 1944–5, but like the Welsh bards in the poem the people have preferred sacrifice to domination. In

Hungary, therefore, the poem speaks a Hungarian truth rather than a Welsh one, but its popularity does at least ensure that Wales has a higher profile in Hungary than in many other countries. Strange to note, therefore, that the Hungarian flag of red, white and green uses the same colours as Wales's Ddraig Goch, or 'red dragon'.

The man behind the brochure I received was László Irinyi, director of Concert Masters International (CMI), a Hungarian concert-promoting agency established in 1994. Since competing in – and winning – the International Eisteddfod at Llangollen with the Budapest University Choir in 1989, László had been passionately interested in links between Hungary and Wales. Like all Hungarians, he studied the epic ballad *The Bards of Wales* and felt that here there was genuine and worthy material for a celebration of the cultures of these two small nations, both desperately dedicated to and always ready to defend their identity whenever endangered or challenged.

The Bards of Wales sheds light on an astonishing similarity between the history of 19th-century Hungary, and that of 13th-century Wales. In both cases, a bitter struggle for independence was waged by people whose unique cultures were threatened by their mighty and hostile neighbours – in the case of Wales, England. The message Arany bequeaths is both timeless and universal: as long as there is oppression or injustice of any kind in our world, we will always need someone brave enough to tell the truth on our behalf – at whatever sacrifice.

László Irinyi wrote:

In order to be able to raise wider awareness of Arany's poem, there was nothing more obvious or inevitable for a concert agent than the need to find an inventive composer of world reputation who could set this strong theme to accessible music. Although an excellent English translation of the original ballad made by Hungarian-born Peter Zollman was already available, I had no idea at all who to approach to do the great job in making my long-cherished and most ambitious dream a reality.

The Leeds Philharmonic Society came to my rescue introducing Jenkins's magnificent music to me first by way of presenting *The Armed Man*'s Polish premiere in Krakow in 2008, which CMI helped organise. Karl's music was passionate love at first hearing, and I simply became obsessed with his unique and overwhelming style, and therefore the yet missing 'component' for a future worldwide success of *The Bards of Wales* was finally found. But how can one approach a celebrated star?

This I learned later, of course, but intrigued and a little irritated by the fact that someone would go to such trouble to present me as the composer of a work of which I had no knowledge, contact was made, a friendship developed and I was commissioned to compose this work for soloists, choir and orchestra. Obviously, I set the English translation by Peter Zollman. Peter had lived near London since 1956, when he came to the UK during the time of the Hungarian uprising against Soviet policies that same year. An eminent academic and a man of science, when the two ends of the Channel Tunnel met in 1990, the man who enabled that meeting to take place through the production of special laser guidance equipment was Peter Zollman. An electrical engineer, he also won three Queen's Awards for technological innovation and export in the industry. He had translated the libretto of Béla Bartók's opera *Duke Bluebeard's Castle* into English, and his translation of 'BOW' was very cleverly done in that the English lay over the Hungarian, rarely necessitating any rhythmic changes to the music to accommodate the text of a different language. Later, a contemporary Welsh Bard, Twm Morys, was commissioned by Rondo Media of

Cardiff to create a Welsh translation of the ballad, so the libretto finally become trilingual: English, Hungarian and Welsh.

The commissioning agreement had already been signed by CMI when the outgoing socialist-liberal Hungarian government most unexpectedly decided to withdraw its support of the project. I believe this was largely because an area of the country was a disaster zone due to flooding, and money was needed. László, completely abandoned by the state officials, had no other choice than to support the project himself but he was fortunate in that an old schoolfriend came on board. László Baradács, CEO of FBZ Hungária, and his wife, Márta Golub, lent massive financial support to see the whole thing through and invest in its future. 'László Number Two', as I called him, is a jolly man and an authority on anything and everything relating to geese, would you believe. Goose liver is enormously popular in Hungary but László's particular 'spin-off' was goose-down feathers.

In addition, John Asquith from Ferndale, Wales, a dedicated conductor, linguist and historian with vision, became a voluntary Director of the BOW Project for the UK, giving a brand-new impetus to the project's future development. Later, HRH The Prince of Wales became its Patron, along with Jim Parc Nest, past Archdruid of Wales.

The world premiere of the English-language version was on 21 June 2011 at the National Concert Hall, Budapest, with the Hungarian-language version being performed at the same venue in June the following year. On 4 August 2012, the National Eisteddfod of Wales saw the first performance in Welsh with tenor soloist Dennis O'Neill singing King Edward. Other notable performances included the American premiere at Carnegie Hall on 20 January 2014, and a performance at the Liszt Academy of Music in Budapest in October of the same year.

Happily, the Hungarian Stone Circle Monument (Gorsedd Hwngaraid) is to be erected by 2 March 2017 to mark the bicentenary of János Arany's birth, in the Tokaj Wine Region – a UNESCO World Heritage site. For my efforts, I was honoured to be awarded the Order of Merit: Knight's Cross by the President of Hungary.

In fact László had some Hungarian red wine bottled as 'Bards of Wales' subtitled 'Karl Jenkins Vintage'! It kept appearing. Even Ken, Joan's husband, I later discovered, knew László, and was given the task recently of bringing me a few bottles back, from Hungary, in his orchestral transport truck.

16

THE PEACEMAKERS

*W*ay back in 1995, soon after the initial success of *Adiemus* in Germany, Austria and Switzerland, I was approached by Ully Jonas and Sat 1 (the first privately owned television broadcasting station in Germany) to arrange and compose a Christmas CD. Entitled *Merry Christmas to the World*, it borrowed from the cross-genre flavour of *Adiemus* and included established carols and Christmas songs, together with some new compositions from me. The canvas was broad, from Bach chorales to gospel music, with much in between. This was recorded in 1995 and the release saw some success in German-speaking Europe, although the languages employed included much Latin and English as well as some German. Fast forward nearly fifteen years and, in 2009, EMI happened to hear a copy of this recording and suggested we re-address the concept, dividing the album into two works: one of music written by me, and the other, my arrangements of established Christmas music. My CD booklet notes at the time explained it thus:

Stella Natalis is the generic title for this album comprising the two works, *Stella Natalis* itself and *Joy to the World*. *Stella Natalis* means 'star of birth' or 'star of origin' and the music conveys the Christmas message of peace, goodwill, compassion and a new beginning while using a wider palette of inspiration than is usual in such treatments. Zulu text, reference to Hindu gods as well as the Old Testament, all make an appearance. The libretto, for the most part, is by Carol together with some established text in Latin and English. *Joy to the World* is a collection of known carols from various parts of the globe.

Apart from Nigel Short's choir Tenebrae, also featured were soprano Kate Royal, trumpeter Alison Balsom and the 2008 'Choirgirl of the Year', Alice Halstead, while as a counterpoint to their 'classical' sound I revisited my past and occasionally featured the ethnic sound of *Adiemus*.

Shortly after reworking *Stella Natalis*, I took on an exciting new project. *The Story of Wales* was a BBC–Open University partnership production: a six-hour series, first transmitted in 2012 on BBC One Wales and subsequently across the BBC Two network. This landmark series tells the story of Wales from pre-history to modern times. Its epic tale runs from Iron Age hill forts and the massive Roman presence in Wales, through Hywel Dda's uniting of the country under one law and the battles of Welsh leaders such as Owain Glyndwr with Norman and English kings. The dramatic and fast-moving story continues with the Welsh at the heart of the Tudor court, takes us through the immense pace of change in the country as coal mines and ironworks flourished, with technological and educational innovations putting Wales ahead of the world in the Industrial Revolution – and climaxes with devolution and the creation of a Welsh government. BBC News presenter Huw Edwards tells this compelling story of the nation, showing how influential Wales has been down the ages. I composed the score and recorded it with the BBC National Orchestra of Wales.

In 2011, I was commissioned by BBC Wales to compose a piece for chorus and orchestra for performance in 2012, coincidentally the year of the Olympic Games in London. I therefore decided to turn to ancient Greece, birthplace of the original Games, and Greek mythology regarding the creation of Earth for inspiration. For text, I considered using my own 'mythical' language, first employed in my *Adiemus* project. I naturally wanted to incorporate the word 'Olympus' or some derivative into the title. Imagine my incredulity when I was told I could not do this. The International Olympics Committee had registered intellectual property rights internationally in the word 'Olympic', including any derivatives, and such branding rights led up to and included the Games. 'Olympus' is not even an English word and is in common usage; this is what Stasi East Germany would have done, the action of a 'police state'.

Due to these frustrating restrictions, I therefore entitled the work *Songs of the Earth*. According to Greek mythology, before earth, sea and sky were created, there existed one warring mass of disparate elements, also perceived as a god, called Khaos. Out of this emerged Gaia, Mother Earth, who, without a mate, gave birth to Ouranus (sky or heavens). Ouranus, in turn, impregnated Gaia who, as a result, gave birth to the Titans, six male, six female, one of whom was Tethys, Goddess of Fountains and Streams. The Greeks imagined the sky to be a dome of brass, decorated with stars at night, whose edges descended to rest on the periphery of a flat earth. Below this were the bowels of the earth, Tartarus, where the Titans were later to be imprisoned. As is often the case with mythology, there are variants of the above. I simply took the one I found to be musically stimulating. *Songs of the Earth* was premiered in Cardiff, again with the BBC National Orchestra of Wales and combined choirs.

However, there were some 'official' cultural events taking place in 2012 under the banner of the Cultural Olympiad. I was asked by the Really Big Chorus, who had applied for and been granted permission for inclusion, to compose a short work. I based this on Greek gods and the piece, with 'official approval', was called *The Gods of Olympus* and premiered at the Royal Albert Hall. What a rigmarole!

My next work was *The Peacemakers* which, at the very least, I could title appropriately. As the name suggests, it is a work extolling peace. One line from Rūmī, the 13th-century Persian mystic poet whose words I have set, sums up its ethos: 'All religions, all singing one song: peace be with you.' Having decided on the concept, the search was on to find messengers of peace. A handful of obvious figures came to mind, figures who have changed the world; others are less well known. I have occasionally placed some text in a musical environment that helps identify their origin or culture: the *bansuri* (Indian flute) and *tabla* in the section inspired by Gandhi; the *shakuhachi* (a Japanese flute associated with Zen Buddhism) and temple bells in that of the Dalai Lama; African percussion in the movement relating to Nelson Mandela; and echoes of the blues of the American Deep South in my tribute to Martin Luther King.

I saw *The Peacemakers* as a continuation of the message and sentiment heard in the last movement of *The Armed Man: A Mass for Peace* – namely, 'better is peace than evermore war'. Having sourced suitable and pithy texts about these remarkable individuals and others, the net was cast to find other 'peacemakers' and then to seek copyright clearance where applicable. Albert Schweitzer (1875–1965) was one who came to mind. A theologian, philosopher, physician and medical missionary in Africa, he was also an organist of some repute. Born in the province of Alsace-Lorraine, at that time part of the German Empire, Schweitzer considered himself French. He received the 1952 Nobel Peace Prize; I had been aware of him as a boy, in part because my organist father had recordings of him playing Bach. Securing the Schweitzer quote was most odd. The line was 'The important thing in life is the traces of love that we leave behind when we have to leave unasked and say farewell.' On approaching his estate, they claimed that this could not, unequivocally, be attributed to him. I pointed out that this line had been used, and so attributed, in a global advertising campaign, for, I believe, some sports commodity. Their response? 'We'd better say yes then!'

Then, there was Anne Frank (1929–45). For most readers, this extraordinarily brave young girl needs little introduction. German born, she was one of the Jewish victims of Nazi persecution during the Second World War. Following the German occupation of the Netherlands, her family went into hiding in a secret annexe at her father's office. After two years, they were betrayed. Anne Frank died of typhus in Bergen-Belsen in 1945; she kept a diary of this period, which has been published in well over fifty languages.

Another 'peacemaker' I chose was St Francis, an Italian Catholic friar and preacher, born in Assisi in 1181 or 1182. He founded the Franciscan Order and is one of the most venerated religious figures in history. In 1228, Pope Gregory IX proclaimed him a saint; he is known as the patron saint of animals. Although associated with him, the text of the Peace Prayer was anonymously written much later and surfaced in France in the early 20th century.

Bahá'u'lláh (1817–92), meanwhile, was born in Tehran and is the founder of the Bahá'í faith. He believed mankind to be a single race that should unite in a global society. His claim to divine revelation resulted in persecution and imprisonment; he died in the prison city of Akka, Palestine (Acre in present-day Israel), after being confined for twenty-four years.

The Peacemakers didn't end there, though. I had previously set texts by Rūmī in my *Stabat Mater* and did so again here. The work obviously needed something from the Abrahamic religions, so there was text from the Bible, the Qur'an, the Torah, and by St Seraphim of Sarov, one of the most renowned Russian monks and mystics in the Orthodox Church. Percy Bysshe Shelley (1792–1822), regarded as among the finest lyric poets in the English language, is represented, while I also quote from the Old Testament Book of Isaiah in my homage to Martin Luther King, just as he did in his 'I have a dream' speech.

When I was composing the work, the structure could not be organic and, indeed, it did not have to be. Copyright clearances, when they were required, were arriving on an ad hoc basis and I was composing when in possession of them. The only problem was that of Martin Luther King where permission was withheld, by the estate, unless an exorbitant fee was paid. This was neatly side-stepped by turning it around to 'he had a dream' and then just quoting from Isaiah, as he did, but correcting his 'mistake' where the words 'mountain' and 'hill' are reversed.

Further text was especially written, by Carol and Terry Waite. Terry, who I am proud to consider a friend, was Archbishop of Canterbury Robert Runcie's Assistant for Anglican Communion Affairs. In January 1987 he was captured in Beirut while attempting to secure the release of hostages. He was kept in solitary confinement for four years and held hostage for almost five years. In addition, *The Peacemakers* also included some anonymous text and one movement where I simply set the word 'Peace' in twenty-one languages.

As usual, we recorded different elements at different times and even at different studios. Jody and I laid down the basic bed of tempi, and percussion where appropriate, before recording at Air Studios with the engineer Nick Wollage. The orchestra was the London Symphony Orchestra, for whom I wrote my concertante, *Quirk*, for its 125th anniversary. The orchestration of the piece is not standard, in that there is no woodwind section as such, nor horns. The woodwind contributions were overlaid by Gareth Davies, the LSO's Principal Flautist, and some 'ethnic' soloists. The *bansuri* player Ashwin Shrivanasan from Mumbai was a friend of Jody, and had worked with him in India, including on a massive 'Western'-style score Jody had written for *Aladin*, a major Bollywood movie featuring Sanjay Dutt, and he added a wonderful layer of sound to the piece. The *bansuri* is effectively an Indian flute and Ashwin, in London working with Nitin Sawhney at the Royal Albert Hall, contributed to the setting of 'I offer you peace' (which also has *tabla* percussion) using the Gandhi text.

Leading the LSO was Carmine Lauri, with whom I had worked before. Carmine is originally from Malta and in the spring of 2013, I was invited by Christopher Muscat to visit and conduct the Maltese Philharmonic Orchestra and Choir in a performance of *The Peacemakers*. Chris, their resident conductor, is also a fine composer. Carmine, who is something of a hero there, returned to lead the orchestra and play 'Solitude' – a movement for solo violin that acts as a kind of bridging point in the middle of the work.

The word 'great' is an overused adjective – but in the case of two jazz musicians who contributed to *The Peacemakers*, it is entirely justified. Soprano sax player Nigel Hitchcock created something truly beautiful, and the guitarist Laurence Cottle provided an intriguing sound with the juxtaposition of the bass guitar and the choir – the fretless bass guitar being used, in the main, as a solo melodic instrument. Despite it being very difficult to perform in tune in the upper echelons of the fingerboard, Laurence played beautifully. The soprano soloist was Lucy Crowe, fresh from the Royal Opera House where she had just sung the role of Sophie in my favourite opera, *Der Rosenkavalier*, and destined for both Glyndebourne and the Met, New York, later in the year. Lucy is a good friend of Jody and Rosie from when they were contemporaries at the Royal Academy of Music. Her husband, Joe Walters, a fine horn player, also runs a wonderful charity called Songbound – a music outreach initiative that uses singing to connect with India's most impoverished children via collaborative projects with schools, choirs and professional musicians worldwide. I am privileged to have been able to make a modest contribution to Songbound where a donation of a few hundred pounds can establish a new choir.

It was important to have two choirs for *The Peacemakers*: a mixed chorus and a children's choir, representing innocence and hope. Choral director Simon Halsey was the perfect choice to oversee and direct this element, in that he had two choirs under his wing that were ideal for this project: the CBSO (City of Birmingham Symphony Orchestra) Youth Choir and the Rundfunkchor (Radio Choir) Berlin. We recorded the Youth Choir at Angel Studios in London. This was the occasion when, with Carol co-producing, we found that many of them had learned the piano with her *Chester's Piano Books*. The Rundfunkchor Berlin was recorded at Teldex Studio, Berlin, in April 2011 with recording engineer René Möller. They are an amazing choir with wonderful breath control; when complimented on their breathing, one chorister said that they were not allowed to breathe until they got home. It was apposite that the Rundfunkchor Berlin is featured on this recording, since its collective history, and that of many members, encapsulates the terrible effect of the struggles of 20th-century Europe and the power of music to transcend boundaries, war and political differences. Formed in 1925, after the Second World War, the choir found itself in the eastern sector of Berlin. Carol had a long conversation with chorister Judith Engel: she was raised in what had become East Germany and became a victim of the Wall. As a child, she was allowed into the Western sector to partake in singing festivals but had to return daily, until one day the Wall was no more and she was free. Some of the choir had Russian, not English, as a second language – a good thing too since one of them corrected the incorrect ending of the Russian word for peace that was part of the text. Their contribution to Leonard Bernstein's 'Ode to Joy' from Beethoven's Symphony No. 9, celebrating the fall of the Berlin Wall in 1989, remains one of the most profound testaments of our time to the power of music.

Two of the movements of *The Peacemakers* – 'Fiat Pax' and 'Anthem: Peace, Triumphant Peace' – feature the Really Big Chorus. This huge congregation of a thousand voices was recorded at Abbey Road Studios, famously opened by Sir Edward Elgar, no less, when he conducted the London Symphony Orchestra there in 1931. Due to the sheer volume of people, we had to record in five shifts of two hundred choristers at a time. The Reverend Aidan Platten provided a rehearsal facility around the corner at St Mark's Church, Hamilton Terrace, and the conveyor-belt recording took place on 18 June 2011. For our recording, the principal conductor was Brian Kay and the participating choirs are listed in the acknowledgements.

Terry Waite very kindly wrote of *The Peacemakers*: 'Music has the capacity to breathe harmony into the soul. *The Peacemakers* breathes the harmony of peace.' My dedication read: '*The Peacemakers* is dedicated to the memory of all those who lost their lives during armed conflict, in particular, innocent civilians. When I composed *The Armed Man: A Mass for Peace* for the millennium, it was with the hope of looking forward to a century of peace. Sadly, nothing much has changed.'

When *The Peacemakers* was released, I took the opportunity to make a public declaration of thanks to Carol, who I very happily described as 'fellow composer, librettist, inspiration, best friend, personal peacemaker and wife of nearly forty years'. I also dedicated one of my favourite sections, 'The Dove', to Astrid May, our first grandchild, born on 5 May 2011 while this recording was in progress.

It was a remarkably large project to be involved in, with five different engineers employed on this recording: Jody, Nick Wollage, Steve Price, René Möller and Simon Changer, who mixed the album. And after writing such a gargantuan work, I really wasn't quite sure what to do next.

In 2011, a major change was taking place in the recording industry in that EMI was put up for sale and Universal was the buyer. Because of monopoly issues, it was decreed that Universal (which already had Deutsche Grammophon and Decca as classical labels) would not be allowed to acquire EMI Classics, which subsequently went to Warner Classics. This long-winded process coincided with the end of my EMI contract and EMI inevitably being in a state of stasis. Mark Wilkinson at Decca was about to become President of DG in Berlin. He had often expressed an interest in us doing something together in the future. This led to me moving to DG, with the iconic 'Yellow Label', for two albums.

Apart from the odd dalliance with a concerto or two, my output over the past decade or more had been with religious, or quasi-religious, texts. I was now ready, in 2013, for a change – and an idea that appealed was to revisit *Adiemus*, a concept born in 1995, but with a Latin–American twist. It meant a certain freedom from the 'shackles' of setting text and by metaphorically 'going to Latin America', an element of plain fun could be introduced. This was by no means meant to be a permanent change of direction, just a musical diversion to revisit an 'old friend' from twenty years back. *Adiemus Colores* is music of fantasy, a sound that, in part, might have evolved if history had taken a different course and the vocal sounds of Africa had travelled, along with the percussion, via the Iberian peninsula to Latin America.

I have always been intrigued by the traditional music of Latin America. I initially came to its exotic and flamboyant world via recordings of Afro-Cuban jazz. Dizzy Gillespie, a major pioneer of modern jazz, had introduced Cuba's greatest percussionist, Chano Pozo, to his big band in New York in 1947. This was the first instance of 'Latin jazz'. Later I came to love the music of the Brazilian composer Antônio Carlos Jobim and also Ástor Piazzolla, who hailed from Argentina. In fact, I had some personal involvement with this music when, with pioneering jazz fusion band Nucleus, we shared the stage with Sérgio Mendes and Brasil 66 at the Royal Festival Hall, and when I wrote some arrangements for singer-songwriter Gilberto Gil (who later became Brazil's Minister of Culture) when he first came to the UK.

I had also produced and orchestrated some music by South American composers for the Dame Kiri Te Kanawa album, of course, as well as the *Bachianas brasileiras No. 5* by the Brazilian composer Heitor Villa-Lobos for *Adiemus: Vocalise*. Another South American spark that helped kindle the flame that became *Adiemus Colores* is the fascination that the people of Wales, me included, have with the romance of Patagonia, that area occupying the southernmost tip of Argentina where there is a Welsh-speaking settlement, dating from 1865. In fact, the Welsh name for this area, Y Wladfa, translates as 'The Colony'.

The two strands of *Adiemus* and the genre of Latin American music come together in *Adiemus Colores*. The movements are named, in Spanish, after various colours, and the mood the colours evoke in me through the abstract medium of music. Here are the titles and what the particular colours were associated with – in my mind, at least – when composing this music:

Canción amarilla (yellow: brightness, flamboyance, panache)
Canción violeta (violet: warmth, fulfilment, geniality)

Canción negra (black: romantic, melancholia, heavy-hearted)
Canción rosa (pink: ebullient, light-hearted, carefree)
Canción azul (blue: cool, funky, 'blue')
Canción turquesa (turquoise: sensuous, ravishing)
Canción naranja (orange: zing, pizzazz, verve)
Canción verde (green: nature, healing, life force)
Canción blanca (white: innocence, kindness)
Canción dorada (gold: optimism, sunny)
Canción plateada (silver: elegance, introspection)
Canción roja (red: passion, intensity, 'hot')

Rhythmically, some movements are Brazilian based, such as the samba; some are Argentinian – the tango, for example; some are Spanish, such as the bolero; and some are a hybrid of different forms and styles. The word *colores* has another relevance here in that, in the tradition of the *Adiemus* concept, I have explored the many disparate sounds and timbres – colours, in fact – of the human voice, from *fado* to the operatic, from African tribal singing to the quasi ecclesiastical.

The main element, in the music, was again the *Adiemus* singers, comprising the wonderful group of performers from Finland, the core of whom I first worked with at the Helsinki Festival in 1997 but with the addition of male voices on this occasion. Some stellar guests are introduced along the way, including tenor Rolando Villazón, guitarist Miloš Karadaglić, and a specially selected orchestra, La orquesta de colores.

Once again, we went round the houses in recording the album, largely due to artist availability and cost. The *Adiemus* singers, led by Säde, laid down their parts at Finnvox Studios in Helsinki; Rolando Villazón, meanwhile, was recorded at Salle Colonne in Paris. Engineered by Rainer Maillard from Berlin, this was done out of necessity like an old-school classical recording, and quite unnerving, in that Rolando, Rainer, Carol and I were all in the same room together, all with headphones, so any discussion or movement during takes would spell disaster. Furthermore, any comment or suggestion couldn't be discussed in the privacy of a control room first. All was laid bare. Rolando was there to record this movement of mine, and to also overdub his part on a duet for a Deutsche Grammophon recording he was making with the great Russian soprano Anna Netrebko. I wonder what the sanctimonious 'how can one hope to have good performances when the music is recorded in different places?' newspaper critic would have made of that?

Miloš was by now quite a star in the world of classical guitar, and touring incessantly, so it was difficult to co-ordinate a date for his recording at *mustache* in London. However, I obviously sent him material in advance, and we managed to fix a session. Cuca, another of the singers, was an absolute delight. A beautiful person in all manner of ways, she was intrigued by the notion of singing 'nonsense words', and worried about the pronunciation. I told her to imagine they were nonsense Portuguese words and just sing naturally. She loved the melody I had written especially for her and said it had the soul of *fado*, the Portuguese musical genre dating from the early 19th century and characterised by mournful tunes and lyrics, and infused with a sense of resignation and melancholia. She flew over from Lisbon with manager Miguel Capucho to record – but not before we enjoyed an exhilarating evening at a Soho restaurant, as we did with Pacho Flores when he arrived from Venezuela.

Pacho had grown up as part of El Sistema and the Simón Bolívar Youth Orchestra, the former providing free classical music education for young people, including impoverished children. The result was 102 youth orchestras, 55 children's orchestras, 270 music centres, and close to 250,000 young musicians. The programme provided four hours of musical training and rehearsal per weekday after school, as well as at the weekend. A brilliant trumpeter, Pacho was now signed as a solo artist to Deutsche Grammophon, but had a slightly different background to most of his countrymen in that his father directed a brass band in provincial Venezuela, a parallel with my friend Tony Small and his son Gareth. Pacho was due to play with Gareth on the world premiere of *Colores* but, due to bureaucracy, he was stranded in Valencia with visa problems. He played both trumpet parts on the album, bringing amazing playing to the project but also that intangible Latin American flavour.

I included this sentiment, attributed to the indigenous Navajo Indian tribe of the USA, in the CD booklet:

Walk on a rainbow trail; walk on a trail of song, and all about you will be beauty. There is a way out of every dark mist, over a rainbow trail.

17

REFLECTIONS

*O*ver the years, I've often been asked for my thoughts and opinions on diverse aspects of music and the music business. As I approach the end of my story, I think this an opportune moment to put them forward. As you may have deduced by now, the idea of categorising anything – in particular, music or people – is never something on which I've been very keen. And, as I look back over my life and career, I believe this has helped me to connect with people all over the world through my work, a fact that moves me greatly.

I often receive letters from people with terminal illnesses, in whose lives my music has made a difference, or correspondence from families of the deceased where certain pieces have alleviated their grief. I even met a lady from Ulster whose mother, tragically, had been murdered one Christmas Day; she told me her family had found solace in my work. It was a genuine and moving utterance of gratitude by which I felt truly humbled, and it speaks of the power of music to heal.

Having lived a life full of music, I now feel more passionate than ever about the right of every child to have the potential to experience what I did. Carol and I were both children in those halcyon days when a family's income was absolutely no barrier to a child's full and happy music education. I grew up in West Glamorgan and Carol went to school in Leicestershire, and both areas had very vibrant, similar approaches to music education in the school system. The learning of instruments was open to every child, no matter what their background.

I went to a grammar school, where I was encouraged to stretch myself, but music provision was certainly not the preserve of grammar schools alone. My father, the deputy head of a secondary modern, saw this first hand. The school had fewer instruments, mostly strings, but at eleven every child would be given the opportunity to play something. And if the instrument the child wanted to try wasn't available, it would soon be found. Peripatetic teachers were on call, and they came to every school. As I experienced on a personal level, there was an established route: school orchestra, West Glamorgan Youth Orchestra, Glamorgan Youth Orchestra, National Youth Orchestra of Wales. And this was replicated right across the UK. Gradually, it's been eroded by different governments of various hues. The reason? Quite simply, because people outside music don't see the benefit. It's well established that skills in music enable children to develop in other fields as well. It's a life-changing medium, but one that urgently needs greater support from those who haven't experienced first hand music's power and relevance. We are reaching a stage, if we haven't already, where youth orchestras are the province only of children from private schools and/or with well-off parents.

My own musical education prepared me very well for a future in music and I cherish the classical training I received. However, I've always tried to go beyond the constraints of genre to find my inspiration.

Combining disparate cultures, both musical and textual, has always fascinated me but it is important that a creative work has integrity, and sounds as though it has 'come from one place' and is not something artificially bolted together. An example of the latter was an album called *Hooked on Classics*, dating from 1981, where a series of popular classical pieces were played continuously without a break at the same tempo to a drumbeat.

I'd like to mention 'time'. This is a word that is alien to many people – but it's a demotic term in jazz. 'Time' alludes to where one plays in relation to the beat, and where the beat is placed. Some don't 'hear' it, which is why they think that all time-based music, like jazz and rock, is identical and therefore banal. A 'good groove is a good groove'; they cannot differentiate the good from the bad. It is interesting that throughout music education, this aspect of music is given short shrift, probably because those in authority have no concept of it. Aural tests relating to pitch abound in music education, but rarely is there any thought or scrutiny given to rhythm and, crucially, 'good time'. One frequently questions the aural ability of critics: I wryly recall *The Times* printing a photograph of its 'house rock band' with its chief music critic at the piano, with his printed music. Needing sheet music to 'jam'? Bless! This reminds me of when someone once 'sat in' with Ronnie Scott. No sheet music is used of course, so having stood aside while the band played the 'head' (the melody before improvisation), he sidled up to Ronnie, saying, 'I don't know this song.' Ronnie's reply: 'You've just heard it, haven't you?'

'Time' is related to rhythm and I find much contemporary music arhythmic. Rhythm is exciting only when related to something, which means an underlying pulse, stated or unstated – which is why many people find ethnic music from Latin America, India and Africa, for example, exciting; not to mention jazz. To make it clear, I am not talking about wonderfully rhythmic composers of genius, such as Stravinsky and Bartók, here, but of a later trend. One rarely hears new fast music either, nowadays, in the 'classical' sphere.

Given a modicum of musical ability, a smattering of serious academic study and some degree of intellectual resource, it is no insurmountable task to construct a piece of music that is architecturally sound and intellectually clever, employing the following techniques that roughly mean the same thing: twelve-tone, dodecaphony, serialism. A 'tone row', or series, of the twelve chromatic notes is selected as a motif. No note is to be repeated (except rhythmically) until all are played, then the motif can be played backwards (retrograde), upside-down (inversion), upside-down and backwards (retrograde inversion). As a mathematical edifice it could be superb, but too often such works are emotionally arid. Apart from Schoenberg, Berg and Webern, I can't think of anyone who has a 'voice', a stamp that makes their music identifiable, who composes in this genre. The fact that so many classical composers working today have left these systems behind and returned to some form of tonality speaks volumes. Many would claim otherwise but it is the nature of this world that twelve-tone pieces are never heard blind with the composer unknown. *Downbeat*, the US jazz publication, used to run an intriguing series called the 'blindfold test', for which a well-known guest jazz musician would have to identify the artists on various recently released records while, metaphorically, 'blindfolded'. Since the musicians were improvising, this held a certain fascination for the reader, and no doubt some nervousness for the subject, an exercise that could not be conducted in the 'atonal' world. Shame!

I might, mistakenly, have given the idea that there is nothing much out there in 'core classical' that I admire but there is. Two fine American composers, John Adams and Steve Reich, for example. Often branded 'minimalists' they are far more than that: accessible and rhythmically exciting, they certainly each have a 'voice'. But brilliant as many are, I feel that no composer of the present, or even of the recent past, will be gaining entry to the pantheon of the greatest composers of history, considering three undisputed 'greats', Stravinsky, Britten and Shostakovich, died in the 1970s.

I feel there has been a seismic shift in music since the Second World War, first with the transformation of the recording studio as a creative tool and then, of course, the revolution in music technology in a computerised age. 'Rock' and popular culture have become 'respectable' and considered 'art', so increasingly, young people of musical talent are looking at other fields in which to express themselves rather than what is perceived as being classical music. There is more to music than the 'straight and narrow' route prescribed by the blinkered and self-appointed cognoscenti. As Bob Dylan wrote, 'The times they are a-changing.' It's an interesting conundrum: whose music will be played and enjoyed more in two hundred years' time? That of Stockhausen or that of Gershwin?

The reader might pick up on the fact that despite my stated aversion to labelling music, I do however occasionally reference styles out of necessity: 'jazz', 'classical', etc. We still need terms of reference to know what we are broadly talking about, stylistically, so I make no excuse for that.

Which brings me to J. S. Bach, considered by many to be the greatest of all composers. In a sense he lived in a bubble, never leaving Germany – and, after his death in 1750, outside Leipzig his music was barely heard again until Mendelssohn resurrected the *St Matthew Passion* nearly eighty years later. Of all composers, Bach's music is the cleverest or the most intellectual of any, on one level, but it is an intellectualism born of the soul, not vice versa, possessing a beauty that goes straight to the heart.

People often ask me about inspiration but it's a term I don't fully acknowledge, and I often cite Bach. He was what one might call a 'jobbing' composer, writing cantatas for most Sundays, and he penned over two hundred of them alone, during the course of his lifetime, essentially for popular consumption. One example of his genius is his use of 'quadruple counterpoint', where music is in four parts and any one of the strands could be melody or bass without compromising contrapuntal rules, yet still sounding sublime. Using serial techniques, one could write a passable piece in an hour; in the style of Bach, never. In a way, it comes down to whether music is primarily a cerebral art or an art of the soul – though it can be both, of course. I think it is an English trait, as opposed to a Celtic one, to shy away from the overtly emotional, to be reluctant to wear one's heart on one's sleeve. Elgar's genius was such that he broke through that reticence.

I don't set much store by much of the airy-fairy nonsense spoken nowadays about music and art (in its widest sense). I heard a debate recently about the orchestration of a certain Baroque work and how many string players the composer intended. The discussion became more and more pretentious, yet no one, probably because they do not live in the real world, mentioned a likely fact of how many players the commissioner (a count? a church?) employed or could afford. It reminds me of when Richard Strauss, a 'down-to-earth' composer, was asked whether the conductor Herbert von Karajan would be allowed to employ extra strings for his *Metamorphosen* for twenty-three solo strings. His reply? 'If Mr Karajan wants more strings, let him have them!'

We all work with the same twelve notes, in the West anyway, and I believe it is possible to write music of integrity and invention within the parameters, or restrictions, of any style. For example, there is no more predictable, or prescriptive, form in music than that of the 'blues'. Twelve bars in length with a basic three-chord structure, when one kicks off, given good 'time' and a fair wind, one knows in advance which chord will be played twenty minutes later. The form can, however, be as relevant today as it ever was, in the hands of musicians of genius. Its very predictability does not, necessarily, preclude its worth or status. That depends on other factors.

During the 1960s, there were some weird and wonderful contemporary performances: aleatoric music, 'happenings', and performance art, where much was left to chance. Carol – who, as a composer, thought she should become involved – told me an amusing story concerning one concert. She went to a Society for the Promotion of New Music event put on by John Tilbury, a fine pianist she knew quite well, at the Queen Elizabeth Hall in London. Come the interval, as everyone was preparing to return to the hall, another composer at the event approached Carol and asked her whether she would like a cup of tea, reassuring her that there was plenty of time. Having agreed, she was led through a door, only to find herself on the stage. Her 'chaperone' invited her to sit on a sofa, in front of which stood a table complete with cups and saucers. In a corner, a kettle was boiling. The piece, it transpired, was something to do with the seasons. John came on, dressed for tennis, holding a racket. He started to play the piano as someone else made the tea. Carol was told to act 'natural' and drink her tea. Sitting there facing the serious few in the audience, she remembers little about the music. One can but guess. Having heard John play Chopin so beautifully in the past, she later asked him, 'Why are you doing this?'

I now turn to address one of the issues that sometimes come up in my conversations with concertgoers and listeners, who can't understand the hostility of music critics to my work. I don't want to overstate the effect on me personally, which is now negligible. But the printed word has a certain authority, and one can easily feel hurt, even when it's claptrap – for example, the first review of *The Armed Man* in 2000, the work that is currently the most frequently performed large-scale work by a living composer in the 21st century.

To my mind, three of the most valueless words in the English language are 'to critical acclaim', the phrase that is trotted out, time and time again, ad nauseam, in biographies and curricula vitae. Have you met any of these people who dispense 'critical acclaim'? The people of whom Kenneth Tynan, a theatre critic himself, once said, '[They] know the way but can't drive the car.' The people whose profession was once described by Elvis Costello as 'a stupid thing to do for a living'. The people who sometimes peer out from the arts pages, with a 'have you seen this man?' kind of snapshot attached to their piece. They then, in common with all arts criticism, to be fair, engage in the puerile activity of dispensing 'stars', from one to five, as though judging a figure-skating competition. It has always been beyond my comprehension that anyone attaches any credence whatsoever to what critics have to say about a discipline in which they have absolutely no talent or ability themselves. As a teenager, I used to read reviews of jazz albums but that soon stopped when I was staggered to learn that most were written by non-musicians. The fact that I once received a 5-star review for *Quirk*, in the *Independent*, has not mellowed my opinion of critics, which is shared by most musicians. One so-called critic described me as 'emotionally manipulative'. Now, by any yardstick, that is a pretty stupid remark. It was meant to be derogatory but what a fantastic compliment to pay a composer – that he can make people cry, laugh, be uplifted, or be sad, at will.

Have you ever been to some of these critically acclaimed premieres of a certain kind of new piece, where 'one man and his dog' comprise the audience? A ripple of polite applause lasting a few seconds follows the performance and stops well before the composer, taking his or her bow, has left the stage (and sometimes before he or she even gets there) – and the piece is never heard again. Still, no matter: it was 'critically acclaimed' ('ravishing' being a de-rigueur word for such reviews), invariably a plaudit for style over content.

I can happily rejoice in the fact that my career has, mercifully, been '100 per cent proof' – critic proof, that is – and I give thanks that I have been able to make a direct emotional connection with my global audience and bring, so I'm told, something enriching to people's lives. It also enables me to say what many think, but dare not utter, for fear of it seriously affecting their careers. It was said that Clive Barnes, a Broadway theatre and dance critic for the *New York Times*, could close a show with one bad review. How ridiculous is that?

In the pantheon of composers, I stand nowhere. Compared to my heroes I am irrelevant, yet I try to write music of beauty and integrity that communicates with people. Clearly, I don't expect everyone to appreciate what I do, but I take exception to being attacked for what I am not and for what I am not even attempting to be. I compose music that draws from cultures and techniques outside the core 'classical' tradition but which could still be written only by a classically trained composer. Much of my music is in simple song form, sometimes 'rondo form', and it eschews the massive monolithic structures of the late-Romantic symphony and a different age. And one problem with composing accessible tonal music is that *everyone* thinks they can do it, just as *everyone* thinks they can write a 'hit' commercial song, until they try. A good tune is a good tune is a good tune – whenever it was written and whoever wrote it.

Critics can be vile, vindictive and ungracious. Perhaps it's something to do with the frustration of them not being able to actually do anything. Not good enough to play professionally and not creative enough to compose but, nevertheless, hugely opinionated. At least many literary critics are writers themselves. Perhaps that's why they are kinder people since they know and understand the trials and tribulations of the process involved. In 2014, the mezzo-soprano Tara Erraught was pilloried by the UK press for, shall we say, 'not being a size 8', when singing Octavian in *Der Rosenkavalier* at Glyndebourne. I thought suspending disbelief was an ineluctable rule when appreciating opera. Apparently, one of these, Richard Morrison of *The Times*, later said he regretted writing it. Too late, mate! I recall a review of a John Tavener concert that included all kind of venom, even dragging in the irrelevant fact that he was, possibly, well off. One thing about Tavener: you knew what you were getting, so if you anticipate hating the music, why go and review it? An opportunity to be vitriolic I suppose, and a chance not to be missed. Anyway, we can be thankful that no statue will ever be erected to a critic, which reminds me of a funny story regarding the composer Rossini. He was told that the local authorities in his home town of Pesaro intended to erect a statue in his honour. On being told of the significant cost involved, he replied, 'Give me the money and I'll go and stand on the plinth myself!'

I can also lay claim to having introduced thousands to core classical music through the gateway of my oeuvre. Perhaps this is a suitable moment for me to mention Classic FM. I feel immensely grateful for the way in which the team there has championed my music over the last twenty years or so, introducing it to millions of people. Much maligned in some quarters, the station has introduced untold numbers of listeners to the classical repertoire, far more so than has Radio 3, which it massively outstrips in listening figures. When compared to the many millions of pounds of public money given to the BBC to champion classical music, it is sobering to consider that Classic FM is a privately owned commercial radio station, with no licence requirement to demonstrate any so-called 'public-service broadcasting', that has opened up this genre to the general public, in a way the BBC could only hope to. The station also does much to extend the scope of the music with its annual Music Teacher of the Year competition and its daily classical music feature for children. It has been criticised for playing single movements from works. What on earth is wrong with that? It still makes people aware of the beauty of great music, some perhaps for the first time, and encourages them to listen to the complete works by buying recordings or going to a concert. I'd wager that any composer looking down on us from above would be thrilled to hear an extract from his oeuvre played to millions of people. Sometimes a movement from a work becomes more well known than the work itself: Samuel Barber's *Adagio for Strings* was but one movement taken from his String Quartet No. 2. Occasionally the opposite happens: Aaron Copland later included his popular *Fanfare for the Common Man* in his Third Symphony. Two examples of compos-ers maximising a gem that they had created. The British premiere of Mahler's Fifth Symphony came thirty-six years after that of the famous 'Adagietto' movement conducted by Henry Wood at a Proms con-cert in 1909. The last movement of Beethoven's 'Choral' Symphony has been performed in isolation. Enough said on this matter. We're plagued by far too much pompous stuffiness from certain, only too predictable, quarters.

Over the years I have collected a few degrees, accolades and 'gongs' for which I am both grateful and by which I feel humbled. Apart from those 'earned' (Doctor of Music for my compositions, Bachelor of Music academic degree, Licentiate of the Royal Academy of Music as an instrumentalist), here are some of the others: Fellow and Associate of the Royal Academy of Music (where a room has been named in my honour); further fellowships at Cardiff University, Swansea University, the Royal Welsh College of Music and Drama, Trinity College

Carmarthen and Swansea Metropolitan University; Classic FM's *Red f* award for 'outstanding service to classical music'; honorary Doctor of Music from the University of Leicester; the Chancellor's Medal from the University of Glamorgan; two honorary visiting professorships, one at Thames Valley University/London College of Music and the other at the ATriUM, Cardiff; Cymru for the World Award; the Hopkins Medal given by the St David's Society for the State of New York; the Order of Merit-Knight's Cross by the President of Hungary; the OBE, by Her Majesty The Queen, in the 2005 New Year's Honours List; and the CBE in the 2010 Birthday Honours List, for 'services to music'.

I'm going to remain on my high horse for a few moments longer, and I hope you'll indulge me as I do so. Writing a book is a wonderful opportunity to share one's views, and when it comes to the role of Master of the Queen's Music, my view is that it is, quite simply, a post not fit for purpose. Duties are not clearly stated, though it is generally expected that the incumbent will write music to commemorate important royal events such as coronations, birthdays, anniversaries, marriages and deaths, and to accompany other ceremonial occasions and not write works that the Queen neither needs nor requests, nor of the kind that she particularly wants to hear. Elgar, Bax and Bliss were previous incumbents, and they all wrote music suitable for such occasions. In recent times, however, it seems there has been a succession of composers who have either been unwilling or unable – not such a fanciful idea as it sounds – to compose accessible memorable music for ceremonial occasions, the position becoming a pointless sinecure.

I am certainly not criticising the creative worth of these composers, but if the incumbent has not even been asked to compose music for a royal occasion, of which there have been a few in recent years, then that is even worse – and an even greater indictment of the post or the suitability of the person chosen. To my mind, the late Sir Richard

Rodney Bennett should have been a shoo-in for this position; he was a fine composer of concert music who also wrote highly memorable film scores, as did another obvious contender: Sir Malcolm Arnold. Tavener is a further name that springs to mind, but all were ignored, perhaps because they were perceived as having a 'lighter' side and therefore lacking gravitas. At least we would have had a march or two from a couple of those! Perhaps it's because, all too often, those in high office or positions of authority believe it's too easy to compose accessible music. There is something intrinsic about music that connects with people very deeply; it is not a skill that any composer, however intellectually or musically able, can simply turn his or her hand to at will, no matter how much one might presume that to be the case. I write music instinctively but it is intuition based on skill and craft, a thorough grounding in the principles of classical music.

To quote the great advertising executive Sir John Hegarty, 'It's quite easy to write a piece of music that some people like but to write something that many people like is much harder.' Is it art? I don't know and I don't much care. Lord Bragg said that if a creative work has 'memorability and durability' then it is art. Some of my music still shows signs of both, over twenty years since I started this facet of my musical life.

By the end of the first decade of the 21st century, my birthday was only a few years away, with me wondering where all that time had gone. Almost each decade had brought a career change that wasn't planned: my twenties as a jazz musician, my thirties as 'prog-rock'/ fusion musician, my forties as a media composer and, from my fifties, *Adiemus* and beyond. Concerts and events were planned, not least the writing of this book, but before that we had to deal with a particularly worrying episode.

18

SEVENTY

*I*n 2010, Carol and I had bought a flat in central London. We were now spending more time in the city again and we needed somewhere with more permanence than a hotel, since we were constantly driving up and down the M4, *really* not knowing whether we were coming or going – and it was proving to be too much. In 2013, a decision was made *for* us in that Carol had a weird experience. I was conducting a concert in Lampeter, West Wales, and we travelled down from Gower with our friends Lorna and Johnny. While I was rehearsing, they took a stroll around the town and I met up with them later. Carol, with a crippling headache and feeling nauseous, asked me where we were, then questioned what we were doing there. The upshot of all this, which was deeply worrying, was that I sent her home the thirty miles or so by cab, with our friends, and did my best to conduct the concert, which was difficult, not knowing how she was and fearing all manner of life-threatening things.

I caught up with Carol later. She felt better but could remember nothing. We were coming back to London anyway, the next day, so we saw our doctor first of all, then a neurologist. Carol was diagnosed with transient global amnesia, which affects a few people in every 100,000 or so, and is brought on by anxiety and stress. People who suffer from migraines, as Carol had in the past, are particularly susceptible to it. This was an immediate diagnosis, which further tests and scans mercifully proved to be right, with nothing organically wrong at all. We discussed the situation with our doctor, Michael Harding, a wonderful man. Agreeing that we had to simplify our lives, we took the decision to sell Noddfa. It was a wrench, for me more than for Carol, since my roots were in the Gower, but it was the right decision. Carol still can't remember those eight missing hours in Lampeter.

That particular experience was one of the most stressful personal situations I can remember – aside, of course, from the death of my parents and Aunty Ev, although when my mother died I was arguably too young at the time to take in the enormity of what had happened.

It brought home how important the family was to me and how it is all too easy to take it for granted. I was happy and grateful to have Carol by my side as I began my seventies.

I suppose we all go through life, marking off each decade with some degree of dread. Up to the 'twenties', all is fine, but I recall 'thirty' as the threshold that marked the beginning of the end rather than the end of the beginning! However, nothing prepares one for seventy. I suppose it's something to do with the biblical 'three score years and ten'. Perhaps it's the morose and melancholic Celt in me. Didn't Oscar Wilde describe the Welsh as being 'like Italians in the rain'? Being a composer means stretching out this birthday year with celebratory concerts, the agony or the ecstasy, depending on one's point of view, but it's been a really rewarding year nevertheless.

The year 2014 began with a recording entitled *Motets* for Deutsche Grammophon to mark my seventieth birthday and fifty years of my career in music. A motet is a piece of sacred music for unaccompanied voices and the collection includes movements taken from my extended works reconceived for this format, together with some pieces that are newly composed. From *The Armed Man: A Mass for Peace* I chose 'Benedictus', 'Agnus Dei' and the closing chorale, 'God Shall Wipe Away All Tears'. 'Healing Light', 'Peace, Peace!' and 'Dona Nobis Pacem' are from *The Peacemakers*. 'Pie Jesu' and 'In Paradisum' are from *Requiem*. 'Ave Verum', written originally for Bryn Terfel, is from *Stabat Mater*. From the same work comes 'And the Mother Did Weep', itself an adaptation of 'Amaté Adea' from *Adiemus: Songs of Sanctuary*. I have also revisited *Adiemus: Songs of Sanctuary* with 'Cantata Domino' and 'Ave Maria', reworkings of 'Adiemus' and 'Hymn' respectively. 'I'll Make Music' and 'Laudamus Te' are from *Gloria*, while 'Lullay' comes from *Stella Natalis*. 'Exsultate, Jubilate' is based on *Palladio*, the 'retro' instrumental piece inspired by the Italian architect of the same name. Of the new pieces 'The Shepherd' and 'Depart in Peace' *(Nunc dimittis)* are taken from *The Healer: A Cantata for St Luke*, which was commissioned by Grayshott Concerts to premiere in 2014. 'Locus Iste' was composed especially for the recording.

When considering the ideal ensemble to sing these pieces, I wanted to approach Stephen Layton and his magnificent choir Polyphony first. I was overjoyed when Stephen said that he was very keen to come on board, remarking that he had found the original *Adiemus* quite addictive. I then had the dilemma of deciding how and where to record. I am very much a studio animal, using all the techniques available in a state-of-the-art modern recording studio. Stephen's preference was to record in a church, one that he knew 'acoustically' and where he had recorded before; more of the traditional approach to 'classical' recording. He also felt happier with his own technical team around him, so we went down Stephen's preferred path and recorded at All Hallows Church in Hampstead,

London, in January 2014, but did the final mix at my *mustache* studio London on 6 February. Adrian Peacock, a very experienced and good-humoured man, produced the recording with Carol and me overseeing everything. Our engineer, David Hinitt, played a crucial role, too, as did Will Brown, who edited and mastered the finished product. Stephen, a brilliant musician, and Polyphony performed this music with integrity, devotion and great beauty. *Motets* is dedicated to my first granddaughter, Astrid May.

The background to the CD cover design is quite intriguing. Late one night in 1997, across a dark and deserted St Mark's Square, Venice, I saw a painting, lit like a beacon, drawing me inexorably to the window of what turned out to be an art dealership, Galleria Ravagnan. It made a deep impression on me, and Carol remarked that it looked like my music sounded. I returned the next day, bought the painting and began a firm friendship with gallery owner Luciano Ravagnan. On a return visit a year or so later I met and befriended the eminent artist Andrea Vizzini, only for us both to discover that he, not knowing who had bought his painting, had been painting to my music! Vizzini's work reflects the ethos of my music: of today but with a traditional core that connects, emotionally, with people. The cover painting, *Il luogo degli angeli* ('the place of the angels'), another of his works that I own, is particularly felicitous for this album of motets and, as Stephen Layton remarked, is 'the perfect doorway to what lies inside'. The album went to No. 1 in the UK Classical Chart.

The first 'birthday concert', in my seventieth year, was my Martin Luther King Day concert at Carnegie Hall on 20 January 2014. Although it predated my birthday by a couple of weeks it was billed as such, and Distinguished Concerts International New York performed my *Stabat Mater* and *The Bards of Wales*, while I conducted the 'Benedictus' from *The Armed Man*. I was presented with a cake, an enormous card signed by several hundred choristers and a letter of congratulation from NYC Mayor, Bill de Blasio, which was read aloud. On my return, I went down to Cardiff on 10 February to conduct the second half of a 'Classic FM Live' concert in a programme of my most popular pieces including *Adiemus*, *Palladio* and 'Benedictus'.

Carol's birthday and mine fall on consecutive days, 16 and 17 February, and we're a year and a day apart. We're the same age on one day each year! Since the 16th was a Sunday (and Carol's sixty-ninth) we decided to go out that night for dinner with Jody and Rosie. We were to meet them at a local Italian restaurant, Café Caldesi in Marylebone, just the four of us. It looked somewhat dark inside as we turned the corner. We struggled in, the lights went on and there were sixty people there to welcome us including 'my little princess', granddaughter Astrid. In fact Carol, together with Jody, had graciously, and selflessly considering it was her actual birthday, organised it for me, it being my seventieth the following day. There were so many people I had not seen for a few years and we had a fantastic evening, a sumptuous repast and some jazz mates played. Having arrived at the actual date, I felt much better about it all.

In April, I visited Sweden for the first time for many years. I had been approached by Rikard Gateau, General Manager of the Västerås Sinfonietta, a fine orchestra, one of the handful of state-sponsored orchestras, from the town of Västerås, about eighty miles west of Stockholm. I was to conduct a performance of *The Armed Man*. The choir was from a school that specialised in music, particularly singing, called Fryxellska skolan. The choir, including some very young children, incredibly, sang the whole work, which lasts for more than an hour, from memory. More importantly, they also sounded fabulous. The trip was an emotional journey. Followed by a UK film crew, I revisited Gävle and some memories: the flat at Brunnsgatan 49 where I had lived for a time, the Baltic Hotel where I dined as a child, and Furuvik, the park bordering the Baltic where I spent many happy summer days.

With regard to singing from memory, I remember Brian Kay, ex-King's Singer and excellent choral conductor and trainer, telling me of an *Armed Man* he conducted at the Royal Albert Hall with the Really Big Chorus, and it *is* big: two thousand or more. A group from Ireland, positioned somewhat to the rear of the aggregation (which means near the roof at this venue), sang it from memory. Brian congratulated them later, after the performance. 'Who are you?' they asked. They had been too far away to recognise him.

On my return from Sweden I went over to Dublin for a concert with the RTÉ Concert Orchestra before returning for my Royal Albert Hall birthday bash on 9 May. This was with the Royal Choral Society and the Royal Philharmonic Orchestra. Again, many of my most enduring and popular pieces featured, including favourite sections from *The Armed Man*, *Requiem* and *Stabat Mater*. We also performed the Euphonium Concerto with David Childs and some new orchestrations of *Adiemus* material. Referred to as 'The Symphonic Adiemus', the collection is scored for mixed choir (as opposed to women's voices on the original) and full orchestra. The original *Songs of Sanctuary* was scored for strings only. Apparently we had a 109 per cent capacity audience, the 9 per cent being those standing in 'the gods' up on high.

The date 7 June 2014 was a momentous day: the birth of our second granddaughter Aminta ('Minty') Jane. Jody was in France, best man at cellist Jonny Byer's wedding, two weeks before the scheduled delivery date. Minty decided not to wait and suddenly arrived two weeks early, the same day as the wedding. Jody beat a hasty retreat on the first flight, having first proclaimed Jonny the godfather. Minty was tiny. Now one year later, she is happily on course and bouncing.

In 2013 I'd been asked by Dave Cottle to become Patron of the new Swansea Jazz Festival, planned for 2014, and I was delighted to accept. My first public forays into jazz had been at the Glandŵr Jazz

Club in Swansea and I thought it a splendid idea for Swansea to have a jazz festival. Although the Cardiff-based BBC National Orchestra of Wales and the Welsh National Opera are national institutions, Swansea is home to no orchestra and no opera and jazz is a vibrant and exciting – albeit undervalued – art form. Dave was seeking support from both the Welsh Government and Swansea City Council as well as from local sponsors. Dave is one of the celebrated and very musical Cottle family and a fine jazz pianist in his own right. Brother Laurence, who played on the original recordings of both *The Peacemakers* and *Colores*, is one of the finest electric-bass players on the planet. For the past sixteen years Dave has put together a weekly programme of jazz events at Swansea Jazzland held at St James Club near the city centre. This community-based, not-for-profit organisation presents over fifty weekly performance events each year with a mixture of international jazz artists and UK-based, including local, musicians. Thankfully, the festival came to fruition over the weekend of 21 June, which was a blissful three days for Carol and me.

On 9 July we performed *Adiemus Colores* at the International Eisteddfod in Llangollen. It was the world premiere. For many reasons, mainly logistical, we couldn't re-form the cast from the album. Trumpeter Pacho Flores almost arrived from Venezuela via Valencia, but could not leave Spain, on the actual day, due to visa issues. Gareth Small, from the Hallé, stepped in at really short notice to play first trumpet, a demanding part that he performed brilliantly. The magical Cuca Roseta, the *fado* singer, came over from Lisbon and we had all the rhythm players from the album. Eilir Griffiths, Music Director of the festival, put an excellent choir together for the event. It's not an easy sing, with a great deal of 'tribal' non-vibrato singing. Many singers cannot lose their 'wobble'.

Then down to South Wales to the Gower Festival and my first ever appearance at my local event on 12 July. It had previously been run by a 'composer' and ex-BBC producer (which says everything) and had a very stuffy atmosphere but there had been a change from 2014 with Gordon Back as Artistic Director. Originally from Neath and a pianist and accompanist of international repute, since 2002 he has been the Artistic Director of the celebrated Menuhin Competition. The Gower Festival holds its concerts in the many beautiful churches scattered around the peninsula but this 'seventieth' concert was held in Tabernacle Chapel where my father had been organist and choir-master and where, in many ways, I had begun my journey. It was pretty soon a sell-out and many were disappointed. ('Some couldn't get in either!' – joke courtesy of Ronnie Scott.) Because of advance orders to 'friends of the festival', many local people missed out on tickets. There was some discussion about beaming the performance to another local venue but this proved both financially and logistically impossible. No one was allowed to sit in the front row of the gallery unless one was less than 4 feet 5 inches tall. This was decreed by the Synod since, at another chapel in South Wales, someone had died falling over a similarly low parapet. Throughout my childhood and adolescence, the front row had been used without any mishap what-soever. The chapel was packed with an audience of three hundred. Gordon interviewed me about my life; Cor Caerdydd sang; Rob Nichols, who as a child had studied piano with my father, played *Trumpeting Organ Morgan*, and three stellar guests played: Catrin Finch, David Childs and cellist Steffan Morris with the Chamber Orchestra of Wales, led by Rhys Watkins from the LSO, in what was the most emotional of all the birthday bashes. The next day I unveiled a new cenotaph in the centre of the village, bearing the names of all those from Penclawdd who were lost in action, including my uncle, Pilot Officer Alfryn Jenkins. In April 2015 I was asked to become the Patron of the Gower Festival.

Back to London and the Queen Elizabeth Hall for my concert

with Soweto Strings. As mentioned earlier, they had especially requested a work from me that used some themes from movements from my choral works in the *Soweto Suite for Strings*. They performed admirably. This concert was a London seventieth birthday event for the orchestra's founder and guiding light, Rosemary Nalden.

August was spent in France, for a few days with all the family before Carol and I went on to Italy. (The ex-footballer Eric Cantona was staying *en famille* at the French hotel. Poolside one day, his trunks were on the ground. Not bothering to bend and pick them up, he put his toe underneath them and flicked them up overhead, catching them on the way down. Very impressive.)

The Armed Man was performed again at the Royal Albert Hall on 28 September 2014. Organised by Anne Renshaw of Sing UK, this was a commemorative performance to mark the centenary of the Great War; a chorus of 600 young voices from the UK, Germany, Belgium and France, all countries involved in the conflict, sang the work accompanied by the Philharmonia Orchestra. Introduced by international best-selling author Kate Mosse, they came together in a spirit of reconciliation and hope to make their own special contribution to the commemorations taking place.

The year 2014 also marked the centenary of the birth of poet Dylan Thomas. Together with Cerys Matthews, Catrin Finch, Bryn Terfel, Michael Sheen, Matthew Rhys, Carol Ann Duffy, Gillian Clarke and Owen Sheers, I was an official ambassador for Dylan Thomas 100 or 'dt100'. I was approached by Huw Tregelles Williams to write an orchestral overture to mark the event. A brilliant organist, for whom I wrote *Trumpeting Organ Morgan*, Huw was a music graduate of my alma mater, Cardiff University, and for many years was Head of Music at BBC Wales. For the past ten years he had been Artistic Director of the Swansea Festival and 2014 was to be his swan song. As my instrumental music tends to be quirky, it was an obvious choice to base this piece, of twelve minutes' duration, on *Under Milk Wood*, the play for radio that the poet wrote in 1954 and which is so redolent of life in my own Welsh coastal village, Penclawdd.

Llareggub is a quirky, surreal and whimsical snapshot, in music, of life in the fictional seaside village where Dylan Thomas set *Under Milk Wood*. The 'Welsh-sounding' name itself betrays Dylan's sense of humour since, when written backwards, it means something else in English. The piece is in three short movements, to be played without a break: 'Starless and Bible Black', 'Eli Jenkins' Prayer' and 'At the Sailor's Arms'.

For the Nonconformist hymn heard hummed by the orchestra, I quoted from the hymn tune 'Burnt Oak', written many years ago by my late father, himself a devotee of the poet who was born and raised in Swansea, not ten miles away from Penclawdd. The programme notes read:

> It is night, 'starless and Bible black'; the town sleeps and dreams. Dawn approaches when blind Captain Cat pulls the 'townhall bellrope' to announce the day. A Welsh Nonconformist Methodist hymn is heard as a prelude to the Reverend Eli Jenkins's bittersweet prayer. Later, at the Sailor's Arms (a public house or bar), locals begin to drop in and do what locals do: chat, gossip, argue, brawl, get happy, and get drunk. Cherry Owen ('who breathes all night like a brewery'), Mr Waldo ('what he'll do for a drink'), Dai Bread ('with two wives, one for the daytime one for the night'), Polly Garter ('who cuddled you when?'), Nogood Boyo ('too lazy to wipe his snout') appear, as well as postman Willy Nilly and occasional barman Sinbad Sailors. Organ Morgan's ('it's all the time organ organ with him') 'full' organ is heard above the clamour and excitement. Chaos ensues before it all settles

down. I claim some poetic licence in inviting some of these characters into the public house.

Llareggub was performed by the Russian State Philharmonic Orchestra conducted by Valery Polyansky. Conducting his outstanding orchestra, Maestro Polyansky entered the spirit of the piece, even simulating a drunk on the podium during a trombone cadenza that reflected some degree of inebriation at the Sailor's. Although the premiere was due to take place on the last night of the Swansea Festival in October, since the orchestra was undertaking a UK tour, they requested that they perform the piece on the previous Monday at Cadogan Hall, London, which they did, thanks to the artistic generosity of the commissioning body.

Sandwiched between these two performances of *Llareggub* was the world premiere of *The Healer: A Cantata for St Luke*, at St Luke's Church, Grayshott. The capacity is only 330 and concerts are always oversubscribed, so we performed on two consecutive nights. The text deals with healing, not only in the Christian and spiritual sense, but also with secular issues such as the 'healing' of our planet, Earth. Apart from the Gospel according to St Luke, there are extracts from the Book of Common Prayer and a poem by William Blake together with contributions penned by Terry Waite, Vivien Harrison, and Carol who researched and collated the text with guidance from Father Tim Ardouin of Llanrhidian Church, Gower. The work was commissioned by Grayshott Concerts, of which I am Patron, and is dedicated to its founders Vivien and Peter Harrison, whose idea this was and whose enthusiasm and belief made it happen. Grayshott Concerts is a volunteer-run not-for-profit community group and, since 2012, a registered charity. Its aim is to provide top-quality classical music performances by renowned soloists, instrumentalists, choirs and orchestras for the people of Grayshott, and surrounding villages, in the area of the Hampshire–Surrey borders. The London Mozart Players is their Orchestra in Residence while pianist and conductor Howard Shelley is Associate Artist. Regular guests include: Classical BRIT Award-winners Chloë Hanslip and Alison Balsom, former Young Musician of the Year Guy Johnston, star violinist Tasmin Little and clarinettist Michael Collins. In 2012, founders Peter and Vivien Harrison were awarded the Lady Hilary Groves Prize for their 'outstanding contribution to music in the community' from the Making Music organisation, which supports over three thousand groups throughout the UK.

The Healer is scored for soprano, baritone, mixed chorus, oboe (doubling cor anglais), strings and percussion. To evoke the atmosphere and the sound of the ancient Holy Land or Middle East, I have occasionally used, as in my *Stabat Mater*, some percussion instruments such as the *riq* (essentially a tambourine) and the *darbuca* (a 'goblet' drum), both associated with those foreign parts. There is also an important role for the solo oboist, which is featured throughout, echoing the ancient indigenous double-reed instruments of that area. I was thrilled to have my daughter-in-law Rosie play this solo part. It was her first 'gig' after giving birth to Minty before returning to the ENO orchestra and her occasional work with the LSO. She played so beautifully. The two excellent vocal soloists were soprano Lucy Knight and baritone Håkan Vramsmo, performing with the excellent local Excelsis Choir and the superb Marylebone Camerata.

In November, I resumed my UK tour with a series of sell-out concerts, first of all at Symphony Hall, Birmingham, and Bridgewater Hall, Manchester, then later a Radio 3 concert with the BBC National Orchestra of Wales from St David's Hall Cardiff: *The Armed Man: A Mass for Peace*, the Euphonium Concerto with David Childs and *For the Fallen*. In between, I went over to Carnegie Hall to conduct a concert featuring Marat Bisengaliev in a performance of two works I composed for him, choir and orchestra based on Kazakh folk themes: *Abai* and *Shakarim*.

Music has given me so much and for some time I had been considering giving something back by way of launching a prize to help aspiring young instrumentalists studying in the UK. I had been looking for a suitable partner and the initial plan was to float this under the aegis of the Worshipful Company of Musicians, where both Carol and I are 'Liverymen'; we therefore have the Freedom of the City of London, which enables us to drive our sheep over London Bridge. That idea foundered, however, so I was fortunate to find a partner in the Arts Club at Dover Street, London and a supporter in Classic FM. The inaugural final of 'The Arts Club – Karl Jenkins Classical Music Award' in association with Classic FM event was held in November 2014. Apart from Carol and myself, the adjudicating panel comprised Emma Johnson (clarinet) and Julian Lloyd Webber (cello), Sam Jackson (Managing Editor, Classic FM) and Kathryn Enticott (Enticott Music Management). One hundred and forty entries, by CD, YouTube or SoundCloud, had been whittled down to the twelve semi-finalists. The semi-finals and the final took place over two weekends in November at the Arts Club.

Violinist Joo Yeon Sir was the winner and awarded the £4,000 cash prize but, in addition, a repertoire piece selected by Joo Yeon, as well as a short work specially composed by me, was recorded in a London studio and broadcast on Classic FM. The runners up, accordionist Iosif Purits and violinist Benjamin Baker, each received a cash prize of £500. During the event, candidates were judged based on their technique, individualism, musicality, interpretation, communication and overall performance.

As usual we spent the New Year under the Eiger at Grindelwald with the family. Carol and I drove down and back, stopping off in Paris on the return journey. We were wandering round that fateful morning of 7 January 2015 when the *Charlie Hebdo* massacre occurred. So much for peace.

Professionally, my seventieth year ended with a return to DCINY where *The Peacemakers, The Healer* and *Llareggub* were performed, the latter two being US premieres. I conducted *Llareggub.*

Many circles were completed this year. Neither my father nor I would have ever imagined when we went to hear the Warsaw Philharmonic Orchestra at the Swansea Festival sixty years ago that, in 2014, a piece written by me and referencing a Welsh Methodist hymn written by him would be performed, honouring Wales's great poet a generation later at this same event. Also my returning to Sweden and reconnecting with that part of my childhood spent there. In 1998 and 1999 I had been composing *The Armed Man* for the millennium, dedicating the piece to the victims of the war in Kosovo, a horrific example of ethnic cleansing and genocide. In March 2015, fifteen years later, I was invited to Priština, the capital, to be presented with the President's Medal prior to a performance of the work before an audience including members of the government and foreign diplomats.

My birthday year ended with me being more relaxed about becoming a septuagenarian, a milestone that Carol was about to pass. Instead of accepting gifts for her birthday she asked party guests to make a donation to Nordoff Robbins, a wonderful charity who, to quote their mission statement, 'use music therapy and other music services to help a range of people with a range of challenges such as autism, dementia, mental health problems, stroke, brain injury, depression and life-threatening or terminal illnesses, such as cancer. All of the people so helped have one uniting factor – music dramatically improves their quality of life.'

In May 2015, I travelled to The Hague in the Netherlands. *The Armed Man* was performed on the eve of Liberation Day, celebrated each year on 5 May to mark the end of the occupation by Nazi Germany during the Second World War. The performance was by the Dutch Jenkins Choir, formed and directed by Hans Matla who has, gratifyingly, conducted a great deal of my music. It was a dramatic and emotional evening. Hans structured the performance so that the cataclysmic ending of 'Charge!' and the ensuing silence coincided, at exactly 8 p.m., with the moment when there are two minutes' silence throughout the Netherlands, followed by the singing of the national anthem, which is what happened here. Instead of the 'Last Post' being played, as in the *Armed Man*, *Taptoe*, the Dutch version, was performed and the work continued to its completion.

After a day back in London, I flew to Kazakhstan for two concerts with 'me old mucker', Marat Bisengaliev. On my return, I went to the studio and found, as I wrote in the opening chapter, the letter regarding the Knighthood.

My reaction: thrilled, bewildered, embarrassed; a thousand thoughts raced through my mind. It was particularly gratifying since it was given to a composer who has never been part of the music establishment, which is unheard of. Perhaps, times *are* changing. I also believe I am the first Welsh-born writer of music of any kind to be so honoured, which tells us something, though I'm not sure what. It also gives me another claim to fame: the first composer so honoured never to have had a note played at the BBC Proms – but *Doctor Who* has! The knighthood, unexpectedly, has also given me a curious sense of a certain degree of validation. I was touched by the hundreds of personal messages of congratulations I received, from royalty and lords to the local shopkeeper.

As I sign off I am writing a work to commemorate the fiftieth anniversary of the Aberfan disaster where 116 children and 28 adults were either crushed or suffocated to death when a coal tip enveloped a school. I am only too aware of the responsibility this entails in writing something that will connect and move everyone affected by the tragedy. Paradoxically, dealing with such a subject, that lies deep in the soul of the Welsh, is both a harrowing and uplifting experience but the journey has been made easier and more rewarding by my travelling companion, Mererid Hopwood, the brilliant Welsh poet, academic and linguist who has written the amazing text.

During the course of writing this book, I have been asked by a few of my friends and colleagues whether I have a 'wish list' of music I still want to compose or anyone I'd like to write for or work with. I'm afraid that, for me at least, it doesn't quite work like that. My music is led entirely by new ideas. I'm not the kind of composer who thinks success is defined by writing a certain number of concertos, symphonies or string quartets. Instead, so long as I'm busy writing a work that I feel confident will connect with people, I'm happy. It is also salutary for me to consider that if I had been a better jazz musician, I might have never left the genre to explore other fields; also a frightening thought in that that would have meant no *Adiemus*, no *The Armed Man*, no book that you are now reading, and no knighthood!

Similarly, the notion of retirement, as one might say with confidence is the case with all 'artists', is an entirely alien one to me. I am blessed to have spent my entire adult life being paid to explore my first love: music. I cannot imagine life without composing; it is what still drives me, every day, and I am extremely fortunate to be married to someone who understands this more deeply than I could wish to imagine. When that cockle-vendor in Penclawdd asked if I was 'still with the mew-sic', I replied with an emphatic yes. If I bump into her again a decade or so from now, I very much hope to be able to answer in a similarly enthusiastic way. Until the day I die, I will always be 'with the music'. And the music will forever remain with me.

DISCOGRAPHY

Adiemus I: Songs of Sanctuary (Warner Classics 1995)
Diamond Music (Sony Classical 1996)
Adiemus II: Cantata Mundi (Warner Classics 1996)
Imagined Oceans (Sony Classical 1998)
Adiemus III: Dances of Time (Warner Classics 1998)
Adiemus IV: The Eternal Knot (Warner Classics 2000)
The Armed Man: A Mass for Peace (Warner Classics 2001)
Adiemus V: Vocalise (Warner Classics 2003)
Requiem (Warner Classics 2005)
Kiri Sings Karl (Warner Classics 2006)
This Land of Ours (Warner Classics 2007)
River Queen: Original Soundtrack (Warner Classics 2007)
Quirk: The Concertos (Warner Classics 2008)
Stabat Mater (Warner Classics 2008)
Stella Natalis (Warner Classics 2009)
Gloria/Te Deum (Warner Classics 2010)
The Peacemakers (Warner Classics 2011)
Adiemus Colores (Deutsche Grammophon 2013)
Motets (Deutsche Grammophon 2014)
Still with the Music: The Album (Warner Classics 2015)
Voices, featuring **The Healer** (Warner Classics 2015)

For a full list of works, visit www.boosey.com/jenkins

ACKNOWLEDGEMENTS

I would like to acknowledge and thank the following, some of whom, although not mentioned in my story, have nevertheless made a massive contribution to my career or else been instrumental in the production of this book.

Sam Jackson for his expertise, patience and good humour in guiding me though the maze that is this, my first – and which shall remain my only – book.

Jennie Condell (Publisher) from Elliott and Thompson for her diligence, friendliness and great skill in putting it all together and to the many at E&T books who made it possible: Lorne Forsyth (Chairman), Olivia Bays (Director), Pippa Crane (Senior Editor) and Alison Menzies (PR).

And Carol, yet again, for proofreading everything, contributing much, and remembering even more.

Steve Abbott, manager since 2008, whose acquaintance with, and knowledge of, music across all genres is unmatched and who is brilliant at the 'big picture'.

Emma Kerr, Head of Promotion at my publisher Boosey & Hawkes, whose wisdom and guidance in my professional life as a composer has been far greater than the job description suggests and who also read a draft of this publication; Senior Editor Jeremy Allen whose expertise in editing and producing my scores has been faultless in its detail; Head of Publishing James Eggleston; and last but by no means least, Managing Director Janis Susskind, an iconic name in music publishing, who engineered my signing to the company in 1995.

In life, one needs lawyers and accountants: Andrew Thompson, partner at Lee & Thompson has been my lawyer since 1995, with Mike Brooks dealing with the litigious matters that, alas, surfaced from time to time. Since my twenties I have been with accountancy firm Lubbock Fine, in particular the partners, Russell Rich and David Levy; the latter, one of the wisest men I have ever met, sadly died just before the completion of this book.

The six Finnish Adiemus singers are: Mervi Hiltunen, Anna-Mari Kähärä, Mia Simanainen, Nina Tapio, Rika Timonen and Säde Barling (née Rissanen) who was the leader of the ensemble. We later added: Pirjo Aittomäki, Merja Rajala, Hanna-Riikka Siitonen. And thanks to Irma Tapio who managed them for a while.

I'd also like to express my gratitude to John Gibbons and his musician wife Rowena. John has many irons in many fires, including conducting the Worthing Symphony Orchestra. He came to enjoy my work, performed much of it and, with Rowena, promoted *Requiem* and *Stella Natalis* UK concert tours, where John and I shared the conducting.

Adiemus Colores: The Adiemus Singers were recorded at Finnvox Studios Helsinki and engineered by Mikko Oinonen. They were: Säde Barling (leader, alto); Mirjam Schulman, Hanna Tuomela, Anna-Mari Kähärä (sopranos); Pirjo Aittomäki, Mia Simanainen, Mervi Hiltunen-Multamäki (mezzo-sopranos); Pia Lönnqvist (alto); Tomas Takolander, Paavo Hyökki (tenors); Sampo Haapaniemi, Pemo Ojala (basses).

The superb rhythm section for *Colores* comprised: John Parricelli (guitars), Ksenija Sidorova (accordion), Danny Evans (piano), Zands Duggan, Jody Jenkins (percussion) and Laurence Cottle (bass guitars).

Thank you to cellist, friend, Minty's godfather and Jody's best man Jonny Byers for 'fixing' (contracting) many fantastic freelance ensembles for me in recent years: The Marylebone Camarata and La orquesta de colores among them.

The massed 1,000 voices on two movements of *The Peacemakers* included the Angmering Chorale, Ashtead Choral Society, Beckenham Chorale, Billingshurst Choral Society, Burgess Hill Choral Society, Camerata Chamber Choir Isle of Wight, Carshalton Choral Society and Holy Cross Choir, Gainsborough Choral Society, Havering Singers, Hook Choral Society, Leatherhead Choral Society, Leicester Philharmonic Choir, Redland Green Community Chorus, Choir of St James Church Finchampstead, and the Tyranno Chorus.

I am also indebted to my friend the judge, Paul Thomas QC, for, as a non-musician, reading the draft of this book to see if it made any sense, and to Welsh Government Minister Edwina Hart MBE for her continuing friendship and support.

And to my record companies: Patrick Lemanski (Head of Warner Classics UK) and Lee Daniel Woollard, who now look after my EMI catalogue, for producing the *Voices* CD box set and *Still with the Music* CD released in conjunction with this book; Mark Wilkinson (President of Deutsche Grammophon) and Christian Badzura (Executive Producer A&R) at DG, Berlin.

Apologies to anyone who feels slighted that they have been omitted. Put it down to a senior moment by an old (*-ish*) Welsh composer.

INDEX

OUT NOW

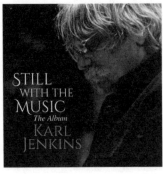

Karl Jenkins: Still with the Music, The Album A companion to this autobiography, a 16-track collection of music from Karl Jenkins's bestselling albums, spanning 20 years of music making from *Adiemus – Songs of Sanctuary* (1995) to *The Healer* (2015).

Karl Jenkins: Voices An 8-CD box set bringing together for the first time the best-selling albums *Adiemus: Songs of Sanctuary* (1995), *The Armed Man: A Mass for Peace* (2001), *Requiem* (2005), *Stabat Mater* (2008), *Stella Natalis* (2009), *Gloria / Te Deum* (2010), *The Peacemakers* (2011). The set also includes a previously unpublished recording, *The Healer* (2015).

WARNER CLASSICS